Carrying Out the City Plan

Frederick Law Olmsted, Flavel Shurtleff

Copyright © BiblioLife

Our goal is to help readers, educators and researchers by bringing back in print hard-to-find original publications at a reasonable price and, at the same time, preserve the legacy of literary history. The following book represents an authentic reproduction of the text as printed by the original publisher and may contain prior copyright references. While we have attempted to accurately maintain the integrity of the original work(s), from time to time there are problems with the original book that may result in minor errors in the reproduction, including imperfections such as missing and blurred pages, poor pictures, markings and other reproduction issues beyond our control. Because this work is culturally important, we have made it available as a part of our commitment to protecting, preserving and promoting the world's literature.

The BiblioLife Network

These books are in the "public domain." They were digitized and made available in partnership with library partners seeking to help in this important mission. We believe that when we undertake the difficult task of re-creating them as attractive, readable and affordable books, we further the mutual goal of sharing these works with a larger audience.

For more info: www.bibliolife.com

BCR's Shelf2Life program grew from a strong desire to help libraries share their vital collections with new audiences. BCR is the nation's oldest and most established library network, and their mission is to bring libraries together for greater success by expanding their knowledge, reach and power. By helping libraries digitize and widen access to their collections, BCR's Shelf2Life program helps libraries increase the visibility, use and recognition of their important collections. In addition, the program is designed to help researchers, collectors and all curious readers by putting these editions within easy reach: in print-on-demand or electronic format.

The University of Colorado at Boulder's University Libraries has a threefold mission. First, to be central to the University community's discovery, communication and use of knowledge by providing materials, information and services that support the University's mission. Second, to serve as a research resource for Colorado residents through support for individual, business, cultural, educational, governmental and other information needs. Third, to share resources with the national and international higher education community. In order to continue to meet this mission and their high level of service to the University, research, higher education, local, national and international communities, the CU Boulder University Libraries continually strive to innovate and adapt their collections and delivery options. By participating in the Shelf2Life Program, the University Libraries provide their faculty, staff, students and researchers access to this important content in ways they have never been able to in the past.

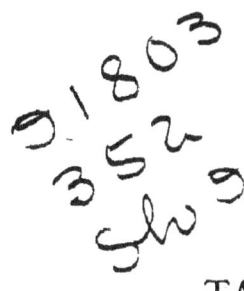

TABLE OF CONTENTS

CHAPTER	PAGE
INTRODUCTION	
I. The Public Ownership of Land	1
II. The Acquisition of Land	22
III. The Distribution of the Cost of Land Acquirement	52
IV. Excess Condemnation	103
V. The Use of the Police Power in the Execution of a City Plan	138
VI. The Work of Administrative Agencies in the Execution of a City Plan	168

APPENDICES

A. Legislation and Decisions	211
B. Extracts from Report on English and Continental Systems of Taking Land for Public Purposes	308
INDEX	335

INTRODUCTION

THE reason for preparing this book is the astonishing variation in the practical efficiency of methods actually employed and prescribed by law or legal custom in different parts of the United States in acquiring land for public purposes, in distributing the cost of public improvements, and in other proceedings essential to the proper shaping of our growing cities to the needs of their inhabitants. Mere variation in method would be of little more than academic interest in itself, but variations that result in obstructing the path of progress in one community and clearing it in another are of large practical importance. The extent and significance of these practical variations have impressed themselves more and more strongly on the writer in the course of an extended practice as a landscape architect, especially in connection with the design and execution of such municipal improvements as parks, playgrounds, public squares, parkways, streets, the placing of public buildings and the improvement of their grounds. Even more notable than the variation in method and in relative efficiency has been the close preoccupation of public officials, especially in the city law departments, with the constantly recurring problem of finding the way

INTRODUCTION

of least resistance for navigating a specific improvement through the maze of obstacles imposed by the existing local legal situation, accompanied by an almost fatalistic acceptance of these obstacles as a permanent condition. There has been evident in most cities a very limited acquaintance with conditions and methods to be found elsewhere, and a general lack of strong constructive effort for the improvement of the local conditions and methods on the basis of general experience. Of late years, however, there has been a growing tendency to break away from this indifference and to face these problems in a larger spirit.

Feeling the importance of stimulating and assisting such constructive local effort by calling attention to the more important of the variations in actual use, and lacking both the time and the legal training to himself prepare a proper presentation of the subject, the writer of this preface urged the Russell Sage Foundation, some three years ago, to provide the funds for making a systematic survey of the field and for publishing its results. The response was cordial and effective and enabled Mr. Flavel Shurtleff of the Boston Bar to devote a large part of his time for two years to the undertaking.

Mr. Shurtleff has done the real work of the book from beginning to end and is responsible for its accuracy from a legal point of view. The writer of this preface has been compelled to limit his collaboration to a general guidance in the gath-

INTRODUCTION

ering and selection of material and its arrangement for presentation, and to a somewhat careful and detailed revision of the manuscript and proofs for the purpose of making the impressions conveyed by the book conform in a common sense way with the observations and conclusions to which he has been led in dealing with actual problems of municipal improvement in many different cities.

There has been no attempt to compile a comprehensive treatise on city planning; and some subjects properly within the title of this volume have not, for many reasons, been examined with as great a detail as their importance may seem to justify. This is particularly true of the subject of building regulations.

Since city building is primarily a question of the acquisition of land by the municipality, or else of the power to regulate its use by others, the search for precedents in codes, reports, and legal text books has been concerned with three well defined subjects: the acquisition of land, the power to tax, and the police power. In respect to these there has been no attempt to compile a complete digest, but only to present the more significant variations revealed by a fairly systematic and intelligent search. The practice of municipal departments has been much more difficult to discover. The examination of state codes and the results obtained from a questionnaire sent to most of the larger cities in the United States

INTRODUCTION

made it possible to determine upon a limited number of states as typical of the rest, and by selecting the most promising cities in each state, to make up a list of cities for study on the ground. The data obtained in one city by consultation with city officials and otherwise often led to the addition of a new city to the list. The following cities were visited for a few days each: New York, Buffalo, Cleveland, Indianapolis, Chicago, Milwaukee, Minneapolis, St. Louis, Kansas City, Denver, Los Angeles, San Francisco, Portland (Oregon), Seattle, Houston, Dallas, New Orleans, Baltimore, Philadelphia, and Pittsburgh. An opportunity to make a more intensive study in one city presented itself in connection with an investigation conducted by the city planning committee of the Boston Chamber of Commerce into the methods employed in extending the street systems in the metropolitan district of Boston, and the information thus secured has been made use of in this report.

The material for the book was gathered between January, 1910, and January, 1912, a time of extraordinary activity in city planning legislation. Some of the text became obsolete before the book was completed and some of the conclusions have been made a basis of legislation during the past year (1913). Thus, Ohio has written into its constitution the power of excess condemnation of land* and the right to assess

* See Appendix A, III, p. 280.

INTRODUCTION

the cost of improvements on territory especially benefited.* Massachusetts, New York, and Wisconsin have amended their constitutions to incorporate the principle of excess condemnation.† The Pennsylvania law of 1907, allowing excess condemnation, has been tested and the supreme court has declared it to be unconstitutional.‡ Plan commissions have been made mandatory in Massachusetts and have been authorized in New York, New Jersey, Pennsylvania, and some cities of Connecticut.§

This activity in the gradual and experimental reshaping of legal mechanism will doubtless continue until it shall have been forged into an instrument of much higher average efficiency than at present for the accomplishment of the social purposes of city planning. It is as a help toward the successful working out of this process that the present book is offered.

FREDERICK LAW OLMSTED.

Brookline, Mass.,
30th April, 1914.

* Constitution of Ohio, Article XVIII, Section 11.
† See Appendix A, III, pp. 248, 278, 279.   ‡ See Appendix A, III, pp. 272, 275.   § See Appendix, pp. 283, 284, 290, 294.

CHAPTER I

THE PUBLIC OWNERSHIP OF LAND

THE ownership of land by the municipality is essential to the execution of many parts of a city plan. Certain acts of private owners which have a tendency to prevent the realization of a plan, either temporarily or for all time, may be enjoined by municipal regulation. Certain other acts in the furtherance of a plan may be induced by persuasion or compelled by administrative pressure. But at an early stage land or rights in land must be acquired for the public, and a municipality will be called upon to consider, first, whether it has a right to acquire or use land for a desired purpose; second, the methods of acquiring the land; and third, the equitable distribution of the cost of its acquisition.

THE RIGHT OF A MUNICIPALITY TO ACQUIRE AND HOLD LAND

It is well to emphasize at the start that the municipal ownership of land is subject to important limitations in the United States. It is customary to cite German examples of town planning and point out that the success of the plan is due to the large percentage of land under municipal ownership. German cities are encouraged to enter into the real estate field for the avowed purpose of checking speculation, and of reducing the over-crowding of lots, by releasing from private ownership land for building purposes. However desirable this may be in German cities, it is not permitted in any municipality in the United States.

In Germany as well as in the United States the purchase money at the disposal of any municipality is but the return from the taxation of the citizens, and the income of all can be spent only for a use that can be shared by all. German cities have reached a broad conception of a "public use" and have emphasized in this conception the rights of the community. The Constitution of the United States, on the other hand, was written when the individual was paramount in philosophy and politics, and the clause which protects the individual at the expense of the community has proved an effective check to the democratic tendencies which would substitute in importance the community for the individual. Consequently a "public use" in the United States has been more narrowly interpreted by the courts.

But new public needs have been recognized by the legislatures and sanctioned by the courts since the growth of great centers of population in the United States. To satisfy recreational needs the appropriation of the community's money has been authorized both for the purchase and the condemnation of land for parks, boulevards, and playgrounds. It is not inconceivable that more radical needs will be recognized by legislatures and courts in the next twenty years. The need for the protection of the community against the selfishness of a few large property owners, for instance, may bring about the creation of a municipal board representing all the people of a community as a factor in the real estate market.

A municipality in the United States may become the owner of land by gift, dedication, or devise, and may use such land for any purpose whatsoever not inconsistent with the conditions of the gift, dedication, or devise. But land or rights in land can be acquired by the municipality out of public revenue only for a specific public purpose, whether the acquisition be by purchase or by appropriation under the power of eminent domain. If the city has acquired a complete ownership in land either by purchase or appropriation, it may make any use of the land so long as that use carries out some public purpose; except in the jurisdictions where it has been held that a city has only a qualified ownership which limits its right of use to the specific purpose for which the land was acquired.

METHODS OF ACQUIRING LAND

1. ACQUISITION BY GIFT, DEDICATION, OR DEVISE

There is nothing to prevent a city from taking and holding land for other than a public purpose, provided the tax payers' money is not spent in the acquisition or holding of the land for the desired purpose. If in any specific case it were desired to grant real estate to a city for a purpose not covered in the city charter, the legislature would usually be found willing to pass enabling legislation. The character of most municipal administrations has not been promising enough to induce large holders of land to create trust estates which cities shall administer for the benefit either of all or of a certain class of their citizens; but there is nothing in legal theory which would prevent the acceptance on the part of a city, as trustee, of either real or personal property which the donor desires should be devoted to a certain use; as, for instance, to the providing of cheap and sanitary dwellings for its citizens. This is but one illustration of what might be done by the city as trustee, but the validity of any such trust would depend entirely on its administration without expense to the city.

2. ACQUISITION BY PURCHASE AND CONDEMNATION

The acquisition of land by the city for an unrestricted purpose either by gift, dedication, or devise is unusual, but its acquisition out of public revenue, for other than a public purpose either by purchase or by condemnation, is prohibited in all cities. In the latter case the city may take a fee, which is complete ownership of land, or an easement, which is the right merely to use the land for a specific purpose and one which will be interpreted as "public." These restrictions on the right to acquire land by condemnation or purchase have a decided influence on a city plan.

RESTRICTION TO A SPECIFIC USE

If land is acquired for specific purposes in accordance with a well conceived city plan, and if the terms on which it is acquired prevent its use in any manner inconsistent with these original purposes, an important safeguard is thereby set up against an ill considered abandonment of the original plan. A subsequent administration can not then sacrifice the deliberate progress made along the lines of the original plan by confiscating any of the land so acquired and diverting it to the service of some new project which may for the moment seem more important but for which the city is unable or unwilling to buy additional land. Clearly this makes for a conservative stability of purpose which is wholly in accord with the spirit of city planning.

On the other hand the normal and healthy modification of the city plan to meet new conditions may be seriously hampered by any restriction of municipal land holdings to a specific use. Owing to the great physical changes due to the growth of a city the use for which land was originally acquired may be entirely outgrown. This situation may arise when land originally transferred to the city for park or school purposes becomes absolutely unsuited for such use and useful for another public purpose or for private corporations or individuals. It is on the one hand undesirable to devote a considerable area to a use which prevents the best all-round development of the city, —commercial, industrial, and residential; it is equally undesirable to allow a decrease in park or school lands except for the best of reasons.

Cities have adopted at times a very shortsighted real estate policy. They have sold their valuable holdings at a low figure, have seen the buyer realize a tremendous profit, and have been obliged to purchase sites at a greatly increased figure when by retaining their holdings they would have had adequate land for their needs. Buildings have been planted in parks in the supposed interest of economy, and by filling up the site the building has been robbed of distinction and the people of needed open space. Such offenses against good taste and true economy, which are two of the compounds of city planning, are committed even now when the need of parks is more fully recognized by the public and is being championed by the press. This mistaken idea of economy probably explains the location of many city halls, in cities large and small, in downtown squares where open spaces should be preserved for the benefit of the community and public buildings arranged to face upon them. Worcester, Massachusetts, used part of its old common for a city hall; Philadelphia appropriated for the same purpose one of the public squares set aside by William Penn; the city hall in St. Louis occupies six acres that were once a public square; Charleston, South Carolina, whose city hall dates from early times, took for its site one of four small parks; Pittsburgh placed on land originally used as a public square two market buildings; Delaware Park, in Buffalo, has been encroached upon by an art gallery and historical building in a manner seriously impairing its value for the purposes which controlled its original acquirement; another five-acre park in Buffalo has been used in part for a school house site.

These are instances where good city building demands the protection of the original purpose through stringent limitations on municipal authority. But it would be unfortunate if park lands or any other public lands which have become unsuited for their original purpose, or which even though still suitable would block a desirable change in the city plan, could not be diverted to a new use without too great expense or delay. Some public lands are easily leased for a long term at good rentals and may thus bring in an income which, if applied to the purpose for which the lands were originally acquired, would accomplish more than the direct use of the land itself. The return from former school house property now in the retail section of Chicago swells the school funds by $637,569 every year.

The appreciation of one lot at the corner of La Salle and Adams Streets, bought for $8,750 for purposes of the water department and now occupied by the Rookery, is $2,142,000.

The trouble comes when, for instance, the plans for a new civic center, as in Cleveland, provide for a union terminal station on park land, or where Chicago wishes to locate a Field Columbian Museum in Grant Park. Controversies aroused by cases like these only after years of delay reach the supreme court for a determination of the conflicting rights of the city and the grantors or their heirs. The principles as evolved from cases that have been decided recognize clearly a distinction founded on the legal character of the ownership of the land in question.

CASE 1.—Where the city has acquired merely a right in the land, for instance a right to use the land for park purposes, and the ownership has remained in the grantor, there is a unanimity of decision that the land must be used for park purposes only, and that any other use operates to leave the land in the ownership of the original grantor free from the incumbrance of the city's use. This reversionary right may be purchased or, if necessary, condemned, since the power of eminent domain is paramount to any kind of ownership, but it must be paid for.

CASE 2.—Where the city has acquired all right, title, and interest in land by condemnation, it is the law in New York, at least, that the legislature may change the use and provide even that land formerly used as a park may be conveyed to private individuals or corporations for a private use.

In the case of Brooklyn Park Commission *vs.* Armstrong, 45 N. Y. 234, the city of Brooklyn had acquired a fee simple—absolute ownership—by condemnation to lands which were to be henceforth used as Prospect Park. Subsequently when the park plans were more fully developed it was found best to include some additional lands and exclude some of those originally acquired. The city sold one lot to the defendant, who refused to take title on the ground that the city could not convey a clear title. The court held that since the title was received in trust for an especial public purpose the city could not convey without the sanction of the legislature, but that it was within the power of the legislature to relieve the city from the trust and authorize it to sell and convey:

"Doubtless in most cases where land is condemned for a special use on the score of public utility, the sequestration is limited to that particular purpose. But this is where the property is not taken but the use only. There, the right of the public being limited to the use, when the use ceases the right ceases; when the property is taken, though a particular use may be abandoned, the right to the property remains." "The public had the right of the land in making payment, and as soon as the owner was paid he was disseised. There is no reverter." "By legislative sanction, it may be sold, be changed in its character from realty to personalty, and the avails be devoted to general or special purposes."

Cases in other jurisdictions which seem to establish a different rule, namely, that the legislature can not divert property held by a municipality in trust for one purpose to another and inconsistent purpose, will be found to depend on the language of the particular statute or to be based on the conception that the complete ownership was never in the municipality.

CASE 3.—The most perplexing situation arises where the land has been dedicated in fee for a particular public use, as for park purposes. The state of the law in this situation is by no means clear. Various state courts have come to different conclusions.

The Ohio court, in the case of Louisville and Nashville Railroad *vs.* Cincinnati, 76 Ohio St. 481, held that when a common, legal title of which was in the city in trust for its inhabitants, was no longer desired or the purpose for which it was dedicated was no longer obtainable, it would revert to the dedicator. But the Minnesota court in City of St. Paul *vs.* Chicago, Milwaukee and St. Paul Railroad, 63 Minn. 330, concluded that in attempting to divert property dedicated in fee simple for a specific purpose, the property would not revert to the dedicator but that the act of the legislature would be a mere nullity.

The most surprising decision on this point is that of South Park Commissioners *vs.* Ward, 248

Ill. 299. The case arose out of an attempt by the South Park commissioners of Chicago to locate the Field Columbian Museum in Grant Park.

The park had been dedicated forever to the use of the public by a platting in accordance with which there had been sold certain abutting lots, some of which had come into the possession of the defendants Ward *et al.* The right of the owners of the abutting lots to keep the park free from buildings was by a special statute of 1861 made enforceable by a bill in equity. Subsequent to 1893 an area many times the size of the original park was added to it by filling into Lake Michigan. The district abutting on the park had also undergone a radical change from its original residential character. The commissioners decided in 1909 to locate the museum on the addition to the park but were enjoined by Ward *et al.* The commissioners then proceeded under an act of 1903 which authorized them to condemn the rights in the park possessed by any lot owners under the original conveyance, but the petitions brought to condemn these rights were dismissed in the superior court.

In sustaining the decision the supreme court of Illinois held:

"If the legislature had no power to change the uses of Grant Park and to disregard the terms of the dedication by authorizing the erection and maintenance of buildings in the park, there could be no condemnation of the rights of the defendant that the park should be kept free from buildings whatever the nature of such rights might be."

CARRYING OUT THE CITY PLAN

This decision is a denial of the sovereign power of eminent domain as is pointed out in the strong dissenting opinion. If the legislature could appropriate by eminent domain the property comprised in Grant Park before it was dedicated, it is impossible to see why it could not do the same thing after it was dedicated. Whatever the rights of the original dedicators or their heirs or those holding contract rights under them, those rights can be taken under the power of eminent domain like any other property right in any other jurisdiction but Illinois.

To avoid legal complications in the event of a change in use it is not enough to have inserted in the original dedication "for the use of the inhabitants as a park *or for any other public use which the duly constituted authorities shall ordain.*" Even under this provision, lands held in complete ownership by the city might become so dedicated to a specific use that the public, and perhaps in some jurisdictions private interests, would gain rights which later must be condemned if the land were desired for a different public use. This was the case in State *vs.* Woodward, 23 Vt. 92. A certain town had full ownership in a piece of land which could be used for any public purpose. An uninterrupted use by the public as a public common for twenty years had been allowed by the town, and the town survey described the land as a common. The court held that these facts amounted to a dedication of the land to the public use as a common, which was irrevocable. Cities must therefore be as guarded in preserving their control of the use of property as dedicators must be in the language of their grant if they wish to avoid restricting it to a special use.

Since such restrictions may either be valuable in maintaining a consistent city plan or may seriously impair the proper flexibility of such a plan, no general rule can be laid down as to their wisdom. They have proved an important protection in the case of many raids on park property, but it would seem that at least some portion of the lands acquired by a city ought to be readily transferable from one use to another without the delay and expense imposed by such a safeguard.

THE ACQUISITION OF LAND FOR A RESERVE ACCOUNT

The procedure in condemnation and the practice in purchasing prevent a city from taking advantage of the many opportunities which it has of becoming possessor of lands at an advantageous price, even though the need for such lands may be only a few years distant. In appropriating land against the will of its owner the purpose for which the land is acquired must be specified, and that purpose is closely scrutinized in some states by a jury which must find that the acquisition is necessary before the city can take further steps. In purchasing, cities usually come into the market for land, particularly for the sites of public buildings, when prices are high, a procedure which no well conducted business corporation would adopt. Bargains in land are taken advantage of only rarely and only indirectly. It is possible to buy small areas for one purpose and later use them for another; but there is little purchasing on the part of cities for what might be called a reserve account, although a very accurate forecast can usually be made of needs for lands for various public purposes based on the direction and rate of growth of the population. Considerable areas, to be sure, may be purchased for park lands and later, by authorization from the legislature, be diverted in part to other uses, thus accomplishing the purpose by indirection; but this is a bad public policy since it makes park lands, even when they become inadequate in area, subject to unlimited inroads in favor of any and every other purpose.

How much money might be saved to the city by purchase of land at favorable opportunities in advance of actual need is apparent in any city from the increase in property values due to growth in population. The congestion commission appointed by the mayor of New York in 1911 looked into the value of 943 city sites and found that the assessed value in 1908 in 537 cases had increased in value over the price paid.

Table 1 shows the percentage of increase in the values of these sites.

PUBLIC OWNERSHIP OF LAND

TABLE 1.—INCREASE IN VALUE, FROM DATE OF ACQUISITION TO 1908, OF 537 PUBLIC SITES IN NEW YORK CITY, ACQUIRED FROM 1812 TO 1900*

Per cent of increase in value of site	Sites which increased in value as specified
Less than 25 per cent	91
25 and less than 101 per cent	154
101 and less than 201 per cent	94
201 and less than 301 per cent	42
301 and less than 401 per cent	43
401 and less than 501 per cent	17
501 and less than 601 per cent	18
601 and less than 701 per cent	10
701 and less than 801 per cent	12
801 and less than 901 per cent	10
901 and less than 1,001 per cent	6
1,001 and less than 1,501 per cent	11
1,501 and less than 2,001 per cent	10
2,001 or more	19
Total	537

The dates of acquisition of the sites considered in the table varied from 1812 to 1900. Of the 406 pieces of property which showed no increase over purchase price, 230 had been acquired since 1900.

The committee pointed out that the city could do a great deal of purchasing for its park and playground accounts, even in comparatively unsettled districts, and these holdings would have influence in the carrying out of a city plan. The same is true of the purchase of land for school

* Report of New York City Committee on Congestion of Population, p. 49 and Appendix. (Appendix is in manuscript.)

house sites. It has been very generally agreed that at least 30 square feet should be provided for every pupil registered in the city schools, but it is safe to say that very few cities have bought land to this amount. In 1905, Manhattan borough, New York City, lacked 65 acres for school houses alone on this basis. Almost 3000 acres were needed for playgrounds in boroughs outside of Manhattan, while Manhattan itself was hopelessly behind its recreation requirements. It would be a very good investment for New York as well as for any other city in the United States to buy school house sites at 43 cents a square foot, the price for which they can be bought in the borough of Richmond, instead of at $10.69 per square foot, which they cost in Manhattan.*

But it is impracticable to determine far in advance exactly which will be the best sites for schools and which for other purposes. All that can be safely said is that the total land needed for miscellaneous local uses will be at least equal to a certain minimum, and the acquirement of that minimum area by the city from time to time as favorable opportunities arise is a wise policy—provided that its ownership by the city does not withhold it for a long time from economic use pending its assignment to definite public service.

Both San Francisco and San Diego have saved considerable money by the inheritance from their Spanish founders of so-called "pueblo lands,"

*Op. cit., p. 56.

which they have in part used as parks and public building sites, in part have sold, and in part retain as an unapportioned reserve. Chicago's investments in sites on Dearborn, State, and Clark Streets are returning large dividends and would yield much more if the rentals were graduated in accordance with increasing ground values. Los Angeles is proposing to use some of its landed inheritance for a housing experiment. If its plan is carried out, the city would loan the land, and the construction and maintenance of the houses be privately financed.

Limitations in law and practice on the power of the city to acquire land are for the protection of the tax payers against official extravagance and corruption. But finance commissions have well checked many kinds of municipal waste, and they can as effectively prevent a misuse of the purchasing and condemning power. City building can undoubtedly be carried out more economically through the purchase of a reasonable amount of land by the municipality for a reserve account.

THE ACQUISITION OF LAND FOR AN ESTHETIC PURPOSE

By an amendment to the charter of the city of St. Louis in 1901, the right was given the municipal assembly of St. Louis by ordinance to "prohibit the erection or establishment or maintenance of any business house or the carrying on of any business vocation" on property fronting on a boulevard which might thereafter be opened.* By an act of the legislature of Massachusetts in 1898, buildings "now being built or hereafter to be built, rebuilt or altered" on land abutting on a public square known as Copley Square, in Boston, were limited to the height of 90 feet.† By a bill presented in the national house of representatives in 1910, the commissioners of the District of Columbia were authorized to designate certain streets or avenues within the District as Class A highways, and on such highways to establish certain special restrictions which might include the prohibition of any kind of business, and might require that buildings should be of certain height, certain materials of construction, and of such architectural design "as shall secure the beautiful and harmonious appearance, as viewed from the public streets, of all structures to be erected or altered on land to which said restrictions shall apply."‡

In all this legislation provision was made for compensation to owners for the right in land thus taken, and herein the legislation partakes of the character of ordinary eminent domain statutes. But the interference with private property which this legislation authorized is at least an unusual application of the power of eminent domain, if not an extension of it for a new purpose.

The condemnation of private property for parks, playgrounds, and boulevards has been upheld as

* See Appendix, p. 211.   † See Appendix, p. 218.
‡ See Appendix, p. 213.

justified in the exercise of the power of eminent domain, but the decisions are for the most part very careful to point out that esthetic purposes were merely incidental, allowing the inference to be drawn that the taking would not be justified for purely esthetic reasons. Under the legislation cited, developments of private property may be to a considerable extent controlled, bill-boards may be abolished, structures may be limited in height, the design of private buildings may be modified, solely in the interest of the public's sense of beauty.

The only precedent that has been cited to support the validity of the right in the public which is asserted in this legislation is the Massachusetts case of Attorney General *vs.* Williams, 174 Mass. 476, decided in 1899. This case arose under the Massachusetts statute of 1898 above cited. The defendants were owners of a building abutting on Copley Square, Boston, which had been built in violation of the statute prohibiting the construction of buildings above 90 feet in height on this square. The action was brought to restrain the maintenance of the building at the height above the statutory line. The court decided that the statute was constitutional and that the height of the building should be made to conform with the statutory provision. The language of the court has been generally interpreted to mean that rights in private land and buildings in the nature of an easement may be taken by eminent domain solely for the protection of the public's esthetic sense.*

"It hardly would be contended that the same reasons which justify the taking of land for a public park do not also justify the expenditure of money to make the park attractive and educational to those whose tastes are being formed and whose love of beauty is being cultivated. . . . It is argued by the defendants that the legislature in passing this statute was seeking to preserve the architectural symmetry of Copley Square. If this is a fact and if the statute is merely for the benefit of individual property owners, the purpose does not justify the taking of a right in land against the will of the owner. But if the legislature, for the benefit of the public was seeking to promote the beauty and attractiveness of a public park in the capital of the Commonwealth and to prevent unreasonable encroachments upon the light and air which it had previously received, we cannot say that the law-making power might not determine that this was a matter of such public interest as to call for an expenditure of public money, and to justify the taking of private property. While such a determination should not be made without careful consideration, and while the growing tendency toward an enlargement of the field of public expenditure should be jealously watched and carefully held in check, a determination of this kind once made by the legislature cannot be lightly set aside."

The court says merely that the taking of private property is justified to promote the beauty of a park and prevent encroachments on its light and air. It is very doubtful if any broader meaning

---
* See text of decision, Appendix, p. 219.

should be given to its language, but, if it is, it is believed that there have been no decisions in other jurisdictions involving the same principle. If the decision is generally followed it will be no great extension of this principle to declare constitutional the legislation previously cited which has been enacted in Missouri and proposed in Washington. It may be as clearly for the benefit of the public to promote the beauty of a street or boulevard, as is attempted by the St. Louis and Washington legislation, as to promote that of a park, which was declared to be one of the aims of the Massachusetts legislation in Attorney General *vs.* Williams. Education may so increase esthetic sentiment as to compel a general extension of the power of municipalities to interfere with the rights of owners for purely esthetic reasons, just as education compelled a judicial sanction of the right to take private property for purposes of public recreation. The framing of an esthetic test which will adequately protect the sense of beauty and still withstand the assaults of property owners, will puzzle the most astute law makers. An impartial administration of the newly sanctioned power will also be difficult. Neither of these difficulties, however, will stand in the way if the public demands a universal recognition that esthetic purposes are sufficient to justify condemnation.

CHAPTER II

THE ACQUISITION OF LAND

THE great obstacle to the execution of any plan, whether for the orderly extension of a city or for the reconstruction of its older sections, is usually the expense of acquiring the necessary land. This difficulty may arise because the cost of the land is excessive, due to bad methods of acquisition, or because the cost of land acquirement is unfairly distributed. Either or both of these conditions will place an excessive burden on the tax payers. If this cost must be borne wholly or mainly by the tax payers at large while a few land owners absorb a wholly disproportionate share of the financial benefit from the improvements, there will result a strong popular sentiment against such improvements, and a city government that is at all responsive will refuse to undertake them, even though the city as a whole may suffer for lack of them in the long run.

We are considering here only well conceived plans, the execution of which will be a real advantage to the community as a whole if the initial difficulties of financing them can be overcome. The execution of any plan which would result in a net damage or loss to a community can not properly be called an improvement. A real improvement is an investment on which the return to the community may be immediate or may be deferred.

The financial problem in acquiring land for any contemplated improvement is, therefore, in the first place, to avoid excessive cost, and in the second place, to distribute the cost in an equitable manner. To determine whether the city is paying an excessive price for land, a careful consideration of the details in condemnation procedure is essential.

PROCEDURE IN THE CONDEMNATION OF LAND

The extraordinary right of the community to take private land even against the will of the owner necessitates extraordinary protection to the individual. This protection is written into every state constitution excepting that of North Carolina, and the clause is interpreted, not as a declaration of the power of eminent domain, which is inherent in sovereignty, but as a limitation on that power. This protection is further guaranteed to the citizens of every state by the Fourteenth Amendment of the Federal Constitution. Private property can be taken for a public purpose only after "due legal process" and the payment of compensation, but the guarantee of the Federal Constitution does not compel uniformity in the provisions of all states. "Due legal process" in condemnation proceedings is satisfied by a great variety of statutory requirements, the only essential being that they shall contain provisions for determining compensation, for giving proper notice, and for hearing remonstrants. On the methods of determining these three essentials depend the simplicity and economy of condemnation procedure.

Most states give the further right to the land owner at some stage of the proceedings of having his compensation ascertained by a common law jury. In the absence of specific language to that effect it is generally held that the owner has no right to a jury in land damage cases, since at common law before 1787, in both England and America, compensation in such cases was ascertained by other tribunals without the right of appeal to a jury of twelve. Constitutions giving in general terms a right of trial by jury are interpreted to refer only to such cases as were tried by jury at the common law. Many states, however, have granted jury trials in eminent domain cases by statute, while other states have construed clauses of their constitutions as applicable to eminent domain proceedings and have allowed a jury trial.

The method of ascertaining the compensation is the first consideration of a municipality endeavoring to reduce the cost of taking land for public purposes, but the other elements of "due legal process" are responsible for much of the delay in condemnation procedure and may affect considerably the amount of compensation. Every hearing requires either a notice to property owners or legal service in hand, by mail, or by publication. After every hearing, time must be allowed for protest and appeals and the report of every hearing must be published. As the hearings grow more numerous the expense of advertising becomes a large item, and every addition to the length or complexity of the procedure involves an increase of counsel and witness fees or other legal expenses. Consequently, the elimination of any one of the steps in condemnation procedure has an important bearing on the question of reducing the size of the city's investment. We may best consider the provisions for notice and hearing together.

PROVISIONS FOR NOTICE AND HEARING

After authority has been given by the proper administrative body, the steps in condemning land for public use are notoriously many before the city can take possession of the land. Property owners are given not one day in court for the protection of their rights, but many days.

1. INITIAL PROCEEDINGS

MILWAUKEE. After the city council passes an ordinance authorizing the taking of land by eminent domain, there must be first, a finding by a jury of 12 that the taking is necessary for public use; second, a hearing before the board of public works on the question of damages; and third, there may be an appeal from this hearing to a jury which reviews the entire evidence. The following docket entries were made in a normal street opening case:

> Sept. 30, 1907, first resolution of common council referred to committee.
> Oct. 14, 1907, first resolution adopted by common council.
> Oct. 15, 1907, first resolution approved by mayor.
> Oct. 28, 1907, second resolution adopted and approved.
> Feb. 17, 1908, third resolution adopted and approved.
> May 7, 1908, proof of publication and service of resolution on land owners returned to court.
> May 16, 1908, list of owners filed.
> May 23, 1908, jury sworn and premises viewed.
> June 5, 1908, jury hears evidence and returns a verdict that the opening is a public necessity.
> July 2, 1908, papers in the case go to the board of public works for award of damages after the hearing of evidence.

Thus, in a typical Milwaukee street opening almost a year elapses before the point of beginning to ascertain compensation is reached.

LOS ANGELES.* The city council passes an ordinance of intent to take private property by eminent domain and sets out the purpose for which the land is to be taken. The ordinance is published and thirty days are given for protest,

---
* For streets, see Acts of California, 1909, Chapter 684.
For parks, see Acts of California, 1909, Chapter 697.

either against the taking or against the district which has been marked out as benefited by the improvement. A protest against the improvement from the owners of a majority of the frontage of property proposed to be taken or damaged puts an end to the proceedings, and the improvement can not be initiated again for at least six months except on petition by the owners of a majority of the frontage. Not until the protests have been disposed of can the city council proceed to pass an ordinance authorizing the filing in court of a petition for condemnation. Sixty days from the time of the passing of the ordinance are allowed for filing the petition, and the details required in the petition are such that even this time usually has to be extended. It is impossible for the city to acquire land in less than a year.

MINNEAPOLIS.* The first hearing on the question of damages under the park procedure in Minneapolis is held before five appraisers appointed by the park commissioners. The second hearing is before the park commission. At the second hearing the park commissioners consider objections to the appraisers' report on the ground either of irregularity in the proceedings or of inadequacy of the award of damages. The third hearing is before the court on the question of irregularity of the proceedings. The fourth hearing is before three appraisers appointed by the court to review the evidence and bring in a report on the question

* Special Laws of Minnesota, 1889, Chapter 30.

of damages. If this appraisal is unsatisfactory there may be even a fifth hearing before three new appraisers, but in the practice of the present counsel for the board of park commissioners, which has extended over several years, there has been only one instance of the court's granting this fifth hearing.

St. Louis. In St. Louis there is a curious anomaly making for delay. Ordinarily the findings of the eminent domain commission are taken up on appeal to a justice sitting without a jury, but a corporation is allowed to appeal to a common law jury on the question of damages although not on the question of benefit. It is not infrequent for the appeal of a single corporation to result in a jury's overthrowing the finding of the eminent domain commission in respect to one item, in which case all the work of the commission goes for nothing. A new commission must be appointed and the evidence must be entirely reviewed. A corporation has the same right in Kansas City but, by statute,* it must exercise that right before the eminent domain commissioners report, and if it elects to have its damages assessed by a jury the commissioners have no jurisdiction over that part of the case, but accept the finding of the jury and incorporate it in their own report.

Denver. In Denver, where in other details the condemnation procedure is satisfactory, there is much time wasted over the formality of notice

---

* Charter of Kansas City, 1908, Article 13, Section 12.

and hearing. After the passing of the ordinance and the formal negotiation by the mayor for the purchase, a petition is brought in the district court. Two months, at least, are required for service on residents, and a month more for publication on absent defendants. The hearing is then begun before the commissioners, who are allowed thirty days to report, but this time can be extended. Thirty days are allowed for the publication of the report and thirty days more for the filing of petitions by parties interested. These petitions are usually tried out by a common law jury, but may be heard by a jury of six. It is impossible for the city to get possession of land inside of a year and, where many property owners are involved, much more time is required.

CHICAGO. In Chicago, where land for streets is commonly dedicated without expense to the city, the only considerable taking for street purposes in the past fifteen years was in connection with the widening of Randolph Street. The docket entries show that the ordinance was passed March 16, 1903, and the petition filed in court in June of the same year. The commission was appointed in July, 1903, and finished its work in September, but the time allowed for petitions and the actual trying of these petitions by jury so delayed the proceedings that an order of possession was not issued to the city until June, 1906.*

* Original papers filed in the case.

OREGON. In contrast with the cumbersome methods illustrated above, the state code of Oregon shows the possibilities of a more direct method of condemnation procedure.* Without preliminary notice or hearing a petition is filed in court and issues may be joined within fifteen days before a common law jury, and even in cases of non-resident owners the interval between the filing of petition and the trial before the jury is not over two months. The city may come into possession of the land within two months after filing the petition, unless the court docket is crowded. Delays are occasioned chiefly because of insufficient judges.

2. APPEALS TO HIGHER COURT

Even after the award of damages is finally determined by a court sitting with or without jury, a hearing on appeal is allowed on questions of law in condemnation cases as in any other civil case. Such appeals are relatively infrequent, because the determination by the legislature that a proposed taking is for a public use is held not appealable, and because a finding of fact by the lower court on the question of damages will not be disturbed unless there is evidence of gross error or fraud. The questions that go up to the supreme court usually are:

1. Is the statutory provision under which property is condemned constitutional?

* Lord's Oregon Laws, Title XLV, Of the Condemnation of Land, Section 6859. Acts of 1909, Chapter 171.

2. What is the legal meaning of the language of the statute?

3. Have the municipal authorities strictly complied with the details of the procedure as outlined by the statute?

4. Is the rule of damages as announced in the lower court inequitable either to the city or to the land owner?

The additional expense of appeals to a court of last resort can not be avoided; but possession of land by the city should not wait on the outcome of this appeal, particularly where the only question in issue is the amount of damages. It is the law of most jurisdictions that ownership of the land passes to the city on the payment of the final judgment in the lower court.

THE TRIBUNAL

1. A SPECIAL BOARD SUBJECT TO REVIEW BY THE COURT WITH JURY

A common law jury is apt to lack the knowledge of real estate values and the experience in handling technical evidence which are important in the tribunal which is to ascertain the compensation in land damage cases, and therefore most condemnation codes provide a special tribunal. Some of the codes also see the necessity of a tribunal as far removed as possible from the influence of the parties to the suit and provide for its non-partisan appointment, usually by the court which has jurisdiction over the proceedings. There is a wide difference in the character of these judicial commissions in different cities and even in successive commissions in the same city.

DENVER. In the opinion of the city attorney's office, Denver gets excellent commissioners, or appraisers as they are called. The procedure is a semi-judicial one from the start. The petition is filed in the district court and three appraisers are appointed by the presiding justice, who endeavors to get men of the highest qualifications for this work. The bill which is submitted by the appraisers for their services is usually allowed without much question. On the average, only 15 per cent of the findings of the appraisers are appealed from. A commission was appointed in 1911 to ascertain damages in connection with the extension of the Denver park system. Property for this purpose was taken to the amount of $2,523,463, as estimated by the report of the appraisers. Of this sum $1,814,539 was paid for land taken for the site of the civic center. Considering the size of the undertaking there were very few protesting owners, and these were for the most part owners of property involved in the taking for the civic center. Out of 50 owners only 18, representing $527,428, protested against the awards, and one of these alone represented $265,000. The common law jury which heard the first protest found against the petitioners, and all the rest of the protesting owners withdrew their appeals.*

* Denver Municipal Facts, Vol. III, No. 20, p. 10.

ST. LOUIS. The same procedure as in Denver is followed in St. Louis, the three commissioners being appointed by the judge of the circuit court presiding over the case. A majority of the commissioners has full power to act and make a report. Unlike the practice in Denver, the compensation is fixed at $3.00 a day. It is not to be expected that excellent men will be attracted by such low pay, and perhaps for this reason some of the commissioners have not given satisfaction. It is reported to be not an unusual thing in cases involving less than $1,000 for the commission to take six months in reaching a decision and then to have its finding overturned on review. On the other hand, there have been notably good commissioners in cases involving heavy damages. The commissioners who sat in connection with the condemnation of the site of the municipal courts building took two days to reach a decision, although the property of 400 defendants was taken and over $1,000,000 in damages was paid. Appeals from the commissioners' findings may be taken to a common law jury only by a corporation land owner—an anomaly in procedure which we have already noticed.*

PHILADELPHIA. The municipalities of Pennsylvania in takings for street purposes replace the commission, which may be regarded as somewhat expert in the knowledge of real estate values, by a so-called "road jury" of three appointed by the judge of the court where the petition is filed.

* See page 28.

Philadelphia, with a population of 2,000,000, and the hill towns of a few hundred inhabitants, have the same procedure.

The awards of road juries are, in the opinion of the city solicitor's office, on the whole satisfactory. Excessive awards to land owners are appealed from by the city, and in a large per cent of these appeals land owners, to avoid the danger of litigation, remit some portion of the award. The following shows the total amount of awards and total remitted in Philadelphia in 1906, 1907, and 1908.

Year	Award	Remitted
1906	$1,786,785	$147,821
1907	2,273,867	118,973
1908	2,719,691	208,173

The appeal from the awards of road juries is heard by a common law jury in the superior court and results, in a considerable number of cases, in a substantial increase over the award. The report of the city law department in 1906 shows that there were 76 cases heard by a road jury in 41 of which appeals were taken. In this same year awards in 130 cases heard in the superior court were increased from $132,054, as fixed by the road jury, to $225,758. In nine cases the amount of the award remained the same and in one there was a decrease of $2,256. The reports of the law department of 1907, 1908, and 1909 do not give the whole number of cases appealed from the road jury, but in the 23 appealed cases heard in the superior court for 1907 there were increases in awards in 17 cases from $49,169 to $91,551; in the 22 appealed cases heard in the superior court for 1908 there were increases in awards in 20 cases from $61,550 to $85,877; in 1909 out of 19 cases there were increases in awards in 14 cases from $119,650 to $153,907.

It is significant that in a considerable number of the cases appealed from a road jury the evidence is heard by a referee, particularly where a large sum is in dispute, and the common law jury acts on his report. Almost half the appealed cases of 1906 were sent to a referee.

PORTLAND, OREGON. In taking land for street purposes Portland does not use the state code, the advantages of which were described on page 30, but follows the provisions of the city charter,* which prescribe a procedure much like that in Philadelphia. Its three "viewers" correspond to the Philadelphia "road jury," except that they are not appointed by the court but by a committee of the common council and usually for political reasons. The result is that a body of professional viewers has developed who are peculiarly open to the charge that their findings may be influenced by the political strength of the parties to the proceeding. The report of the viewers goes to the city council which usually adopts it as the easiest course to pursue. At any time within twenty days from the confirmation of the report of the viewers by the council, an appeal may be made to

* Charter of Portland, Chapter VI, Section 348 ff.

the court sitting with jury, the only questions open to appeal being the amount of damages and, where assessments for benefit are also made, the amount of the assessment. Since any number of persons may join in the appeal the proceeding is so complicated that the jury is ordinarily glad to confirm the report as a whole and avoid the rather difficult task of revising it. Two out of three recent cases had that result.

There are two types of commission which for convenience will be placed in this group, though they differ essentially from the Denver and St. Louis commissions. The first is illustrated by the street commissioners in Boston, or the board of public works in Milwaukee; the second, by the Chicago commission specially appointed under the local improvement act. Like judicially appointed commissions, those of Boston and Milwaukee conduct hearings, but unlike judicially appointed commissions they sit as arbiters in a case in which they, as representing the city in the capacity of administrative bodies, are interested parties.

BOSTON. In proceedings for the condemnation of land needed for streets, and for school houses and other public buildings in Boston, awards of damages are made by the street commissioners after public hearing. The street commissioners are elected for three years and receive a fixed salary. There may be much or little significance in the fact that appeals are frequent from the awards of this elected commission which is apt to be regarded as closely allied with the city administration. Before the jury the city undoubtedly is handicapped by the fact that the awards of damages have been made by a department of the city administration sitting as a tribunal in a cause in which the city is an interested party. The number of appeals from the findings of the Boston street commission compares very unfavorably with those from the St. Louis and Denver judicially appointed commissions, or even with the Indianapolis park commission, a board which, like the Boston street commission, is a department of the city administration. The different result in Indianapolis may be due altogether to the strong demand for the completion of the park system and to the conviction in the minds of land owners that parks create land values; but contributing factors to this result are doubtless, first, the strictly nonpartisan character of the Indianapolis commission, which serves without compensation, and its reputation for fair dealing; second, the elimination of the jury in cases appealed from the park commission; and third, the assessment of the cost of land taking on the property specially benefited, which compels the interest of the land owner "specially benefited" in every verdict for land damages and makes appeals to increase verdicts extremely unpopular.

Data in 35 proceedings for street openings, widenings, and relocations in Boston, taken at random from the records of the last fifteen years, show that in 31 cases the awards of the street commissioners were not accepted by the owners. In 28 of these cases there were 1,065 parties to the proceedings, of whom 462 refused to accept awards. Approximately 175 of these claims for additional compensation were settled by the street commissioners, 287 were entered in court and either tried by jury or settled by the law department. Thus 26 per cent of all owners interested in the proceedings appealed to a common law jury and a considerable portion of these appeals were actually tried. Complete figures were obtained from the records of the street commissioners in 12 proceedings and are given in the following table:

TABLE 2.—DAMAGES AWARDED, PARTIES INVOLVED, CLAIMS FOR INCREASE, AND CLAIMS COMPROMISED OR SETTLED, IN 12 PROCEEDINGS FOR STREET IMPROVEMENTS. BOSTON, 1895 TO 1913

Location of improvement	Amount of damages awarded	Parties involved	Claims for increase	Claims settled by street commissioners
Huntington Ave..	$230,353	58	34	26
Audubon Rd.	26,472	1	1	..
Columbus Ave.	926,986	177	122	92
Boylston St..	10,039	8	7	..
Brighton Ave.	103,165	26	26	23
South Huntington Ave.	56,195	11	1	..
Dorchester St.	307,193	52	5	5
Walter St.	6,000	33	14	6
Brookline Ave.	26,000	20	9	2
Tremont St..	12,000	25	8	1
Cambridge St.	30,000	25	12	..
Queensbury St.	112,904	7	6	..
Total .	$1,847,307	443	245	155

MILWAUKEE. Although in Milwaukee the board of public works is the tribunal before which evidence is presented on the question of damages on account of the taking of property for public purposes, a finding that a taking proposed is necessary and that the purpose is a public one must be made by a jury of twelve men before the case gets to the board of public works. From the awards of the board of public works appeal is allowed to a common law jury, but in the last eight years every appeal has been settled before the case reached trial. It may be said in this connection that there have been no very extensive takings for either street or park purposes.

CHICAGO. The second type of commission is provided for in the procedure for street improvements in Chicago. Like the Denver and St. Louis commissions, it is judicially appointed but is more in the nature of a board of advisory experts to the jury, since its report is made without a hearing and on the basis of its own appraisal of valuations. The court frequently follows the suggestion of the city attorney in making the appointments to this commission. The report of the commission is filed in court, summonses are immediately issued to all persons whose land is damaged or taken, and the trial proceeds before a common law jury. There have been so few cases of takings for street openings, widenings, and extensions in Chicago that the data are insufficient to form the basis for an opinion as to the merit of the Chicago method of ascertaining compensation. The only proceeding that has involved considerable land taking within the past twenty years was the widening of Randolph Street, in which case the work of the commission was on the whole well done, if judged by the result of the review by the court. Many owners were concerned in that proceeding, but the finding of the commissioners as to compensation for land taken or damaged was increased only from $314,000 to $367,000, and the finding of the commissioners that there "was no public benefit" and that, therefore, the total expense of the improvement should be assessed on private owners was not altered on appeal. For their services in this case, the commissioners received $1,000 each.

2. A COURT WITH JURY HAVING ORIGINAL JURISDICTION

Although an appointed commission is more likely to consider intelligently the evidence and to come to a fairer conclusion than if the proceedings are brought directly before a jury, this advantage may be more than offset and the preliminary hearing be a waste of time if the commission's findings are overturned by an inexperienced jury of twelve men. It is therefore not surprising to find in several jurisdictions where the right to a jury is granted in eminent domain cases that the expense of a first hearing before a commission is entirely eliminated. This is so in the state codes of Louisiana, Ohio, Washington, and

California. In the city of Chicago for some public purposes, and in Portland, Oregon, for all public purposes except street openings, widenings, and extensions, the same procedure is followed.

CLEVELAND. In Ohio, the procedure in appropriating land for all public purposes is regulated by the state law.* When an ordinance authorizing the appropriation of land is passed by a two-thirds vote of the common council of any city, the city solicitor makes application to the court of common pleas, to a judge in vacation, to the probate court, or to the insolvency court, for the appointment of a jury to award compensation, giving five days' notice of such application to the owners of property affected by the ordinance. The judge applied to sets a time for the hearing of evidence by the jury and the trial proceeds as in other civil actions. Appeal lies from the finding of the jury, but the right to take and use the property condemned is not affected by the appeal. Upon payment of the judgment or upon depositing the money in court, a fee simple vests in the city unless a lesser estate is asked for in the ordinance of appropriation.

In Cleveland, when the state insolvency court was legislated out of existence by operation of the federal bankruptcy law, that court took over jurisdiction in juvenile and condemnation cases. The docket of the court is not overcrowded and a speedy trial is assured in every case. So rarely

* General Code of Ohio, Section 3677 ff.

have the offers made by the city been exceeded by the jury's findings that owners have learned the economy of accepting the city's offer in the first instance and avoiding the delay and expense incident to litigation. The result is that less than one-tenth of the land needed for public purposes is acquired by condemnation procedure.

CHICAGO. Chicago gets practically all of its sites for school houses by condemnation. The offer of the school board to purchase land desired is hardly more than formal, and on its rejection the petition for condemning the land is brought immediately in court and evidence of the value of the site is presented directly to the jury. This method has been in use for some years and counsel for the board, who has served during the history of this method of procedure, is convinced that the city is in substantially as advantageous a position as a private buyer. During the past five years (1907–1912), with an average of at least 20 cases a year, the jury has, with practically no exception, accepted the valuation of the site as fixed by the law department of the school board. Settlements with property owners have consequently been much more common. Ten years ago 90 per cent of the cases involving condemnation for school purposes in Chicago were tried through to a verdict. Today more than 90 per cent are settled and subsequent proceedings are merely formal, to perfect the title.

THE ACQUISITION OF LAND

SAN FRANCISCO.* In San Francisco, too, the procedure is begun by filing a complaint and issuing summonses thereon in the superior court. If the owners affected by the process do not demand a trial by jury it is waived and three appraisers are appointed by the court to ascertain the compensation. In practice, however, more than 80 per cent of the land needed in San Francisco for public purposes is acquired directly by deed from the owners without resort to condemnation procedure.

3. A COURT WITHOUT JURY HAVING ORIGINAL OR APPELLATE JURISDICTION

NEW YORK.† When the board of estimate and apportionment of New York City authorizes the taking of land for street or park purposes, application is made to the supreme court for the appointment of three commissioners of estimate and assessment, to determine the compensation to owners and to assess as damages the cost of the proposed improvement, or such a proportion thereof as the board of estimate and apportionment directs, on lands deemed specially benefited. After hearing evidence an abstract of the report of the three commissioners or of a majority of them is filed in court at least thirty days before being presented formally to the court for confirmation, in order that petitions in writing against the

---

* California Code of Civil Procedure, paragraph 1243 ff.
Acts of California, 1909, Chapter 684.
† Greater New York Charter as amended in 1901, Section 970 ff.

confirmation of the report may be filed. The court gives a public hearing to remonstrants who have filed their written objections, and confirms or modifies the report, or in some cases sends it back to a new commission. The commissioners are directed by the statute to complete their work within six months unless granted an extension by the court for good cause. Their compensation is $10 a day.

This procedure was long regarded as unsatisfactory. In 1911 it was characterized by the New York press as "inordinately expensive," because of the financial interest of the commissioners in protracting the proceedings; "generally inefficient," because of the many incompetent commissioners selected for political reasons; and open to "flagrant abuse," because the commissioners thus selected were likely to favor property owners who had political influence. By the adoption of a constitutional amendment at the general election November 4, 1913, the legislature is permitted to pass an act which will give to a justice of the supreme court the power to dispose of all matters concerning condemnation formerly in the hands of the commissioners of estimate and assessment.* In the opinion of the corporation counsel, Archibald R. Watson, "A justice of the supreme court with undivided responsibility, with no interest to prolong the proceedings,

---

* Amendment to Constitution of New York, Section 7, Article 1. For text see Appendix, p. 248.

not susceptible to influence and generally of high grade character and capacity, should be able to dispose of condemnation matters with results far preferable than by means of commissioners."

MINNEAPOLIS. We have already described the procedure in appropriating lands for park purposes in Minneapolis up to the time of the confirmation of the awards by the district court.* The results are on the whole quite satisfactory. The appraisers are usually competent men and, although appeals are taken from their awards as confirmed by the board of park commissioners to the district court sitting without jury, the percentage of such appeals is not large, not more than 15 per cent in any proceeding, and the increase in awards on appeal is often merely nominal and rarely more than 20 per cent. There seems, however, little justification for two preliminary hearings, one before the appraisers and one before the park commissioners, on the question of land awards. The appraisal could as well be done by the park commissioners through the agency of a competent clerical force, as in Indianapolis, and the expense of appraisals and reappraisals would be avoided.

KANSAS CITY. In Kansas City, Missouri, the petition for taking land for street purposes is brought in the municipal court which sits with a jury of six appointed by the presiding justice.†

* See p. 27.
† Charter of Kansas City, 1909, Article 6, Section 1 ff.

The verdict of the jury is confirmed by the common council of the city and appeals are allowed to the circuit court. In practice not more than 25 per cent of such actions are appealed from the municipal court. In the newer procedure for the taking of land for park purposes a saving of both time and expense, by eliminating the preliminary trial in the municipal court, is brought about by allowing the petition to be filed directly in the circuit court.* As in St. Louis, a corporation is allowed a hearing on the question of damages for land taken before a common law jury, but in Kansas City corporations do not demand common law juries. When the procedure was new, a corporation tried the experiment and the result was so disastrous that it is said never to have been attempted since. Presiding justices both in the municipal and circuit courts take care to appoint competent men. That satisfactory jurors can be obtained for $2.50 a day, which is the compensation allowed, is ample evidence that jury service in these cases is regarded as a civic duty and not as a desirable "job."

INDIANAPOLIS. In Indianapolis the board of public works in takings for street purposes, and the board of park commissioners in takings for park purposes, have the same duties which in Kansas City are performed by a jury of six men. All objections to the taking, awards for damages, and the size of the specially benefited area as

* Charter of Kansas City, 1909, Article 13, Section 8 ff.

marked out by the commissioners, are disposed of in one hearing.* From the findings of the commissioners appeal lies directly to the circuit or superior court sitting without jury, and the amount of the judgment as found on appeal is final. The businesslike practice which has been adopted by the park commission under the act of 1909, appeals to the sense of fairness of the property owner and has proved most helpful in arriving at awards. In every taking the park board has the assistance of real estate experts as an advisory committee, and is kept in close touch with valuations by a complete card catalogue system which registers the actual consideration in transfers of property.

Although the act is only three years old, there has been at least one considerable taking in each park district. In the North Park there have been two, one involving an expense of $154,420 and the other $131,662. In all the takings for park purposes under the new act involving over $600,000 worth of property and several thousand owners, there have been only four appeals from the findings of the board, two of which have been decided by the superior court. In one an award of $10,000 was increased to $17,000 and in the other an award of $6,925 was increased to $9,800. In one proceeding alone there were 1,600 owners involved and only 50 were present at the hearing given remonstrants.†

* Acts of Indiana, 1911, Chapter 231, Sections 17 and 19.
† Records of Indianapolis Park Commissioners.

CONCLUSIONS

The New York constitutional amendment provides the simplest method of ascertaining compensation. Owners of land are given one day in court in which all questions concerning the regularity of procedure and the amount of compensation are determined. There is in such a procedure the least chance for waste of time or money in preliminary hearings, and all the responsibility for decisions is put on the justice who presides in the case. But no judicial decision has sufficiently tested whether the land owner's rights are properly safeguarded. The procedure in Indianapolis has had the advantage of a thorough testing. Its results are satisfactory enough both to the city and to the land owner to recommend its adoption in any jurisdiction contemplating a change in procedure. But where a common law jury is prescribed by the constitution the adoption of the Indianapolis procedure in its entirety would not be possible without a constitutional amendment. No comment is necessary to emphasize the difficulty of passing such an amendment, and there is considerable question whether it would be necessary or expedient in the light of experience in Chicago and Cleveland where the awards of common law juries have been fair both to the municipality and to property owners.

The worst that can be said of the jury in condemnation cases is that in some jurisdictions it has a lively prejudice against the city as a petitioner in eminent domain cases. The opinion is also generally held by those who have had experience in the presentation of evidence to a jury that the usual uncertainty in a jury's findings in any civil case is only increased by the technical nature of the evidence presented in condemnation cases. The jury is asked to estimate land values without having had any previous experience. It must depend entirely on its view of the premises and on the opinion of real estate experts for its decision. About all a fairminded jury can do in such cases beyond striking a mechanical average of the widely divergent expert testimony is to discount the several claims in proportion to the impression made upon the jury by the individual experts,—and the jury is asked to measure the relative elasticity of conscience of experts after a too meager character study.

Where condemnation cases must continue to be tried before a jury, the important question in revising methods of procedure is whether there is any advantage in a preliminary hearing, either before a permanent board or before a board specially appointed for each case. From the data which we have just reviewed it is obvious that however excellent the preliminary tribunal, it results in increased cost and delay in those cases where its findings are not accepted by the land owners. But it is just as clear, first, that before a preliminary tribunal well constituted and acting under favorable conditions, the procedure is simpler and less expensive; second, that appeals from its findings are few; and third, that not infrequently its awards are sustained on appeal. Thus the preliminary hearing at its best has the positive merit of being the means in a great majority of cases of a large saving in time and expense, and, even in cases that are appealed, of influencing the jury's verdict. In jurisdictions where preliminary boards are unsatisfactory, changes in method of appointment or in minor details should be tried before the principle of a preliminary hearing is condemned. If the tribunal has a political bias or is too closely affiliated with either of the parties to the proceeding, it should be replaced by a strictly non-partisan tribunal appointed by the court. A tribunal of permanent tenure is likely to handle cases with more dispatch, because of longer experience, than one appointed for each case. A properly paid tribunal is a surer guarantee of competent service than one paid an entirely inadequate sum or one induced to prolong its deliberations by a per diem compensation.

Whatever reason may justify the continuance of commissioners in eminent domain cases is not applicable to procedure in Philadelphia and other cities and towns of Pennsylvania and in Portland, Oregon. There seems to be no good reason for allowing damages to be ascertained in the first instance by a jury indifferently qualified to pass upon the evidence and then to have the same evidence reviewed by a larger jury that is if anything less qualified to reach a fair verdict.

Even where it can be shown that awards of commissions of acknowledged excellence are generally appealed from and are increased by a jury on appeal, the reform that is needed is likely to be more fundamental than the abolition of the commission. A very large factor in determining the attitude both of the general tax payer and of the owner of land, and consequently in determining the number of appeals from a commission's findings and the advantage or disadvantage of the city's position before a common law jury, is the method of distributing the cost of an improvement. A summary of these methods in several jurisdictions should, therefore, indicate ways and means to reduce the initial investment of capital in the land required for an improvement, the problem which has just been considered, as well as the way of providing capital, which will be discussed in the next chapter.

CHAPTER III

THE DISTRIBUTION OF THE COST OF LAND ACQUIREMENT

CITIES may pay for improvements as they go along, appropriating the funds out of the general tax levy, or they may make special issues of bonds from time to time, and draw upon the general tax levy gradually for the interest charges and the redemption of the bonds. The income applicable to improvements derived from the tax levy, both directly and through the sale of bonds payable out of the tax levy, is likely to prove inadequate in almost any city in the United States, since a limit to the borrowing ability of a city is usually fixed in the state constitution at from 2 per cent to 10 per cent of its assessed valuation, and the amount available from taxation is just as effectively limited by the inelasticity of the tax rate above a certain figure. The most obvious way out of the financial difficulty is to remove the limitation on borrowing power, and there are precedents for this in nearly every progressive city. It is in fact the usual thing when comprehensive plans are proposed involving considerable financing, for the legislature to allow a bond issue and provide that it shall not be reckoned in determining the amount of the municipal indebtedness.

DEVICES EQUIVALENT TO BORROWING OUTSIDE THE DEBT LIMIT

The city of Milwaukee employs a somewhat different expedient in stretching its borrowing ability. The constitution of the state of Wisconsin allows cities to incur indebtedness up to 5 per cent of their valuation,* provided that the bond issue is approved by the people at a special election. Counties are also given the right to become indebted up to 5 per cent of their valuation and no approval of the people is required. These provisions give Milwaukee the right practically to borrow money up to 10 per cent of its assessed valuation, since most of the county's valuation is included within the city's limits. Improvements are construed whenever possible to be county improvements in order to give the city a greater borrowing power and avoid the submission of the bond issue to the people.

But Milwaukee and other cities of Wisconsin have also worked out a method of purchase of land by contract, which amounts really to purchase on the instalment plan, as a further relief from the exigencies of the financial situation. The same practice is sanctioned by legislation in Minnesota and is employed at least in Minneapolis.

* Constitution of Wisconsin, Article XI, Section 3.

This method is useful where a city is close up to its limit of indebtedness. The legislation of both states specifically provides that the contract shall not create a corporate liability or constitute a pledge of the general credit of the city. In construing this language the supreme court in both states has held that there is no obligation on the part of the city to meet unpaid instalments, since the city has merely an option to purchase, with the right of possession till default in payment.*

It was argued in Burnham *vs.* Milwaukee, 98 Wis. 128, that a land contract was merely a scheme to evade the constitutional limitation on municipal indebtedness, but the supreme court sustained the contract, holding that in spite of the weight and persuasiveness of the argument the legal meaning of the statute was definite and could not be twisted or enlarged. Its conclusion was, "that the unpaid instalments upon the park land contracts do not constitute a corporate indebtedness within the meaning of the constitution because the payment thereof is entirely optional on the part of the city." To the same effect are Perrigo *vs.* Milwaukee, 92 Wis. 236; Milwaukee *vs.* Milwaukee County, 95 Wis. 424; and in Minnesota, Kelley *vs.* City of Minneapolis, 63 Minn. 125.

Cities often have opportunities to secure a tract of land at a low figure subject to immediate ac-

---

*Acts of Wisconsin, 1891, Chapter 179, Section 8. Special laws of Minnesota, 1889, Chapter 30, Section 2.

ceptance of the offer. The offer will not stand until a bond issue, which must be submitted to popular vote, has been secured, and the amount of such an issue might increase the indebtedness beyond the limit of the borrowing power. In such an emergency the cities of Wisconsin and Minnesota may enter into a contract with the owners of land, paying 5 per cent of the purchase price at the date of contract and the balance in annual instalments. A piece of land costing $100,000 may be paid for by an initial instalment of $5,000 and 19 annual instalments of $5,000 each. In providing for these payments, the city issues bonds each year, bearing 4 per cent interest, the issues being for twenty years, of which 5 per cent is redeemed each year. The amount of each bond issue is made up of the annual instalment of $5,000 and the interest on the balance of the purchase price at 4 per cent. The last bond in the issue will be redeemed forty years after the purchase of the land. Each year the amount required for sinking fund and interest charges on each annual bond comes out of the tax levy.

There are several advantages in the contract method of paying for land: First, the payment is distributed over forty years without the necessity of legislative sanction for a long term bond; second, desirable tracts of land may be purchased at any time during the year at an advantageous price and the city is not compelled to wait for the time-wasting formality incident to bond issues;

third, the city's borrowing power is in effect considerably extended.

Leaving out of consideration financially self-sustaining municipal investments, like many municipal water works, which are usually reckoned apart from the municipal debt and which do not impose a burden upon the tax payers as such, the temporary relief from financial difficulties secured as above described, by extending the limit of a city's borrowing power or by expedients such as the contract method of paying for land, leaves the ultimate burden on the municipality and substantially distributes it over the whole of the taxable property of the city in accordance with valuation. Conservative policy will never allow a very great stretching of the debt limit, and any considerable increase beyond the customary annual tax rate is bitterly resisted. Sources of municipal revenue other than the general property tax are practically negligible in this connection in American cities. It is therefore very important to relieve the general tax payer of a portion of the cost of public improvements wherever they can be found to be of so much special benefit to the owners of a limited area as to justify a special assessment.

SPECIAL ASSESSMENTS

1. DEFINITION

"A special assessment is a compulsory contribution paid once for all to defray the cost of a special improvement to property undertaken in the public interest and repaid to the government in proportion to the special benefits accruing to the property named."*

Though a special assessment is an exercise of the taxing power, it differs from a tax in two particulars: First, the nature of a special assessment makes it a charge for a real benefit to property and one which can be more or less accurately measured in money values; second, it has been almost uniformly held by judicial decisions that special assessments need not conform to the constitutional requirement that taxation shall be equal and uniform.

The equity of this species of taxation is defended on the theory that the individuals of the community whose holdings have been made more valuable by the expenditure of the community's money should repay at least some portion of that outlay. Specific application of the principle may produce an unfair result. If an assessment for street improvement is figured by the front foot, it is unfair to the man with a long, shallow lot. If it is levied in accordance with the area of lots, it is unfair to the land with much depth and small frontage. It is impossible to devise any method of taxation which distributes the financial burden automatically with perfect and indisputable justice. If a lot which was worth $1,000 before a public improvement can be sold for $1,100 after

* *Quarterly Journal of Economics*, April, 1893.

it, and if the lot is assessed any amount up to $100, the method of arriving at this amount is immaterial, since the result is just enough.

2. HISTORY

A special assessment law enacted for New York City in 1691 is said to be the first true special assessment law in the United States, and to have been based on a law passed in 1667 to aid the rebuilding of London after the great fire of 1666.* This law of 1667 was one of three special assessment laws enacted in Great Britain before 1900 and their use was very infrequent. But in 1658 the general court of Massachusetts appointed a committee "to lay out the way through Roxbury lots to Boston farms, and to judge what is meet satisfaction to the proprietors for the way, and that they have power to impose an equal part upon all such of Boston or other towns as shall have benefit of such way."† Whatever may have been the origin of the principle, because of its general use and extensive development in the United States it is recognized even in Great Britain as an "American device."

The New York law of 1691 assessed the cost of street pavements and sewers on the property specially benefited, in proportion to the benefits received. Pennsylvania passed a similar law in 1700: "To defray the charge of pitching, paving,

---

* Colonial Laws of New York, Vol. I, pp. 269–271.
† 4 Massachusetts Colonial Records, Part I, p. 327.

graveling, and regulation of said streets . . . each inhabitant was to pay, in proportion to the number of feet of his lots . . . . adjoining, on each or either side of the said streets."* Massachusetts in 1709 and 1761 provided that "Persons receiving any benefit from common sewers, either direct or remote, were obliged to pay such proportional part of making or repairing the same as should be assessed to them by the Selectmen of the towns."† The old New York law was little used until 1787 when it was amended and made somewhat more definite.‡

The adoption of the principle was extensive after the war of 1812. The following dates indicate about the time when the legislation was passed in different states and territories, the dates usually indicating the incorporation of the principle in the charter of some city, followed usually by court decisions in the main upholding the assessment. The active use of the special assessment principle may be considered as dating in New York from 1813; Kentucky, 1813; Michigan, 1827; Pennsylvania, 1832; Louisiana, 1832; New Jersey, 1836; Ohio, 1836; Illinois, 1837; Maryland, 1838; Connecticut, 1843; Wisconsin, 1846; Indiana, 1846; Mississippi, 1846; California, 1850; Oregon, 1851; Missouri, 1853; Rhode Island, 1854; Iowa, 1855; Delaware,

* Cited in Hammett *vs*. Philadelphia, 65 Pa. St. 158.
† Ancient Charters of Massachusetts, pp. 389, 651.
‡ Tenth Session Laws of New York, Chapter 88, p. 544.

1857; Kansas, 1864; Massachusetts, 1865; District of Columbia, 1865; Virginia, 1866; Vermont, 1868; West Virginia, 1868; Minnesota, 1869; New Hampshire, 1870; Texas, 1871; Maine, 1872; Nebraska, 1873; Florida, 1877; Georgia, 1881; Nevada, 1881; Washington, 1883; Alabama, 1885; North Carolina, 1887; North Dakota, 1887; South Dakota, 1887; Montana, 1887; Idaho, 1887; Wyoming, 1887; Utah, 1888; Colorado, 1889; Oklahoma, 1890; North Mexico, 1891; Arizona, 1893.[*]

In early times special assessments were most frequently used only to defray the cost of construction of improvements, but the language of the first Massachusetts act is broad enough to allow also an assessment to cover the cost of land acquirement. It is only the use of special assessments to defray the cost of land acquirement with which we are concerned in the present survey, although a special assessment for a more restricted purpose is based on the same principle.

3. SPECIAL ASSESSMENTS IN ACQUIRING LAND FOR PARK PURPOSES

It is generally agreed that parks judiciously acquired in a city are a benefit to the whole community, but the use of some of them, especially of small parks, is confined almost wholly to the people of the locality in which they occur, while other

---

[*] Theory and Practice of Special Assessments. Transactions. American Society of Civil Engineers, Vol. 38. Paper 817.

parks, especially the large ones, may be used by people from all parts of the city.

It is also a real estate axiom that residence property contiguous to parks commands a higher price, other things being equal, than similar property several blocks away. We should therefore expect the cost of park acquisition to be distributed, first, by an assessment on such property as really receives a special increase in value because of the nearness of the park; and second, either by assessment on a much larger area assumed to include practically the whole public served by the park as a local institution, or else by general taxation on the whole city.

In the case of small parks, it is logical and fair to subdivide a large city into local "park districts" or "improvement districts" and to make each district pay for its own local park. This practice is not only fair but extremely salutary. It forces a clearer understanding of what each dollar of the tax payer's money has gone to secure, thus checking a loose extravagance in the acquirement of park lands, and at the same time makes it possible for a progressive and prosperous locality which is in need of parks to proceed with their acquirement unhampered by the resistance of other parts of the city which are satisfied with the existing situation or are really unable to afford further taxation for park purposes. The principle is the same as that which justifies the subdivision of a state into municipalities for the localization of taxes required for local purposes, and it becomes more and more important, as the size of municipal units is increased, for dealing with affairs that affect large groups of contiguous communities having many conflicting interests.

But although the amount and kind of benefit resulting from large and small parks is about the same in all cities similarly situated, the practice in paying for the cost of park areas shows the greatest divergence. It is usual in the United States to assess no part of the cost of acquiring park lands on property specially benefited. In some cities the law does not permit such assessment. In other cities the assessment is made in so limited a way as to give the community little relief from the financial burden. In several cities, notably Seattle and Portland of the western cities, and Baltimore in the east, which assess private property very liberally for street improvement, including the cost of land takings, there is no assessment for the acquisition of land for parks.

In the cities of Ohio, it was illegal up to 1912 to raise the cost of land acquired by condemnation by a special assessment. The case that establishes this law in Ohio is City of Dayton *vs.* Bauman, 66 Ohio St. 379. In that case the city appropriated land for the extension of two streets and assessed the cost on abutting lots. In deciding against the validity of the assessment the court based its decision entirely on Section 19, Article I of the Ohio constitution, holding that a special assessment was an indirect method of evading that constitutional limitation. This section provides:

"Private property shall ever be held inviolate, but subservient to the public welfare . . . where private property shall be taken for a public use, a compensation therefor shall first be made in money, or first secured by deposit of money, and such compensation shall be assessed by a jury without deduction for benefits to any property of the owner."

The court said:

"The limitation of Section 19 goes to the full extent of prohibiting the assessment of compensation, damages and costs of land appropriated upon any real estate whatever. In short, money cannot be raised by assessment to pay such compensation, damage and costs, but such money must be raised by taxation. The *public* appropriate land for *public* use, and the *public* must pay. Nothing less than the *public* can appropriate lands by legal process for *public* use. If an assessment district should be formed and a petition filed by such district to appropriate private property for the use of such district, or the public, a demurrer to such petition would be sustained on the ground that the constitution gives no power of appropriation of private property to such assessment district, such district not being the public and the power of appropriation being given by Section 19 by the public only.

"The power of appropriation being given to the public only and only for the public use, it follows that the *public*, the taker, must pay for what it takes, because he who takes from another should himself make restitution, not compel others to pay for what they have not taken."

CARRYING OUT THE CITY PLAN

The language of the decision is given since it is believed to be the most pointed judicial expression of the chief argument against the validity of special assessments. It is in substance a decision that a tax, unless uniformly levied, amounts to an illegal taking of private property. In this respect the decision is contra to the great weight of authority in the United States.

In 1912 the people of Ohio ratified the following constitutional amendment which makes the law of Ohio uniform with that of the rest of the country:

"Section 11. Any municipality appropriating private property for a public improvement may provide money therefor in part by assessments upon benefited property not in excess of the special benefits conferred upon such property by the improvements. Said assessments, however, upon all the abutting, adjacent, and other property in the district benefited, shall in no case be levied for more than fifty per centum of the cost of such appropriation."*

In Missouri we find St. Louis making no special assessment for the cost of taking park lands, but in the same state Kansas City assesses the entire cost of park acquisition on the land specially benefited.

In Massachusetts, since 1882, park commissioners have been allowed to assess an amount not exceeding one-half of the special benefit, but no

* Constitution of Ohio, with Amendments proposed by Constitutional Convention of 1912, Article XVIII, Section 11.

assessment can be laid upon any land except such as abuts on a park or on a way bounded by a park.* Whether because of official inertia, or because of the ineffectiveness of the legislation due to its cumbersome machinery or to the limitation on the assessment area, special assessments have been rarely levied. Inquiry in ten of the largest cities in the state shows that only in two has there been any use of this power, and that quite infrequent. In takings by the Metropolitan Park Commission of Massachusetts, the practice is to levy no assessment; but where owners are compensated for land taken or damaged, the amount of their compensation is reduced by the amount representing the special benefit to the land remaining by reason of the improvement. Owners whose land is not taken may be equally benefited, but the benefit is not assessed.

The New York practice shows interesting changes from the time of the acquisition of Central Park to the present. Both the creation of Central Park in 1853 and of Prospect Park, Brooklyn, in 1865 were considered to benefit property in the vicinity, and that benefit was held to diminish with the distance from the park. Of the entire land cost of Central Park, $1,657,590, or 32 per cent, was assessed on property specially benefited, and the assessment was collected in one instalment. Of the entire cost of Prospect Park,

* Acts of Massachusetts, 1882, Chapter 154, Section 7.

$1,236,655, or 38.5 per cent, was assessed on private property specially benefited.

The report of the park commissioners for 1867 does not give the valuation of the property in the area assessed because of special benefit due to the creation of Prospect Park, and it is now possible only to approximate the proportion of increase in value which the special assessment represented. Roughly, the special assessment district in the Prospect Park case included 30 per cent of the area of ward 8, 12 per cent of ward 9, and 20 per cent of ward 20. The value of the assessed portion of ward 8 in 1865 has been reckoned at 30 per cent of the entire valuation of the ward, or at $1,200,000. The increase in value in the area assessed in ward 8 is estimated to be 400 per cent as against an increase in value of 100 per cent in other parts of the city since 1865. At this rate its assessed value in 1905 would be $6,000,000; estimated value at the ratio of increase of the rest of the city, $2,400,000; increase in value assumed to be largely due to the improvement, $3,600,000. Since the entire assessment over the three wards was only $1,236,655, we may conclude with due allowance for inflation of values and inaccuracy of estimates that the special assessment was not in excess of the special benefit to the property.*

The figures for Central Park are even more

* Report of the Chief Engineer of the Board of Estimate and Apportionment, October 19, 1907, pp. 15 ff.

·striking. Value of land assessed for benefit (half the valuation of wards 12, 19, and 22), $13,250,-000; estimated value of land of this same area in 1873, $118,000,000; estimated value at the ratio of increase of the rest of the city at 100 per cent, $26,500,000; increase in value due to the improvement, $91,500,000; amount of special assessment, $1,657,590. Here, too, the valuations are probably inflated and the estimate of the valuation of assessed property is no better than a rough guess, but the margin of increase over the special assessment is wide enough to justify the conclusion that land owners were not unfairly burdened by the share of the cost of the improvement levied against their property.*

From the consolidation of Greater New York under the charter of 1901 to the year 1907, there was a legal reason for the city assuming the entire cost of acquiring title to parks, since a resolution of a "local improvement board" was considered necessary before any part of the expense of acquiring land could be assessed as a special benefit on a local district. The decision of the court of appeals of March 5, 1907, seems to change the impression in this regard. The case was Rose Reis *vs.* City of New York,† which is held to have decided that the board of estimate and apportionment has the right to initiate local improvements and to provide for the assessment of their cost

* Op. cit. pp. 20 ff.
† Rose Reis *vs.* City of New York, *et al.*, 188 N. Y. 58.

against property deemed to have received a special benefit. Following this decision the board of estimate and apportionment resolved that property specially benefited by parks should be assessed for their cost. Previous to that time requests for parks frequently had come from local sources, and the first striking result of the action of the board was the falling off in such requests.

Legislation of 1911 gives full recognition to the benefit theory by allowing the board of estimate and apportionment to determine what portions of the costs of park lands shall be paid by the city of New York, what proportion by one or more boroughs, or parts of one or more boroughs, and what proportions by owners whose land is particularly benefited.*

In Minneapolis the board of park commissioners determines what percentage, if any, of the amount required for the acquisition of land for park purposes shall be assessed on the land specially benefited. The fixing of the area of benefit and the determination of the amount which each lot benefited shall pay are the duty of the three park assessors appointed by the district court. After hearing evidence the assessors make findings and file them in the district court, which has power to hear objections and confirm or revise the assessment or send the case to new assessors.† It is the practice for the courts to confirm assessments,

* See Appendix, p. 249 for text.
† Special Laws of Minnesota, 1889, Chapter 30, Section 4.

unless satisfied that the assessors have been governed by improper motives or have proceeded on erroneous principles, or have based their findings on a mistake of facts. The percentage which private land owners have paid under park takings has varied greatly under this procedure.

4. PARK DISTRICTS FOR ASSESSMENT PURPOSES

In the comparatively recent practice of some cities "park districts" have been laid out, each treated as a separate entity, both for the purpose of locating park areas and for assessing the cost of their acquisition.

KANSAS CITY. In 1908 the entire city was divided into six park districts, administered as one system by three commissioners appointed by the mayor. The commissioners' duties are to devise and adopt a system of parks, parkways, and boulevards, and to select such lands as are appropriate for these purposes within or without the city limits. They must provide at least one park in each park district. Responsibility for the selection of areas is left with the park commissioners, since only on their recommendation can the common council provide for the acquisition of the necessary land by ordinance, and it is made the duty of the common council to carry out the park commissioners' recommendation.*

The cost of acquiring land outside of the city limits must be paid out of the general tax levy or

* Charter of Kansas City, Article 13, Section 8 ff.

by a bond issue which is a charge on future general tax levies; but within the city limits land for parks, parkways, public squares, and boulevards, whether acquired by purchase or condemnation, may be paid for by special assessment on the land specially benefited. Special assessments are also used to defray the cost of construction of boulevards and park roads on which private property abuts and are levied directly on such property, as in an ordinary street improvement. The remainder of the cost of construction and all the maintenance cost is met by a tax not to exceed 2½ mills levied over each park district in accordance with its valuation, and by a special maintenance tax of 10 cents a front foot on the property which fronts on parkways, boulevards, roads, or avenues.* The funds of each district are kept separate.†

Kansas City is fortunate in the provisions of its law regarding condemnation proceedings and special assessment for benefit. The ordinance of council following the recommendation of the park commission describes all the properties to be acquired for the proposed improvement or group of improvements and the area which is deemed specially benefited. This area may include one or more park districts or a part or parts of such district or districts. The proceedings are initiated by petition of the city in the circuit court, and when the parties have properly joined issues the

---

* Charter of Kansas City, Article 13, Sections 33 and 34.
† Charter of Kansas City, Article 13, Section 23.

DISTRIBUTION OF THE COST

case is heard by a jury of six which ascertains the compensation for property taken and for the damage sustained by property not actually taken. The same jury assesses the benefit of the improvement, first charging to the city that portion of the cost which represents the benefit that accrues to the city at large, and then distributing the balance of the cost by special assessment against the parcels of private property found specially benefited. The verdict of the jury is reviewed by the circuit court and may be appealed from to the court of appeals on any question; but, curiously, only corporations have a right to appeal to a common law jury and this right is almost never taken advantage of.*

In legal theory the assessments are approximately in proportion to and not exceeding the special benefit, and if the cost of land acquirement should exceed the estimated special benefit the difference would be paid by a general tax on the whole park district or on the whole city. As a matter of practice the assessing juries have with almost absolute unanimity found that the entire benefit from the acquisition of park land is to private property. The right to assess the entire cost of a "public improvement" on a specially benefited area—to find, in other words, that there has been no "public benefit"—has been declared constitutional in several cases.† The city, through its right to have the proceedings discontinued at

* See p. 28.   † See Appendix, p. 250.

any time before the first assessment is paid into the city treasury by repealing the ordinance of condemnation,* is protected against the finding of a jury that the benefit is entirely a public one and that no assessment shall be laid against the private property.

The special assessment method as applied in Kansas City makes unnecessary an appropriation by the council or a bond issue, both of which would increase the general tax rate. Payments for the purchase of land are met either directly by park fund certificates or these certificates are sold to provide purchase money at a price not less than the face value of the amount of special assessment, excluding interest. The payment of special assessments is usually by instalments, and distribution of the amount collected is made at least semi-annually to certificate holders who are entitled to the proportional share of the special assessment represented by their certificate with interest at 6 per cent.†

The Kansas City park system has not been secured any more cheaply than other park systems, with the exception that the simplicity of condemnation procedure has probably resulted in some saving in the cost of land, but the financial burden has been distributed with more fairness. Practically the entire amount of special assessments has been collected. From the beginning of the

---

* Charter of Kansas City, Article 13, Section 19.
† Charter of Kansas City, Article 13, Section 24.

DISTRIBUTION OF THE COST

history of the park system in 1892 to April, 1911, its cost was $10,372,876. Of this sum, $500,000 was raised by a bond issue in 1903; $496,181 was appropriated for construction and maintenance in Swope Park, the city's largest park; and $651,776 which was spent for miscellaneous items entirely separate from the expense of acquiring the land or improving it, was also appropriated out of the general tax levy. Deducting these three items, there is left $8,724,919, representing the funds raised by special assessment.*

The significant thing about the Kansas City method of financing its park system is that 85 per cent of the total cost was distributed over the district which received the benefit, and that the entire cost of acquiring the land was assessed strictly on the land found to be specially benefited.

DENVER. By the charter adopted March 29, 1904, Denver was divided into four park districts administered by an appointed commission of five, one from each district in addition to the chairman. The cost of acquiring land for parks is met, as in Kansas City, by a special assessment based entirely on the benefit theory, and the cost of improving the park areas is covered by a uniform park tax not to exceed two mills. Occasionally the park fund is increased by the revenue from other sources of taxation. Compared with Kansas City, Denver is at a disadvantage in

* Report of Board of Park Commissioners, 1909, Table 22.

choosing one commissioner from each district, since this method is too much like that of electing representatives to the city council from each ward and is apt to result in the same difficulties. Where the make-up of the commission emphasizes separate localities rather than the whole city, the distribution of park areas and the distribution of appropriations for improvements over these areas may present troublesome questions.

The second important difference is in the procedure for acquiring land and assessing the cost on specially benefited property. The board of park commissioners in Denver prepares a preliminary estimate of the cost of acquiring the land for each improvement. This report, which contains a full description of the property to be taken and the estimated special assessment on each lot in the entire park district, is formally served by publication on all owners whose property is affected either by being taken or by being assessed to pay for the improvement. If the owners of 25 per cent of the area thus affected object, in writing, to the report, the project may be defeated for at least a year. Upon the certification to the city council by the board of park commissioners that the objections are insufficient in number, the council proceeds to pass the ordinance of condemnation. The ordinance of council has been held to be a finding of fact conclusive on every other tribunal that the land is acquired for a public

DISTRIBUTION OF THE COST

purpose and that the protests of land owners are insufficient.*

It is noteworthy that the park commissioners are the judges of the amount of assessment to be levied against each parcel of property. No assessment in excess of those fixed in the preliminary report can be levied, and if the estimate of cost proves too low the difference must be assumed by the city or the project abandoned. After the petition for the land taking is in court, three appraisers are appointed, corresponding to the jury of six in Kansas City, except that their duty is merely to appraise the damages caused by the taking. Their report is reviewed by the court, which may modify their awards for damages and at the same time may declare inequitable the rule of assessments as fixed by the park commission.

Instead of issuing park certificates as in Kansas City, the park commissioners in Denver are authorized to issue bonds for the cost of land. The cost of construction is met by appropriations from the park fund, and in Denver the proceeds of taxation for park purposes in one district may be used in any other; which again is unlike the rule in Kansas City, where the funds of each district are kept separate for that district's needs.†

In 1911 Denver finished the condemnation of

---

* Londoner vs. City and County of Denver, decided November 22, 1911.

† Denver Municipal Facts, 1911, Vol. 23, p. 14.

land for the completion of its park system. All the land included in the petition lies in the East Denver Park District, and consists of park areas, playgrounds, parkways and boulevards, and a civic center site. In August, 1909, the board of park commissioners reported an estimated cost of land for the whole project of $2,780,000, and assessed this entire amount over the East Denver Park District. The district was for this purpose subdivided into 38 parts, each assessed a varying amount depending on its distance from the various improvements, the unit of assessment being a standard Denver lot of 25 feet by 125 feet. For instance, District No. 1, being the nearest to the civic center site, was assessed a maximum of $96 each year for ten years on some lots, and from this amount the sums varied down to $10 a year for ten years on lots least benefited. In District No. 36, on the other hand, which is most remote from any of the proposed improvements, the average assessment was 30 cents a lot each year for ten years.* The first instalment of the assessment was made payable five years after the passage of the assessing ordinance. On November 23, 1909, the park commissioners certified to the city council that protests of the property owners were insufficient, and on December 23 the council passed the ordinance of condemnation. Meantime an action had been brought in the district court to restrain the city council from passing the ordinance

* Op. cit. Issue of March 11, 1911, p. 8.

on the ground that the charter provisions under which the land for park purposes was acquired were unconstitutional, and further, that the commissioners' apportionment of the cost was inequitable. The city demurred to this action and the demurrer was sustained in the district court, from which decision the property owners appealed to the supreme court of the state. In November, 1910, appraisers were appointed by the district court, and on March 2, 1911, they made their report, estimating the total damages for the acquisition for lands in the East Park District at $2,523,463. Of this sum $1,814,539 was for the civic center site.

Considering the size of the undertaking, there were very few protesting owners and those for the most part owners of property involved in the taking for the civic center. Out of a total of 50 owners whose lands were taken for any of the purposes set forth in the council's ordinances, only 18, representing $527,428, protested against the awards and one of these alone represented $265,000. In May, 1911, the first protest was heard by a common law jury, which found against the petitioner. All the other protesting owners then withdrew their petitions. In November, 1911, the state supreme court sustained the decision of the lower court above referred to* and on March 2, 1912, "civic center bonds" for $2,696,600, which amount included the cost of appraisement,

* Londoner vs. City and County of Denver.

the cost of survey, and other incidentals, were offered for sale.

In spite of the bitterness of opposition from some interested land owners, the time from the initiation of the proceedings to the advertising of the bond issue was short, but this was not so much because of the simplicity of the procedure, which suffers in this respect by comparison with that in Kansas City, as because the civic center project and the plans for the completion of the park system had the backing of public opinion and of the strongest organization in the city of Denver.

INDIANAPOLIS. The most recent park law which provides for payment of land acquirement by the special assessment method was passed by the legislature of Indiana in 1911 for cities of 100,000 or over. Under the provisions of this act the entire area of Indianapolis is divided into four districts administered by a commission of four appointed by the mayor. Only such features of practice as are peculiar to Indiana are here noted.

The park commissioners have the duties which in Kansas City were given to a jury of six and in Denver to three appraisers. Without action on the part of the city council the board of park commissioners may adopt a resolution for the condemnation of land and the assessment of its cost on private property.* Opportunity is given to land owners to defeat the undertaking by the

* Acts of Indiana, 1911, Chapter 231.

written remonstrance of a majority of the resident land owners in the proposed benefit district.* If the commissioners find the protest insufficient they prepare a roll in which are included the estimated damages for land taking, the estimated cost of construction, and other miscellaneous items. To this amount 5 per cent is added to cover any delinquency in the collection of assessment. This entire amount is then spread as a special assessment over the area which in the judgment of the park commissioners is specially benefited by the improvement. This may be an entire park district or may be limited to a few blocks. The act provides that no assessment of benefits may be made in excess of 15 per cent of the value of the land so assessed, exclusive of the improvement conferred upon it.† The roll must show in separate amounts the damages awarded and the benefits assessed in the case of each parcel of land.

After the roll is made up, a notice describing the location of the lands appropriated, the character of the improvement, and the boundaries of the district to be assessed, is published once a week for two weeks in some daily newspaper. This notice also names a day, not earlier than ten days after the date of the last publication, for hearing remonstrants, and states that the assessment roll with

---

* Ibid., Chapter 231, Section 14. Parts of the text are given in Appendix, p. 254.

† Acts of Indiana, 1911, Chapter 231, Section 17.

the names of the owners to whom damages have been awarded and against whom assessments have been made is on file in the office of the board of park commissioners. A written notice is served upon the owner of each piece of land which is taken or damaged and a notice is mailed to the persons against whom assessments have been made.

After the hearing, the assessment roll is confirmed with or without changes by the park board, and aggrieved owners then have fifteen days to perfect an appeal to the superior court. This is the first important difference between the procedure in Indianapolis and that in Kansas City and Denver, and is one of the reasons for its extraordinary effectiveness. Land taking in Kansas City and Denver is from the start a court proceeding, but in Indianapolis the details of procedure, such as the making up of the award of damages and the spreading of the special assessments, are almost entirely taken care of by the clerical force connected with the board of commissioners. Only rarely is a judicial tribunal called upon to exercise jurisdiction. Even in appeal cases the jurisdiction of the superior court is limited.* It may decide whether the park board has properly taken jurisdiction by the observance of the formalities imposed in the act; it may review awards of damages and assessments for benefits; but there is no appeal from the finding of the park com-

* Acts of 1911, Chapter 231, Section 19.

missioners that it is necessary to take private land, and that it is necessary to take the particular land included in their resolution.

Owners of land which is taken or which is assessed for benefit have no constitutional or statutory right in Indiana to have their damages or their assessments fixed by a common law jury, but in its discretion the superior court in appeal cases may appoint a small board of appraisers to pass upon the evidence. This is the second advantage in procedure.

Finally, in Indiana the superior court is a court of last resort in condemnation cases under the park act. By the terms of the act the judgment of the superior court can not be appealed from,* and there is no other legal process in the state by which a case can be reviewed by a higher tribunal. The court of appeals said in the case of City of Indianapolis *vs.* L. C. Thompson Manufacturing Co., 40 Ind. App., 535:

"In this state since the adoption of the code of 1852, the use of the right of certiorari has not been authorized and the only procedure by which the judgment of a lower court may be reviewed by the court is by way of appeal . . . . Judgment, in a proceeding where the right of appeal is specifically denied by the legislature is not reviewable by the supreme court or this court. . . . Whether the lower court committed error in the measurement of damages, the admission of testimony in assuming jurisdiction over the

* Acts of 1911, Chapter 231, Section 20.

person or subject matter, or in any other matter, is not subject to our review on appeal. . . . There is no vested right in an appeal and the legislature has the power to grant or deny appeals as it deems best."

Besides possessing the advantages in legal procedure which eliminate the usual delay and expense in land taking, the Indianapolis park commission has adopted a businesslike practice which is most helpful in arriving at awards and which appeals to the sense of fairness of the land owner. A complete card catalogue of owners and valuations is kept in the office of the commission, and in the case of every taking the commission has the assistance of real estate experts as an advisory committee on valuations.

Although the act is only three years old, there has been at least one considerable taking in each district. In the North Park District there have been two, one involving an expense of $154,420 and the other $131,662. In takings involving over $600,000 worth of property and several thousand owners, there have been only four appeals from the findings of the park board, two of which have been decided by the superior court. In one an award of damages of $10,000 was increased to $17,000 and in the other an award of $6,925 was increased to $9,800. In one proceeding 1,600 owners were involved and only 50 were present at the hearing of remonstrants.

All these advantages contribute to excellent results under the park act, but a factor which is quite as positive in its influence is the effect on the community of distributing the cost of land acquirement by levying it as a special assessment entirely on the district specially benefited. Petitions either to have damages for land takings increased or to have assessments decreased are not popular when the bill is to be paid not out of the returns from the general tax but out of the pockets of the petitioners' neighbors.

The combination of a simplified legal procedure, a wise business practice, and an equitable method of distributing the cost of an improvement has made it possible for the city of Indianapolis to take land needed for public use at a fair price and with little delay. The park board is, however, limited in its activities by the terms of the act which provide that the aggregate amount of benefits which may be assessed against property in a ten-year period can not exceed $1,250,000, and that in any one year it can not exceed $200,000.

5. SPECIAL ASSESSMENTS IN ACQUIRING LAND FOR STREET PURPOSES

The right to levy a special assessment for such street improvements as do not involve the taking of land, such as grading, paving, curbing, and sidewalk construction, is almost universally granted to municipalities by legislation in the United States. But the use of the special assessment, although common in New York, New Jersey, Pennsylvania, and the central and western states, is most limited in the cities of the South and in New England. It is practically unknown in New Hampshire; and in the other New England states only the cost or a portion of the cost of some one improvement, very often the construction of sewers, is assessed specially on private property. There is, to be sure, in Massachusetts, a rather general practice of accepting streets as public highways only after they have been brought by the abutters to an established grade.

Speaking generally, in street improvements which require the taking of land, as in openings, widenings, or extensions, more often than in takings for parks, the cost of the land is defrayed by a special assessment. The practice in this regard is likely to follow the practice in defraying merely construction cost. We have already seen that the cities of Ohio are prohibited from employing such assessment; in other cities, of which Philadelphia and Boston are the best examples, although the right to levy a special assessment is given to the municipality, in practice little if any of the cost of land taking gets assessed, because in Philadelphia juries are averse to finding a benefit, and in Boston the right to assess specially is limited and the procedure ineffective. Where assessments are made, the practice is as varied as in assessments for the acquisition of land for parks.

AGENCY WHICH ASSESSES THE BENEFITS. Ordinarily the same agency which awards damages for land taking determines the amount of the special assessment which is to be levied for the special benefit resulting from the improvement, whether that agency be a small board of appraisers, commissioners, or viewers, as in New York, Chicago, St. Louis, Kansas City, Portland (Oregon), and other cities; or a department of the city administration, as in Milwaukee, Indianapolis, Los Angeles, and Boston. The usual practice is to assess the benefits at the same time that the damages are awarded and thus offset the benefits against the damages wherever possible. In cases where the damages awarded are increased or assessments are decreased on appeal, either the city must assume the deficiency or the assessing board must find more benefited territory on which to spread the required amount.

The street commissioners of Boston, however, and boards with like powers in the other cities of Massachusetts, are compelled by statute to postpone the assessment of benefit until the completion of the improvement,* a practice the disadvantage of which is evidenced by the difficulty in collecting the assessments, as will be seen later.

In Seattle and other cities of Washington, the special assessments are apportioned by eminent domain assessors, a different tribunal from that which awards damages.† Sometimes a year elap-

---

*Acts of Massachusetts, 1906, Chapter 393; and Revised Laws, Chapter 50, Section 1.

† Acts of Washington, 1907, Chapter 153, Section 20.

ses from the time of the final award for damages to the appointment of assessors, and during this year the amounts of the award are bearing interest. The eminent domain assessors review the same evidence that was heard by the jury in the land damage cases. An amendment has already been proposed which will allow the board of eminent domain assessors to award damages and apportion assessments at one hearing.

THE PROPORTION ASSESSED. It is the general practice to leave the proportion of the cost of land which is to be assessed on the municipality and the proportion which is to be assessed on property specially benefited to the discretion of the board which levies the assessment, limited only by the provision that the special assessment shall not exceed special benefit and shall not exceed a certain percentage of valuation of the property assessed. But in New York the board of estimate and apportionment is given this duty in all cases,* and in Boston† the proportion which private property shall pay is fixed by law, not to exceed 50 per cent of the cost of improvement,‡ which cost includes both the amount awarded for land damage and the cost of construction. Theoretically, the proportion assessed on the municipality at large and on private property should depend on the extent to which the improvement,

* Charter of New York City, 1901, Article 950.
† Acts of Massachusetts, 1906, Chapter 393, Section 5.
‡ Changed by Chapter 536, Acts of 1913.

as, for instance, the widening or opening of a street, serves a general or a purely local purpose. Practice does not follow theory. Some jurisdictions assess specially the whole or a large portion of the cost of all ordinary street openings on the property particularly benefited. In Milwaukee it is the unwritten rule to assess two-thirds of the cost on private property. In Kansas City it is the exception for the city to pay any part of the cost of street improvement out of its general revenue.

The history of special assessments for street purposes in New York and Boston furnishes an interesting comparison. Previous to 1902 the policy of the board of estimate and apportionment in New York City was to assess the entire cost of opening proceedings on the property specially benefited, and subsequently to grant relief, depending usually on the skill with which property owners were represented at the hearing. The result was that almost all the expense of opening streets over 50 feet wide was borne by the city.* The city's bonded indebtedness was greatly increased and it became impossible to execute important improvements.

From 1902 to 1907 the opening and widening of streets 60 feet wide and under was regarded as a purely local benefit and the entire cost assessed on property benefited; but for streets over 60 feet in width† there was a different distribu-

* Report of Chief Engineer, Board of Estimate and Apportionment, October 19, 1907, p. 3.
† Ibid., p. 14.

tion of cost. In the case of new streets the city assumed one-third of the cost due to the excess in width over 60 feet. Where the streets were old and were widened to over 60 feet, the city assumed one-half of the cost due to the excess width. During these years the city was called upon for a contribution of $9,471,550 toward the cost of widening and opening streets, which put upon the city a greater burden than the old method where assessments were reduced on a plea for relief. The board of estimate and apportionment found also that this method was inequitable to the owners of land abutting on the 60-foot street. A street over 60 feet in width was held to be of more general benefit than one of narrower width, and the area over which the assessment could be spread was bounded by a line midway between the widened street and the nearest street of the same or greater width. Thus in widening a street to 80 feet, after the payment out of the general municipal revenue of one-third of the cost due to excess width and after the assessment on property in the benefit zone not abutting on the widened street, it was found that abutting property was paying only the equivalent of the cost of a street 51 feet wide. For this reason, therefore, and because of the greater burden on the municipality, the rule adopted in 1907 was to assess the entire cost of the acquisition of land for street purposes on the property specially benefited, in so far as a special benefit could be established, provided that the amount assessed would not result in confiscation of the property.*

In Boston previous to 1891 special assessments to defray the cost of street improvements were levied entirely according to the discretion of the board of street commissioners, whose practice was to assess private property only in the case of improvements which had more than a local character and to pay for strictly local street improvements out of the general appropriation. In 1891 a board of survey was created and that board in its discretion was allowed to assess on abutting property the entire cost of improvement.† In practice the board used this right only on purely local streets, applying the theory that on such streets the general public received no appreciable benefit. In 1902 large land holders and their representatives insisted on changing the law and were helped by the decision in Lorden *vs.* Coffey, 178 Mass. 489, which declared unconstitutional that part of the board of survey act which allowed the assessment of the entire cost of improvements, holding that a special assessment might exceed the special benefit to property under the provision of the act. There was no finding that the entire cost could not be assessed on a benefited area, and had the board of survey act included the words "but no assessment shall be

* Report of Chief Engineer, Board of Estimate and Apportionment, October 19, 1907, pp. 5 ff.
† Acts of Massachusetts, 1891, Chapter 323, Sections 14, 15.

levied in excess of the actual special benefit to the property" the law would probably have been declared constitutional. The statute of 1902* limited the amount of a special assessment to 50 per cent of the cost of an improvement, no matter what the width or the use of a street.

The evolution in New York is toward a proper rule of apportionment, and in Boston, away from it. Either the assessing board should be given discretion in the matter of assessments, with the usual limitation that there should be no special assessment exceeding special benefit, or a system of apportionment should be adopted based on the width of streets as evidence of their character and use and as a measure of their public and private benefit.†

THE AREA OF SPECIAL BENEFIT. The determination of the specially benefited area is left to the discretion of the assessing board, with very few exceptions. In Philadelphia this area is limited to such properties as abut on the improvement; in Boston‡ it is fixed by the statute of 1902 to 125 feet on either side of the improvement;§ in Milwaukee it is limited in practice to 1,000 feet on either side of the improvement. Under the boulevard law in St. Louis only the

---

* Acts of Massachusetts, 1902, Chapter 521, Section 14.

† Acts of Massachusetts, 1913, Chapter 536, gives the street commissioners discretion and removes the limit of 50 per cent.

‡ Acts of Massachusetts, 1902, Chapter 521, Section 1.

§ This restriction was removed by Acts of Massachusetts, 1913, Chapter 536.

properties abutting on boulevards can be assessed specially for their cost.* The improvement known as the "King's Highway" was assessed under this law with the result that the city would have had to pay 80 per cent of the total cost of improvement, and was forced either to abandon it or to repeal the law. Subsequently the King's Highway was opened as an ordinary street with the same assessment provision as in street openings, which leaves the benefit area to the discretion of the commissioners.

Though it may be generally stated that the size of the benefit district and the amount of the special assessment levied are both legislative questions which are finally determined by the body to which is delegated this duty, and that in the absence of special constitutional limitation the legislative finding will not be reviewed by a court unless there is evidence of gross error or fraud, judicial decisions in several states have held that this legislative authority is not unlimited. Courts on appeal have asserted the right to review the apportionment of the assessment and declare it invalid.

(1) Where the benefit of an improvement is entirely general: Hammett *vs.* Philadelphia, 65 Pa. St. 146; Thomas *vs.* Gain, 35 Mich. 155; Detroit *vs.* Daly, 68 Mich. 503.

(2) Where the rule of assessment would be inequitable for any reason: In re Washington Av.

---
* Charter of St. Louis, 1901, Act VI, Section 1.

69 Pa. St. 352; Scranton *vs.* Pa. Coal Co. 105 Pa. St. 445; Chicago *vs.* Learned, 34 Ill. 203; White *vs.* Gove, 183 Mass. 333.

(3) Where the special assessment exceeds the special benefit: Seely *vs.* Pittsburgh, 82 Pa. St. 360; Lorden *vs.* Coffey, 178 Mass. 489; Norwood *vs.* Baker, 172 U. S. 269.

THE RELATION OF SPECIAL ASSESSMENTS TO AWARDS FOR LAND TAKINGS

In our review of the practice in special assessments we have seen that in some jurisdictions the determination of awards for land takings and the apportionment of the special assessment are distinct functions performed either by the same body or by different bodies at times which may be widely separated. Thus in Denver the park commissioners spread the assessment which is based on their estimate of the land cost before the appraisers who determine the land awards are appointed; in Boston the street commissioners have both functions, but assessments can not be levied until the completion of the improvement. In Seattle three assessors, or three eminent domain commissioners, levy the special assessment at least a year from the time when the jury's awards for land takings have been finally confirmed; under the Minneapolis park procedure assessors are not appointed by the court until the cost of land is finally determined by confirmation of the appraisers' report. In other jurisdictions both the awards for land and the assessment for its cost are functions performed in the same proceeding by the same body. Thus in Kansas City a jury of six, and in Indianapolis commissioners, have these duties.

The disadvantage of deferring the time of levying the assessment is generally considered to outweigh the advantage of a more certain knowledge of the amount of the land awards, which is the largest item of the cost to be assessed. But the necessity of keeping separate the items of awards for damages and of assessment for special benefit, though they may be best fixed at the same time, appears from the methods in very general use of offsetting benefits against damages in arriving at verdicts in condemnation cases.

In Pennsylvania the jury in condemnation cases must find:

1. The value of the premises before the taking.
2. The value of the premises after the taking, which includes the benefit to the premises by the taking. The difference is the compensation to the owner.

In Portland, Oregon, a verdict is made up of:

1. How much, if any, less valuable the land will be rendered by the taking.
2. The damage to the improvements; that is, to buildings, and so forth.

Both of these rules of damage are open to either of two objections: First, in some jurisdictions juries are averse to finding any benefit, in which case a much greater sum than is just is spread over a benefit district, and owners who have justly received as damages large sums for land taken or damaged pay entirely inadequate assessments for the special benefit which they have received. Second, if the jury gives full consideration to the benefit which a piece of property receives and subtracts the full amount of benefit from the compensation awarded for damages to the property, the owner has a decided grievance because he may be paying $100 for one hundred dollars' worth of special benefit, but his neighbor on the other side of the street whose property has not been taken is paying in a special assessment only 25 per cent or 30 per cent of the special benefit to his property.

The commissioners appointed in street cases in Minneapolis are directed to find:

1. The value of land taken.
2. The damage to the land or buildings not taken.
3. The special benefit which accrues to each parcel.

The owner of the property receives as compensation the excess of compensation for damages over the special benefit. This rule is open to the second objection which we have discussed above and only in a less degree is the code of California objectionable which requires the finding of:

1. The value of the land and buildings taken.
2. The damage to the land and buildings not taken.

3. The benefit to the remainder, which must be deducted from (2).

Thus in California the owner of property taken will have as damages at least the value of the land taken, whereas in the Minneapolis street procedure it is conceivable that the owner might not receive as compensation the value of the land taken.

The better rule in these cases is illustrated by the Kansas City procedure where the jury must find:

1. The actual value of land or easement taken.
2. The actual damage to land or buildings remaining.
3. The assessment which is to be levied against the city at large.
4. Special assessment against each parcel of land found specially benefited.

Only this special assessment (4) may be deducted from the owner's compensation for damage (1) and (2).

THE EFFICACY OF SPECIAL ASSESSMENTS

It is clear that the value of the special assessment method differs considerably in different communities and depends greatly on local conditions. The land owners of Kansas City and Denver pay special assessments practically without litigation, and as a general rule, in most cities, collection of assessments is attended with little difficulty, even where the burden is heaviest on the land owner.

The process of collection in New York City, for instance, is very effective. Like most cities where the cost of street improvement is assessed wholly or in part on property specially benefited, the owners of the land assessed may pay the entire assessment at once or in annual instalments. On the failure in payment of any instalment, the land becomes charged with the city's lien. For three years the owner may pay interest on the amount he owes the city, but at the end of this period the city's lien for all charges against the land is sold at auction to the person who bids the lowest rate of interest for which he will pay the face value of the lien and carry it three years more. Thus the city gets its money and the land owner merely has, in addition to the face of his assessment, an interest charge which is apt to be ridiculously low since the bidding in on city liens is usually active.

Boston is one of the few exceptions to the rule in the collection of special assessments. Property owners contest special assessments wherever a contest is made worth while by the size of the special assessment, and reductions in assessments by juries on appeal go far to destroy the effectiveness of this method as a means of providing funds for the acquisition of land; and yet land owners in Boston are treated much more leniently under the law of 1906 than they are in New York, Kansas City, Denver, or Indianapolis. One explanation of the unpopularity of the special assessment principle is that the funds used for improving the old city and opening and widening the streets were taken out of the general appropriation, and property owners, therefore, in the newer sections, or property owners in older sections where openings and widenings are necessary, are opposed to any innovation which puts on them a heavier burden. But the ineffectiveness of the special method in Boston is due chiefly, first, to the statutory limitation on the discretion of the assessing board; and second, to the provision which postpones the apportioning of the assessment until after the completion of the improvement.

The fixing of the proportion which the city must pay irrespective of the character of the street in question and the narrow limitation of the benefit area, work together to place upon a very few owners an altogether disproportionate burden. These are the unfair features of the Boston assessment law: (a) The city must pay 50 per cent at least of the cost of a purely local street, even a street 30 feet in width, the only direct benefit from which is to abutting properties; (b) the city in practice pays as high as 80 per cent of the cost of such streets, because in the opinion of the commissioners the value of the property within 125 feet on either side is sometimes so low that to assess 50 per cent on it would amount to confiscation; (c) the property that receives the most benefit is assessed nothing, particularly in the case of a widened thoroughfare where the benefit accrues certainly no more to the abutters than to the termini of the thoroughfare, or to abutters on the streets leading off from the thoroughfare whose property has been made more accessible.

The time which is allowed to elapse between the opening or widening of the street and the levying of the assessment is a further handicap to the success of special assessments in Boston as to a less degree in Seattle. The chance of offsetting benefits against damages is lost, and consequently the labor of collection is increased. Property owners who get their damages for land taken, alienate the property, and the owner not a party to the condemnation proceedings who has paid to his predecessor in title an increased price on account of the improvement to the property, naturally opposes payment of a special assessment. That most of the action under the law is a perversion of the special assessment principle has been recognized in recent Massachusetts special legislation, where the limitation on the assessment area has been removed and the size of the area left to the discretion of the street commissioners.*

A comparison of the returns from special assessments in Boston, in Seattle, and in Minneapolis, may be made by means of the subjoined tables:

* Acts of Massachusetts, 1913, Chapter 536, removes both limitations on the discretion of the Boston street commissioners in the special case covered by the act.

DISTRIBUTION OF THE COST

TABLE 3.—RETURNS FROM SPECIAL ASSESSMENTS ON STREET IMPROVEMENTS. BOSTON, 1895–1906

Location of improvement	Year	Cost of improvement	Amount assessed	Amount of reduction	Amount paid
Lauriat Ave.	1895	$45,779	$41,201	$34,811	$6,390
Brighton Ave.	1895	201,699	117,270	42,506	74,764
Columbus Ave.	1895	1,818,901	373,127	[a]	[a]
Peterboro St.	1896	187,264	95,457	78,983	16,474
Queensberry St.	1897	196,568	87,565	32,448	55,117
Charlestown St.	1898	696,673	212,229	81,830	[b]
North Harvard St.	1898	70,443	23,721	11,162	12,559
Bennington St.	1899	831,816	54,812	[c]	[c]
Florida St.	1903	16,120	4,392	2,668	1,724
Columbia Rd.	..	1,792,891	296,493	13,307	[d]
Hyde Park Ave.	1906	225,000	28,000	About 50 per cent	About 50 per cent

[a] Fifteen petitions for reduction of assessment are pending and no payments have been made.

[b] Thirteen petitions for reduction of assessments and two writs of certiorari are pending. The latter question the validity of the assessment.

[c] Acts of 1912, Chapter 537, compels the street commissioners to reduce this assessment. See Appendix, p. 268, for the text of act.

[d] Sixty petitions for reduction of assessments are pending. Acts of 1912, Chapter 339, authorized a reduction of assessments. See Appendix, p. 267.

There have been remarkably few contests on any assessments in Minneapolis. The park board has been able to pay every instalment on every certificate as it matured without a moment's delay. All the assessments are collectible as a part of the annual tax for state, county, and city purposes.

In Minneapolis, Kansas City, and Denver the amount collected shrinks but little from the

CARRYING OUT THE CITY PLAN

TABLE 4.—RETURNS FROM SPECIAL ASSESSMENTS ON STREET IMPROVEMENTS. SEATTLE

Location of improvement	Cost of land taking and land damage - Regrading	Cost of land taking and land damage - Widening	Cost of construction	Total cost	Amount assessed on property specially benefited [a]	Amount paid out of general appropriation
Second Ave. from Pike St. to Denny Way	$20,501.00	$32,165.00	$91,579.06	$168,100.97	$144,245.06	$23,855.91
Third Ave. from Yesler Way to Pike St.	27,959.00	1,533,888.00	42,175.55	1,612,074.55	1,604,022.55	8,052.00
Fourth Ave. from Washington to Park St.	64,007.00	623,158.00	299,547.16	987,212.16	986,712.16	500.00
Fifth Ave. from Washington St. to Madison St.[b]	217,824.56	....	155,058.92	377,461.48	372,883.48	4,578.00
Pine St. from First Ave. to Twelfth Ave.	54,871.50	592,773.36	108,297.68	761,065.68	755,942.54	5,123.14
Dearborn St. from Seattle Boulevard to Rainier Ave.	15,945.00	277,509.50	343,063.18	678,218.11	636,517.68	41,700.43
Total	$401,108.06	$3,059,493.86	$1,039,721.55	$4,584,132.95	$4,500,323.47	$83,809.48

[a] For each specified improvement the amount assessed on property specially benefited equals the sum of the cost of land taking and land damage and of cost of construction. Amounts are those used in making assessment roll.

[b] Widening not yet done.

DISTRIBUTION OF THE COST

TABLE 5.—RETURNS FROM SPECIAL ASSESSMENTS ON IMPROVEMENTS. MINNEAPOLIS, 1889–1908

Location of improvement	Year	Cost of improvement	Amount assessed	Amount paid
Glenwood Park	1889	$295,825	$100,000	$100,000
Van Cleve Park	1890	75,348	75,000	75,000
Loring Park	1890	343,693	105,000	105,000
Powderhorn Lake Park	1891	262,387	145,099	145,099
Columbia Park	1892	220,447	213,041	213,041
St. Anthony Parkway	1893	150,337	102,911	102,911
The Parade	1904	280,225	103,127	72,189[a]
Kenwood Park	1907	162,846	162,187	64,875[b]
The Gateway	1908	634,510	634,510	126,902[c]

[a] Three instalments unpaid.
[b] Six instalments unpaid.
[c] Eight instalments unpaid, January 1, 1912.

amount assessed. In Indianapolis and in Chicago a five per cent delinquency is figured in the amount of the total assessment, so that the return adequately meets the cost of the improvement. Indianapolis has collected in the past three years (1909 to 1912) by the assessment method $476,487. Kansas City has collected $8,724,919 in twenty years.

CONCLUSION

Special assessments as an equitable method of distributing the cost of land acquisition have the great advantage of a thorough testing. Judicial decisions universally sustain their legality. Ample precedents prove their practicability as financial expedients. Several cities in the United States are so completely satisfied with the results of an experience of from five to fifteen years with this "American device" that the suggestion of experimenting with the European method of distributing the cost known as excess condemnation meets with little enthusiasm. It remains, however, to consider the applicability of excess condemnation to American conditions.

CHAPTER IV

EXCESS CONDEMNATION

EXCESS condemnation, or the taking by a public agency under the power of eminent domain of more land and property than are needed for the actual construction of a contemplated public improvement with a view to selling the excess at such increase of value as may result from the improvement, offers, as suggested in the last chapter, a method of relieving the burden of the tax payers at large, and it is this feature that is likely to be emphasized in any discussion of the merits of the excess condemnation principle; but, entirely apart from its financial aspect, it has an importance in the execution of plans which is too little considered. We have seen in the first chapter that a serious obstacle to the realization of plans for improvement is the universal constitutional limitation on the power of eminent domain through the provision that land can not be taken unless it is "necessary for the public use." The usual narrow construction of this phrase allows a public agency to take only the land or rights in land required for the actual use of the public. When a comprehensive plan of reconstruction involves the widening of a built-up street or the opening of a new street cutting through improved property, the municipality is allowed to take just enough land for the actual construction of the street irrespective of the size or shape of the lots left on either side of the improvement.

The disadvantage to the municipality is both physical and financial. The land owner receives as compensation both the value of land actually taken and the damage to his remaining land, and consequently often gets as much for a part of his lot as he would for the whole of it. Even where special assessment laws work effectively it is often impossible to show ground for such an assessment against a remnant that is distinctly inferior to the customary marketable lot in size or shape. In the absence of any effective control over remnants left by the construction of the improvement, the new highway is likely to be bordered by ugly vacant lots of irregular shape and size which are totally unsuited for use and likely to remain vacant until they can be brought under the same ownership with parts of adjacent lands so as to provide adequate building lots. One of the most marked instances of this was in the widening of Delancey Street to make a proper approach for the Williamsburg Bridge in New York City, where lots were left in some cases less than 10 feet deep. The plan for the establishment of a new traffic thoroughfare between the north and south terminal stations in Boston shows remnants, the entire length amounting to 48,274 feet, absolutely unsuited for independent development.

EXCESS CONDEMNATION

In so far as remnants are unsuited for proper development a use of them is induced which robs an improvement of much of its effectiveness. Financially the city loses because the sort of development which will increase assessed valuations is prevented. Esthetically the city suffers because it can not protect its streets, its parks, and boulevards by an effective control over the abutting land, and its show places are disfigured by a use of this land not in keeping with the character of the surroundings. It is for this reason that cities have been forced to see approaches to public buildings lined with ill-assorted structures, and park areas surrounded by unsightly dumps and bill-boards. The net benefit to the city of a given expenditure for park purposes may easily be reduced by these means to a small fraction of what was reasonably expected when the investment was made. To overcome these disadvantages and to secure the maximum of benefit from an improvement appears to be the primary aim of excess condemnation legislation in the United States.

It will clear the way for a discussion of the subject to point out the nearest substitute for the excess condemnation method which is ordinarily available in America today. The absorption by the public of the increase of property values directly resulting from an improvement made at public expense, at least up to an amount equal to the cost of the improvement, may be more or less successfully accomplished by special assessments as set forth in Chapter III. The control over property adjacent to a public improvement just in so far as that control is needed to enable the public to get the full use and enjoyment of the public property, may be obtained without acquiring title by the purchase or condemnation of easements. The combination of the two is believed by the more conservative thinkers on the subject to afford all the power that is necessary without the dangers of excess condemnation.

THE HISTORY OF EXCESS CONDEMNATION IN THE UNITED STATES

The Massachusetts legislature of 1903* provided for an examination and report upon legislation needed to enable a city, town, or state commission to take in fee, to purchase, or otherwise to acquire for public purposes and in connection with any public work all or any part of the land within certain defined limits, and after appropriating as much of the land as necessary to sell or lease the remainder. The commission subsequently appointed by the governor did a thoroughgoing piece of work and their conclusions, embodied in two reports to the legislature of 1904, both now out of print, contained very valuable contributions on a subject on which there is scant literature.†

* Resolves of 1903, Chapter 86.
† Several of the conclusions are found in the Appendix, pp. 308 ff.
  House Document No. 288 of 1904.
  House Document No. 1096 of 1904.

EXCESS CONDEMNATION

The commission found no precedent and little of value on the subject of excess condemnation in this country, and in the cities of Europe they found the principle applied in two very different ways. In France, according to the letter of the law, only remnants of such size and shape as to be unsuited to the erection of buildings could be taken in addition to the land actually needed for the construction of the improvement. In England, Belgium, Switzerland, and Italy, municipalities were allowed to take all the property within certain bounds in the neighborhood of a proposed work, to use what was necessary, and to dispose of the remainder by sale or lease. In the bill which was submitted by the Massachusetts commission, the French method was adopted as sufficiently broad to carry out the purposes of the municipality and as being more fair than the other method cited to the property owner whose land would be taken. The draft of the bill was passed with modifications by the Massachusetts legislature of 1904 and is known as the "Remnant Act," the principle of which is contained in the following clauses:

Section 2. The Commonwealth, or any city in the Commonwealth . . . may take in fee by right of eminent domain the whole of any estate, part of which is actually required for the laying out, alteration or location by it of any public work, if the remnant left after taking such part would from its size or shape be unsuited for the erection of suitable and appropriate buildings, and if public convenience and necessity require such taking.

Section 15. The Commonwealth or the city, as the case may be, shall determine within six months after the completion of any public work for which land is taken under this act, or within six months after the filing of a final decree on an appeal taken under this act, whichever shall happen later, with which of the adjoining properties the public interests require that each parcel of land, if any, taken outside the boundaries of the public work should be united; and shall, within said six months, notify the owner of such adjoining property, if his address is known, of this decision by registered letter mailed to such owner, and shall annex to the notice a copy of this section.

Section 16. If such owner or some person on his behalf shall within two weeks from the mailing of such notice notify in writing the Commonwealth or the city that such owner wishes for an appraisal of such parcel, the Commonwealth or the city shall cause such parcel to be appraised by three competent and disinterested persons, one of whom shall be appointed by the Commonwealth or the city, one by said owner, and one by the superior court for the county: *Provided, however,* that the Commonwealth or the city and said owner may in writing appoint a sole appraiser. Said appraiser or appraisers shall forthwith after his or their appointment view the property and determine the fair value of such parcel, and shall make written report to the Commonwealth or the city of the same. The reasonable fees and expenses of the appraiser or appraisers shall be paid by the Commonwealth or the city. The Commonwealth or the city shall forthwith by writing mailed to such owner offer such parcel to such owner at the value as determined by the report of a majority of such appraisers, or by that of the sole appraiser in case of the appointment of one appraiser.

Section 17. If such owner shall in writing accept said offer within two weeks after the date when the same is mailed to such owner, the Commonwealth or the city shall convey such parcel to such owner on payment of the purchase money to the Commonwealth or the city, as the case may be, within thirty days after the acceptance of the offer. The conveyance shall be by deed, with or without covenants of title and warranty, executed and acknowledged in the name and behalf of the Commonwealth or the city by the officers or board which have or has taken such parcel, or by their or its successors or successor, and may be made subject to such restrictions as the Commonwealth or city may in writing have notified the appraisers or appraiser at the time of their or his appointment would be imposed on such parcel.

Section 18. If such owner fails to accept the offer within the time limited, or having accepted it fails to make payment or tender of the purchase money within one month thereafter, the Commonwealth or the city, if it does not take said adjoining property under the provisions of section twenty-nine* may at any time thereafter sell such parcel at public auction.

Section 29. If the owner of property adjoining a parcel taken under this act and outside the boundaries

* It was evidently intended to insert in section 29 a provision under which the Commonwealth might condemn the whole or any portion of the "adjoining property" if the owner of it failed to effect a purchase of the remnant offered for sale by the Commonwealth,[1] but the provision was not included in the act as passed.

[1] See draft of proposed act, House Document No. 288 of 1904.

of a public work fails to accept an offer to sell such parcel to such owner made under the provisions of section sixteen, or, having accepted such offer, fails to make payment or tender of the purchase money within thirty days thereafter, the Commonwealth or city shall cause such parcel to be sold by public auction, subject to such restrictions as the Commonwealth or city may impose. Land sold under this section shall be conveyed to the purchaser in the same manner as land conveyed under the provisions of section seventeen.*

In Ohio† and Maryland‡ the principle is incorporated in legislation for the protection of parks, parkways, and approaches to public buildings and, as far as the language of the acts indicates, excess taking can be made only for these specific purposes. The Virginia Assembly of 1906 passed an act§ giving the power to condemn and take more land than is necessary "when the use of the land proposed to be taken would impair the beauty, usefulness, or efficiency of the parks, plats, or public property, or which by the peculiar topography would impair the convenient use of a street or render impracticable without extra expense the improvement of the same."

The nearest approach to the European idea of excess condemnation is found in the acts of Con-

* Acts of Massachusetts, 1904, Chapter 443.
† Acts of Ohio, 1904, p. 333. See Appendix for text, p. 268.
‡ Acts of Maryland, 1908, Chapter 166. See Appendix for text, p. 269.
§ Acts of Virginia, 1906. Chapter 194. Approved March 14th. See Appendix for text, p. 271.

necticut, 1907.* The language of this clause puts no limit on the amount of land which can be taken. Unless the courts establish such a limit a broad power is given. The city is allowed, in fact, to embark on a real estate speculation. By No. 315 of the acts of Pennsylvania, 1907, cities are allowed to acquire by appropriation private property within 200 feet of the boundary of parks, parkways, and playgrounds. This act also allows the resale of surplus land with restrictions in the deed.

The Massachusetts act is the only one directed specifically to the acquisition of remnants which are made practically unsalable because of the taking for public use, but only on this ground is it to be distinguished from the other legislation above cited. In all this legislation the purpose is to provide a more effective method of accomplishing an improvement. A primary purpose in every case is either to lay out or widen a public street or to acquire or protect parks, parkways, or approaches to public buildings. All of these purposes are without question public, and the taking of excess land is but an incident to an acknowledged public purpose; namely, to insure a more useful wide street or a more attractive parkway. There is no suggestion either directly or by inference in any of this legislation that the excess taking is anything more than an incident to a public purpose and a means of securing the more perfect and successful realization of that purpose.

* Special Acts of Connecticut, 1907, No. 61. Section 7.

CARRYING OUT THE CITY PLAN

THE CONSTITUTIONALITY OF EXCESS TAKING

The Pennsylvania act is the only one which has been tested by judicial decision.

In July, 1912, the City Council of Philadelphia authorized the taking of excess land under the legislation of 1907, in connection with the proposed parkway from City Hall to Fairmount Park. The question of the constitutionality of the act was squarely raised and the lower court decided in favor of its validity, but this decision was reversed by the supreme court of the state.*

That the "remnant act" of Massachusetts would be declared constitutional is suggested in the answer of the Massachusetts supreme court to a question of the legislature in 1910. The question arose out of the necessity for a traffic thoroughfare between the north and south terminal stations in Boston. It appeared to the legislature impossible to construct a direct thoroughfare between these stations, unless a power of eminent domain were given which would allow the acquirement and reallotment of the land adjacent to the thoroughfare in lots suitable for mercantile buildings. As presented to the court the question was as follows:

"Is it within the constitutional power of the legislature to authorize the city of Boston, or such other public authority as the legislature may select, to lay

* Pa. Mutual Life Ins. Co. *vs.* Philadelphia, argued April 15, 1913. See Appendix, p. 275.

EXCESS CONDEMNATION

out such a thoroughfare and rear streets, and to take not only the land or easements necessary for the same, but also such quantities of land on either side of said thoroughfare or between the same and said rear streets as may be reasonably necessary for the purposes hereinbefore set out, with a view to the subsequent use by private individuals of so much of the property taken as lies on either side of said thoroughfare, under conveyances, leases, or agreements which should embody suitable provisions for the construction on said land of buildings suited to the objects and purposes hereinbefore set out and for the use, management and control of said land and buildings in such manner as to secure and best promote the public interests and purposes hereinbefore referred to; assuming that the act provides just compensation for all persons sustaining damages by the said takings."*

The supreme court interpreted the question briefly as meaning "Can land be taken with a view to its subsequent use by private individuals?" and its holding is that where the purpose of excess taking is primarily the creation of lots suitable for use of private individuals, such a taking is clearly unconstitutional. The court seems to make a distinction near the end of the opinion between cases where the excess taking is merely incidental to the main purpose, and cites the remnant act as such an example. We have therefore the suggestion that the remnant act might be found to be a constitutional exercise of power. The suggestion is of course of no value as a precedent, but

* Massachusetts Decisions, Vol. 204, pp. 606 ff.

is helpful as showing the sentiment of the justices of the supreme court of Massachusetts.

The doubtful constitutionality of the acts containing the excess-taking principle and the dissatisfaction with the limitation on the exercise of the power of eminent domain, have resulted in the effort to modify the limitation on the powers as now contained in state constitutions by constitutional amendment. Both the Massachusetts and New York legislatures have passed such amendments, which were submitted to the people of both states in the fall of 1911. The New York amendment was defeated† but it is valuable for purposes of comparison. The Massachusetts amendment was passed by a large vote, and at the legislative session of 1912 a special act gave the city of Worcester the right to take excess land for a street widening.‡ The people of Wisconsin and Ohio in 1912 adopted amendments containing similar wide powers§ of excess condemnation.

The New York amendment provided that when private property was taken for public use by a municipal corporation "additional adjoining and neighboring property may be taken under conditions to be prescribed by the legislature by gen-

* See Appendix for text, p. 279.

† The second attempt to pass such an amendment succeeded in 1913, but it is much more restricted in scope than that proposed in 1911. For text see Appendix, p. 248.

‡ Acts of 1912, Chapter 186.

§ Wisconsin amendment to Article 11 of Constitution adopted November 4, 1912. See Appendix, p. 279. Ohio amendment to Article 18, Appendix, p. 280.

eral laws; property thus taken shall be deemed to be taken for a public use."

From the viewpoint of the believer in excess taking as an easy means of correcting a defective street system and as the handmaiden of reconstruction, the amendment offered in 1911 which was not accepted by the people of New York was ideally phrased. Any excess taking which the legislature saw fit to authorize was made constitutional, whether that taking was a mere incident to a better realization of a public purpose or whether it was primarily a speculation to recoup the city's investment in reconstruction. It is not an answer to the extreme radicalism of the amendment to say that the legislature would probably hedge the power of excess taking with limitations. Radical legislation even in New York is not impossible, and a most radical act of a radical legislature would have had the stamp of constitutionality placed upon it by this amendment if the people had accepted it.

The Massachusetts amendment, on the other hand, limits both the application of the principle and the extent of the excess taking. It applies only to the "laying out, widening or relocating of highways" and the amount of land in excess which may be taken is "not more in extent than would be sufficient for suitable building lots on both sides of such highway or street." The amendment leaves open for dispute the question of what shall be "a suitable building lot," but this can best be defined by special act when the peculiar needs of each improvement are considered.

The Wisconsin amendment makes constitutional an excess taking of neighboring property for streets, squares, public parks, parkways, civic centers, and playgrounds and their surroundings, and after the improvement surplus land may be conveyed with restrictions to protect the improvement.

Before these amendments to the constitution were proposed, court decisions were frequent that it was the province of the legislature to determine whether a proposed taking was necessary for the public use. When once the legislature had so determined, only in case of a manifest injustice or where the legislature had obviously overstepped the bounds of the constitution would the supreme court interfere with the legislative action. The amendments take away the limitation set in the state constitution and therefore leave no constitutional question for the state judicial tribunal to determine. Whether the federal courts would take jurisdiction of such a case from the state court on the ground that property is taken without due process of law in violation of the fourteenth amendment, is still undetermined.

THE EXPEDIENCY OF ADOPTING IN THE UNITED STATES THE EXCESS CONDEMNATION PRINCIPLE

We are not here considering the value of excess taking where the sole or even primary purpose is to recoup the municipality's investment in a public improvement. Such a use of the power would probably not pass the constitutional test, would be too open to abuse, and would tend to draw municipalities into such large speculative holdings of real estate as might easily overstrain their credit. But in the cases where excess taking is made primarily to secure the greatest physical benefit from the improvement, the community is able incidentally to reap a portion of the increase in values caused by the investment of the community's money through the sale of such land as is not actually needed for the improvement. This method of distributing the cost of an improvement is supposed to produce a larger financial return to the city than the special assessment method, and at the same time to avoid the expense of litigating with property owners the question of benefit.

1. FINANCIAL VALUE OF EXCESS CONDEMNATION

In cities where special assessments to cover a large portion of the cost of acquiring land are levied and collected, and the tax payers are not restive, there is little enthusiasm over the European method of financing reconstruction. But cities in which special assessments are ineffective or non-existent, as in Boston, Philadelphia, and cities of Ohio, see in excess condemnation an opportunity to get for the community a large portion of the increment resulting from reconstruction with less chance for litigation by the land holders. No city in the United States has yet experimented with such condemnation,* but precedents from abroad are confidently cited as establishing its financial value. To determine the soundness of this opinion would require an analysis of European reconstructions in which excess takings have been made, and such an analysis depends for its value so much on a first hand acquaintance with many various sets of local conditions that to attempt it here is impossible. A review of the available sources of information on the subject does not make out an overwhelming case for the financial success of excess condemnation.

FINANCIAL RESULTS IN FRANCE. From 1852 to 1869 new streets were laid out in Paris which required a total surface of 2,726,000 square yards.

---

* We refer to clear cases of the deliberate use of the method, especially in connection with street laying out. In the case of parks and parkways an entire lot is systematically condemned by certain boards whenever they find themselves compelled to take so costly a portion that the whole would be a better bargain. Even though a portion of the lot taken might lie entirely outside the line of any proposed construction a park commission could claim if pressed that its acquirement and planting were properly incidental to the park purpose of the improvement; and courts are very slow to upset an administrative decision on such a point. After acquirement the administrative authority can decide that the remnant is not needed by the public after all, and if properly authorized by the legislature may proceed to "abandon" or sell it for a suitable consideration.

In the case of the Burnt District Commission, created in 1904 (Acts of Maryland, 1904, Chapter 87), to deal with the emergency caused by the Baltimore fire, there was definite provision for the condemnation of entire lots in case a portion was needed for a public improvement and for the sale of the remnants at public auction. It is reported that this power was used in at least one case and that a remnant almost unusable alone was bought by a speculator at public auction and used in a manner calculated to extort blackmail from the owner next in the rear.

EXCESS CONDEMNATION

Under the law, the authorities were allowed to take in excess of actual need for street purposes only when the lots left after the taking were unsuitable in shape or size for the erection of proper buildings; but the policy of the French government allowed a very liberal construction of the law, and 'remnants' were taken in some cases 5,000 square feet in area. Remnants which were at the time of the taking considered unsuitable for building purposes were subsequently subdivided into at least two lots, each of which was sold for a building lot. Just how much excess land was taken for the purpose of new streets in this period is not known. In 1869 the sales of such land had totaled $51,800,000, and there was still on hand 728,400 square yards, valued at $14,400,000. The cost of all the land taken was $259,400,000. Valuing the excess taking at $66,200,000, the land actually used for street purposes cost $193,200,000.* "In other words, the sale of lands purchased in excess of the requirements for the purpose of making new streets, together with the sale of 390,000 square yards obtained through the discontinuance of old streets, yielded only 25.5 per cent of the original outlay upon land—$259,400,000. That means that the efforts to secure a part of the increase in values resulting from the laying out of 56.25 miles of streets proved unsuccessful."†

* *Le Journal Officiel de l'Empire Français*, June 18, 1868, January 13, 1869, November 28, 1869.
† Massachusetts House Document No. 288, 1904, p. 58.

CARRYING OUT THE CITY PLAN

No period offered a better opportunity for a successful test of the principle of excess taking as a method of recoupment. The years from 1852 to 1869 were marked by rapid increase in values. The prices received by the city for the sale of surplus land were considered excellent, but the initial cost of all the land condemned had been enormously heavy and for this the juries were responsible. M. Brelay, a former member of the Commission des Indemnités, a body established by the state for the purpose of bringing together without recourse to the jury, public authorities and owners of land says: "The proceedings before the juries are among the most discouraging symptoms of the day. In these proceedings cheating almost has come to be honorable; the juries willingly accept scandalous statements as to value and inventories and leases prepared by lawyers and expert valuers who display a profound knowledge of the extent to which human folly will go in the person of the juror." In 1890 awards were so excessive to owners of land that an award of 50 per cent more than the fair market value was commented upon as honest by Brelay in his survey of public improvements in Paris.* Awards to tenants, whether merchants or householders, were even more excessive. In 1888 the city took 48 houses occupied by tenants who paid an average rental of $54 a year. The owners of property

---

* *L'Economiste Français*, May 31, 1884, June 18, 1887, September 9, 1903.

had the right to dispossess the tenants on three months' notice. The tenants' holdings were therefore worth $13.50—three months' rent; the juries awarded an average of $169.* In another case the city offered housekeeping tenants $700;† the jury awarded $13,000. The offer of the city to tenants with trade interests was increased by the jury from $486,560 to $935,120.‡ To one tenant, with no trade interest or lease, the city offered $7.40; the jury gave him $600.§ "The city had authorized the construction of the Bourse de Commerce on the assumption that the compensations for taking for public use would aggregate $5,000,000; in September, 1887, the compensations awarded aggregated $8,000,000."‖

The avowed purpose in the liberal takings between 1852 and 1869 was to reduce the expense of street improvements. There was no satisfactory law under which the cost of land for streets could be assessed on benefited properties, and only by the sale of excess lands could the expense be reduced. The failure of the method resulted in a change of policy by the Council of State which, from the time of the establishment of the present republic, opposed any excess takings simply for the purpose of resale. When the Trousseau Hospital was removed the Council of State refused to approve the taking of any remnant whose area

* *L'Economiste Français*, September 1, 1888. See also Massachusetts House Document No. 288 of 1904, pp. 60 ff.

† *L'Economiste Français*, August 23, 1890.   ‡ Ibid., June 18, 1887.
§ Ibid., June 18, 1887.   ‖ Ibid., September 10, 1887.

exceeded 650 square feet, even though it was admitted that the controlling purpose of the city authorities was not recoupment.* Approval was given for the taking of small remnants on the ground that the additional cost of acquisition was trifling, and small remnants were readily sold at a price which more than compensated for the additional cost.

As a result of the experience, both before and after the establishment of the present republic, it is the consensus of opinion among those who have had experience with both methods, that extended excess taking *for the purpose of securing a profit* from the resale of surplus land is neither desirable nor profitable.†

FINANCIAL RESULTS IN BELGIUM. The law which permits excess taking in Belgium was passed at the instance of Brussels and to satisfy a peculiar need. The old city of Brussels had no street system worthy of the name, and the jumble of narrow, crooked streets and blind alleys resulted in a most unsanitary condition. Lots, as a rule, were small, in some cases ridiculously so, one plan showing lots with areas of 150 to 175 square feet. Through the center of the lower part of the city flowed the River Senne which was little better than an open sewer. The improvement made possible by the law of 1867 was to carry the river

* Massachusetts House Document No. 1096 of 1904, p. 5.
† Ibid., p. 6.

underneath the city and to build over the old river bed a broad central thoroughfare, which is now the main business street of the city. The law fixed no limit to the extent of land which could be taken in excess of actual needs, and Brussels used the law most liberally.

In addition to the heavy outlay for land, the authorities incurred extraordinary expenses in order to induce a rapid and yet proper development of the new streets. Several public buildings were constructed by the city on the new boulevard; loans were made to contractors to the extent of one-half of the estimated cost of buildings; surplus land was sold on very easy terms, the only requirement being the payment of 4.5 per cent per annum on the purchase price for sixty-six years, payments which were calculated to "extinguish the principal of the debt at the end of that term while giving the city an income on the amount unpaid of $4\frac{1}{5}$ per cent."* These terms proved altogether too tempting and the speculation that resulted brought about wholesale failure of contractors and purchasers. In the end the city was forced to complete the construction of the new boulevard at an expense greatly in excess of the original estimate, to complete unfinished buildings on which loans had been made, and to foreclose through the failure of purchasers of lots. Today the city is the owner of nearly 400 buildings on this thoroughfare known as the New or Inner

* Massachusetts House Document No. 1096 of 1904, p. 12.

CARRYING OUT THE CITY PLAN

Boulevard. The increase in debt occasioned by this and other improvements was enormous. At the beginning of the year 1867 the debt was less than $8,000,000; by the year 1879 it exceeded $50,000,000; and when refunded in 1886 it was about $56,000,000. The city in the early 80's was on the verge of bankruptcy.*

In 1902 it was estimated that the properties acquired by the city in connection with the new boulevard had cost approximately $6,400,000. "The value of the properties at the time of acquisition was fixed either by expert appraisal or the foreclosure sale at $5,200,000." In 1902 they were believed to be worth about $6,400,000; but on the basis of the income which the city receives they would not sell for much more than $5,500,000, and the city is satisfied to keep the properties which are yielding more than enough "to meet interest and sinking fund requirements† on the amount of debt which could be retired through their sale."

Authorities of the city of Brussels without exception consider that excess taking is the only method which could have produced the Brussels of today, and the burgomaster, in 1904, was even of the opinion that the method had been a means of reducing the expense of street improvements. Other cities of Belgium, by avoiding the extraordinary expense connected with the building op-

---
* Massachusetts House Document No. 1096 of 1904, p. 14.
† Ibid., p. 13.

erations under loans undertaken in Brussels, are reported to have secured a profit out of the sales of excess lands. This is notably so in the case of Liege. Despite the financial strain through which Brussels went from 1875 to 1886, it is probably true that the peculiar conditions of Brussels justified the extraordinary methods adopted for its improvement; but whatever may be the consensus of opinion about the success of the experience of the city with excess condemnation it can not be advantageously cited as a precedent for the adoption of excess condemnation as a means of reducing the expense of reconstruction in the United States. The experience with excess taking in Paris and in the cities of Belgium shows conclusively that a considerable period must elapse before real estate contiguous to the improvement increases to any great extent in value* and this experience is confirmed by that of London as shown below. It has, with surprising uniformity, been at least eight years in all three countries before such increase has been noticeable. As an element of the cost of excess condemnation, therefore, the interest on the outlay for the acquisition of land and buildings must be figured for a period of eight to ten years.

FINANCIAL RESULTS IN LONDON. From 1857 to 1889 the Metropolitan Board of Works of London made 14 miles of street widenings and

* Massachusetts House Document No. 1096 of 1904, p. 15.

thoroughfares, for the most part in the central portion of the city, in order to "supply the deficiencies resulting from centuries of neglect and to keep pace with the wants of an ever increasing population."* During these years the policy of the board was most conservative, and in this respect it differs from both the practice in Paris and the practice in Belgium. The taking of costly buildings was avoided even at the expense of the appearance of the street, and such takings as were made were strictly limited to those properties the whole or a part of which were required for the actual improvement. The cost of the land taken for street improvements was $58,859,000, and there was subsequently recovered from the sale of surplus lands $25,607,000 or 43.5 per cent.† The exact amount of land taken or the land sold is not given in the History of London Street Improvements, but in connection with each street the total cost and the total return from sales are given; and of the 54 separate improvements made by the Metropolitan Board of Works only one, namely, Northumberland Avenue, shows a profit from the entire transaction exclusive of cost of construction. The cost was £711,491 and recoupment from sales, £831,310. The profit in this street improvement is variously accounted for.‡ In evidence

*Edwards, P. J.: History of London Street Improvements, 1855–1897, p. 11. London, P. S. King & Son, 1898.
† Massachusetts House Document No. 288 of 1904, p. 65.
‡ Edwards, op. cit., p. 17.
See also Report of the Massachusetts Commission on the Right of Eminent Domain. House Document No. 288 of 1904, p. 68.

given before the select committee of the House of Lords the case of Northumberland Avenue was cited as entirely exceptional, because the Duke of Northumberland had given the land at a price which was calculated to leave a profit from the improvement. Moreover, the land was not occupied by buildings and there were no tenants with trade interests. It is these two factors, representing a dead loss to be charged against any increase in land values, which are largely responsible for the poor financial showing of excess condemnation.

Out of a total of 57 streets, those in which the recovery exceeds 35 per cent of the cost are given in the following table:*

TABLE 6.—COMPENSATION FOR LAND, GROSS COST, RECEIPTS FROM SALE OF LAND, AND NET COST FOR IMPROVEMENTS MADE BY THE METROPOLITAN BOARD OF WORKS IN CASES IN WHICH THE RECOVERY EXCEEDED 35 PER CENT OF THE COST. LONDON, 1857–1889

Street	Compensation for land	Other payments reckoned	Gross cost	Receipts from sales of land	Net cost
Garrick	£106,691	£16,521	£123,212	£89,072	£34,140
Southwark	476,238	108,692	584,930	218,860	366,070
Queen Victoria	2,055,408	245,112	2,300,520	1,224,233	1,076,287
High St., Shoreditch	184,184	27,519	211,703	89,887	121,816
Shaftsbury Ave.	1,004,990	131,466	1,136,456	377,569	758,887
Mare St., Hackney	54,175	5,827	60,002	24,340	35,662
Tooley St. Extension	68,673	7,233	75,906	45,388	30,518

* Edwards, op. cit., pp. 134, 135, 136, 137.

Most of the remaining streets show a recovery from the sale of surplus land of less than 20 per cent, and doubtless in many of these cases if the taking had been limited to the land necessary for the street there would have been a saving in the net cost. In the case of Gray's Road Inn, for instance, a simple street widening, the land alone cost $2,017,000 and from sales $422,000 was recovered, which made a net cost of $1,595,000. "Had the board bought only the land needed for street purposes the cost would have been $1,264,000."*

The Metropolitan Board of Works was criticized for not making more liberal takings, and in the history of its successor, the London County Council, many bills were proposed which authorized a more liberal taking of land solely for recoupment purposes. The London County Council, however, continued the policy of the Metropolitan Board of Works and favored as an additional method of paying for the cost of the improvements a special assessment for benefit.

The relative advantages of excess taking for "recoupment" and the levying of an assessment for benefit were the subject of investigation during the history of the London County Council. Members of the old Metropolitan Board of Works were uniform in condemning excess takings as a method of reducing the cost of improvements.†

* Massachusetts House Document No. 288 of 1904, p. 67.
† Op. cit., pp. 67–68.

EXCESS CONDEMNATION

In 1894 Mr. Charles Harrison, vice-chairman of the London County Council, said that recoupment as carried out in London had been unsatisfactory and had tended to result in a net loss. Mr. W. H. Dickenson, deputy chairman of the London County Council, was of the opinion that past public improvements had produced a rise in prices which would have made the recoupment operations yield a certain profit had that profit not been eaten up before it had been obtained. Mr. J. F. Moulton, member of the London County Council, gave evidence that "recoupment is almost always a loss, and increases the cost unless you are going through comparatively unoccupied property or property which is used for habitation and not for purposes of trade." H. L. Cripps, twenty-five years a member of the Metropolitan Board of Works, said, "It may be taken generally that in no single case, according to the opinions of competent surveyors, has recoupment turned out other than an extravagant operation." As a result of its own experience and that of its predecessor, the Metropolitan Board of Works, the London County Council took the position before every investigating committee of Parliament that the practice of recoupment by the sale of excess lands should give way as both less desirable and less practicable than an assessment for special benefit.

From 1890 to 1898 Parliament refused to grant to the Council the power to assess for special bene-

CARRYING OUT THE CITY PLAN

fit, and in this period practically no large improvement schemes were initiated by the Council. In 1899 the power was granted and was incorporated in the legislation which made possible the King's Highway improvement from Holborn to the Strand. This is probably the most important large improvement of recent years, and in it are united both the principles of excess condemnation and of assessment for betterment. It has been cited in this country as the strongest illustration of the advantage of excess taking as a method of recouping the cost of an improvement.

It is impossible to get accurate figures on the net cost of this improvement since much of the excess land taken is not yet sold or leased, and since it is not certain what portion of the original cost has been returned to the city by sale of excess land and what portion has been returned by assessment for benefit. The cost of land taking and improvement is variously estimated from £4,862,500 to £7,000,000. The last figure includes approximately £2,000,000 for interest charges covering a period of at least fifteen years. The most favorable estimate of the return is £5,000,000, which includes the return from the benefit assessment, making the net cost of the improvement approximately £2,000,000, or the amount of interest charges during the period of development.*

*Manuscript Report of London County Council Improvement Committee, 1910.

EXCESS CONDEMNATION

In analyzing these figures it must be remembered that they were submitted by a political party opposed to the one which initiated the scheme, and items of cost are included which are more than offset by indirect gains that are not easily reducible to figures. The physical results accomplished by the King's Highway would have been impossible without the very liberal use of excess taking. The very satisfactory financial result may be due in a large measure to the advantageous lease of surplus land, but, considering the opinion of best informed authorities in London and the history of London street improvements from 1859 to 1900, and considering further that some part of the return in the case of the King's Highway is the result of betterment assessments on property not acquired, it seems unwise to lay too great stress on the King's Highway improvement as a precedent for the use of excess taking merely as a method of recoupment.

The causes of the general failure of excess taking to give satisfactory financial returns in London are much the same as they are in France:

First, the cost of acquiring excess land is great because of extravagant jury awards and because of the practice of paying for trade interests and for the "goodwill" of such businesses as are obliged to seek other locations. Mr. Harrison, vice-chairman of the County Council, is of the opinion that recoupment cases show not that there is a loss on the land which is acquired, but that the loss arises exclusively from buying what can not be resold (trade interests), and represents great waste, legal costs, and other items of expenditure attached to each interest.* Mr. Dickenson, deputy chairman of the County Council, believes that even if the fee simple alone were taken and the leasehold and subleasehold interests allowed to run out, extravagant prices would be paid and that it would be best to "intercept the benefit" by means of a betterment tax. The fee simple alone would cost at least 10 per cent more than the market value, and to that sum must be added much more in costs.†

Second, the effect on values of an improvement is uncertain. In every country where excess taking is practiced it is the common experience to find that occupation of all kinds adapts itself slowly to a considerable change in the street plan. This phenomenon is not dependent on racial characteristics. In Paris, in the cities of Belgium, and in London at least eight years, as has been noted, were necessary before the city or property owners received the benefit expected from the change.

Third, the large power entrusted to administrative boards, both in the awards for damages and in the negotiation and sale of excess land, is open to great abuse. Charges of maladministration in the Metropolitan Board of Works were

* Massachusetts House Document No. 288 of 1904, p. 76.
† Ibid., p. 76.

made the subject of investigation by a royal commission in 1888, and in spite of the finding by the commission that the board was not corrupt, a great deal of uncontradicted evidence of dishonest practice was offered.

DIFFICULTIES IN THE UNITED STATES. In considering whether excess condemnation is justifiable on the ground of securing to the city such profit from the resale of excess land as will enable it to recoup a large part of the cost of the improvement, it must be borne in mind that "failure of administration" is as likely to defeat expectations in the United States as in Europe. Certainly jury awards in many jurisdictions, and particularly in older jurisdictions, where reconstruction is most necessary, are excessive, and municipal administrations in the United States are no more above temptation than was the London Metropolitan Board of Works.

2. PHYSICAL VALUE OF EXCESS CONDEMNATION

Irrespective of its value as a financial expedient, excess taking allows the municipality to secure the greatest physical benefit from an improvement. The widening or relocating of a built-up street is likely to involve a complete rearranging of lot lines, particularly in older cities where the lot line is irregular and the depth of lots varies greatly. To limit the taking of land to that actually acquired for the construction of the street results inevitably in remnant lots, and the one effective way to unite these remnants with larger parcels is to put their control in the hands of the municipality, and to provide for an impartial appraisal of their value. It should be an exceptional case where the owner of the lot adjoining the remnants would not take the land at its appraised value, but even if the remnants remained unoccupied their control by the municipality would be more likely to prevent their use for undesirable purposes than if they were left in private ownership.

Control over remnants is possible with a very limited right of excess taking. If the right is enlarged and the municipality permitted to take on both sides of a widened business thoroughfare land enough for suitable building lots, the construction of buildings can be secured which will fit the thoroughfare and will yield the highest possible return in taxation. It is equally desirable for the municipality to control land abutting on parks, parkways, and approaches to public buildings, both to prevent a use of the land which would be disfiguring and to induce by restriction in the deed of sale of such land a type of construction which would harmonize with the public purpose.

Those who oppose the radical extension of the power of eminent domain believe that control over development by the municipality can be as effectively gained by the acquisition of easements in the land abutting on streets, parks, and parkways, which would prohibit certain uses of the land and prescribe the character and even the style of architecture of the buildings constructed upon it. Much has been accomplished by such easements. They may do no more than require an open front yard or garden of minimum depth on the private property* or fix an arbitrary height limitation on buildings,† or they may require approval in detail by a public authority of the designs of buildings in case they are built above or beyond certain limits.‡ In theory at least they may curtail the freedom of the land owner to any extent which might be found necessary to secure to the public completely satisfactory use of the adjacent public improvement. But practically they are limited by the fact that if they diminish too far the freedom of control which the owner of the fee can exercise over the development and use of the property they will establish a divided responsibility which is fatal to efficiency and initiative, and which absolutely destroys much of the economic value of the property. The fear of such a result may raise the damages for the acquirement of extensive easements almost to the full value of the property. In addition to this practical limitation upon the taking of easements in connection with special assessments as a substitute for excess condemnation in those cases to which the latter is specially applicable, it is to be

---

* Customary easement along parkways in many cities.
† Copley Square case, see pp. 19 ff.
‡ Restrictions on certain Boston parkways.

noted that one important function of the excess condemnation method is not provided for at all; namely, the prompt readjustment of such serious disturbances of the normal size and shape of lots and of the normal relation of property lines to streets as may have been caused by the public action in forcing through an improvement. These disturbances constitute a situation as full of injustice to the owner of the lots as it is unsatisfactory from the point of view of the public.

CONCLUSIONS

1. In the absence of more convincing precedents too much reliance should not be placed on excess condemnation as a method of distributing the cost of public improvements. Where the maximum physical benefit from an improvement can be secured under the present restricted power of eminent domain, excess taking should not be resorted to except in rare cases where it would involve few expensive buildings and where the land value is so low that the inevitable tendency is upward. Rather than introduce excess taking for the purpose chiefly of recouping the city's investment, the highest possible return should be sought by the American method of special assessment, already proved an eminently successful method of distributing the cost of the acquisition of land for public purposes.

2. But the use of excess taking to protect the value, both economic and esthetic, of a business

thoroughfare, park, or parkway is sometimes essential to the full success of a great improvement. Only by its use in some cases can the full advantage of an improved thoroughfare be secured by providing abutting lots of size and shape adapted for suitable structures. Only by selling surplus land under restrictions can the city most effectively control the fringe along the widened thoroughfare. Whether its use results in a net financial profit or not is a secondary consideration if it accomplishes a necessary result more completely and efficiently than can otherwise be done.

CHAPTER V

USE OF THE POLICE POWER IN THE EXECUTION OF A CITY PLAN

THE control over city building by reason of land ownership is not peculiar to a governmental agency, nor does it depend on legislative authority. Possession of land is the only essential, whether that possession be in a municipal corporation, or in a private corporation organized as a land company for the sole purpose of directing the development of the whole or parts of a city in accordance with a plan.

The type of control over city building which we are now to consider, however, is peculiar to a governmental agency. It grows out of the duty of the administrative body representing all the people to protect the rights of all from individual aggression. Through the process of acquiring lands and rights in land, the city merely by wise use of its possessions and without the exercise of governmental authority may induce the kind of development which is desirable. This process is gradual and may escape public notice. But in acting as the guardian of the community the city says to the individual, "Thou shalt not," and by ordinance it restrains him from doing things on his own land which would damage the health, safety, or morals of the community.

In exercising this power the city council passes an ordinance, and the court determines whether the purpose of the ordinance is confined to those matters which have a real and substantial relation to the public welfare and whether the ordinance is reasonably calculated to carry out this purpose. These are the only tests applied. In a limited field this power of restraint is exercised without question, and ordinances have the strength of custom and legal decision behind them. In a still larger field it is assumed that restraint can not be exercised. But the doubtful ground between is constantly being encroached upon either by ordinances restraining the power of the individual or by decisions denying the power of the community. The law as made and as interpreted by the courts is constantly changing as the sentiment of the community changes.

A too intensive use of land is the chief contributing cause to poor housing, and shares with poor street planning the responsibility for economic losses consequent on every kind of street congestion. A use of land either for buildings unfit structurally for habitation or for other purposes offensive to the occupants of surrounding land reacts upon the use of the latter, tends to instability in values, and may blight a district otherwise adapted to a higher economic use, as for residence or retail trade. A well built city would control by means of segregation the use of land for purposes that would seriously conflict with those of other owners, and would insist on sanitary and structural excellence for its homes. Public control of all such matters on private land is accomplished directly under the police power. A complete catalogue of municipal regulations which limit the use of private land is not within the scope of this chapter, since many such regulations have little or no influence on the physical development of the city; but those which most affect the city plan will be considered under (1) limitations on the degree to which the intensive use of land may be carried, and (2) limitations on the degree to which the offensive use of land may be carried.

LIMITATIONS ON THE DEGREE TO WHICH THE INTENSIVE USE OF LAND MAY BE CARRIED

1. LIMITATIONS ON THE HEIGHT AND SIZE OF BUILDINGS

Most modern building codes interfere with the use of land by provisions limiting the amount of the lot which can be occupied and the height to which certain classes of buildings can be erected. Some cities impose an absolute height limit beyond which no building of whatever class of construction can be erected.* Ordinances of this character are generally sustained by the courts on the theory that they provide a reasonable method of protect-

---
* See Appendix, p. 242.

ing the safety and health of the community. This is particularly true of some provisions which require a specific allowance of space between non-fireproof structures. The serious nature of the "conflagration risk" involved even in buildings of fireproof construction as established by the Baltimore and San Francisco fires would make this theory applicable even to non-combustible structures because of the combustible material which they contain. Thus the absolute height limitation of 125 feet imposed in Boston on buildings of all classes was sustained in Welch *vs.* Swasey, 193 Mass. 373:

"The erection of very high buildings in cities, especially upon narrow streets, may be carried so far as materially to exclude sunshine, light, and air and thus affect public health. It may also increase the danger to persons and property from fires and be a subject for legislation on that ground. These are proper subjects for consideration in determining whether in a given case rights of property in the use of land should be interfered with for the public good. . . . Merely because the commission has come to a conclusion different from that to which the court may come is not in itself sufficient to declare the result of the work unconstitutional."

The decision of the state court was sustained by the supreme court of the United States in Welch *vs.* Swasey, 214 U. S. 91.

It is believed that this is the most extreme ordinance on the subject of height limitations of buildings in the United States which has received judicial approval by the highest courts.*

How much further an ordinance could go and still be held within the police power can be decided only by framing the ordinance and getting it tested. Any other answer to the question would be a guess which is likely to be wrong. City planners ask, "Can buildings be limited to a height not greater than the width of the street between property lines?" Building regulations in Washington, D. C., provide that no building shall exceed in height the width of the street or be constructed to a height over 90 feet on a residence street or 110 feet on a business street, except that buildings may be erected to 130 feet on avenues 160 feet wide. In New York the case of People vs. D'Oench, 111 N. Y. 359, indicates the probable answer to the question, if the kind of buildings is limited to those used or intended to be used for dwellings of more than one family. The question presented to the court in that case was whether the act of 1885 applied to hotels. The act provided that "the height of all dwelling houses and of all houses used or intended to be used as dwellings for more than one family shall not exceed 80 feet in streets and avenues exceeding 60 feet in width." The court found that there was no doubt of the competency of the legislature in the exercise of the police power under the constitution to pass such an act, but that the act did not apply to hotels.

* See pp. 146 ff. for further discussion of this law.

USE OF THE POLICE POWER

Can wooden buildings used for residence be limited to two stories? Building regulations of 1909 for Memphis contain just that provision and there is little doubt that the ordinance would be sustained.

Regulations governing the size of a building in relation to its lot are not so generally adopted and are much more limited in application. An examination of the building codes of the 51 cities of over 100,000 population shows that at least 18, and among them three of the 10 largest cities in the country, have no ordinances on the subject. In several others the regulation is of the mildest kind; as, for instance, in the tenement house act for cities of Massachusetts (Acts 1913, Chapter 786) which provides that no tenement house of third class construction shall be erected nearer than 5 feet to adjoining lot line; but it may be constructed to the lot line if protected by a fire wall. A provision found in several codes limits the size only of tenement houses and apartment houses by specifying the proportion of lot which may be built upon, varying in the case of a corner lot from 75 per cent to 95 per cent, and in the case of an interior lot from 60 per cent to 80 per cent. The building code of Baltimore provides that there shall not be less than 20 feet between frame buildings, and no other building of any kind shall be built within 20 feet of any existing frame building on the next lot.

A bill presented to the legislature of the state

of Washington in 1911* proposed a considerable extension of the right to regulate the use of private property by requiring that in every newly developed area containing five acres or more there should be a reservation of 10 per cent of the land for public open space, after deducting such land as would be required for street purposes. It is clear that a most liberal interpretation of the police power would not justify a regulation which in reality amounts to a taking of private property without compensation.

That the courts will not sanction any and every legislative regulation is clear in several decisions in which the validity of ordinances specifying the degree of intensity with which property should be used have been successfully attacked. The supreme court of California in 1910, in the case of Wilson *et al. vs.* City of Alhambra, 158 Cal. 430, enjoined the enforcing of an ordinance which compelled the owner of six acres of land to lay out a street over his land not less than 50 feet wide. The street in this case was an extension of an existing street which was only 40 feet wide. The court held merely that to require an owner to build a street wider than many of the existing streets in the town was an unreasonable exercise of the police power.

* House Bill No. 81, 12th Session. (The bill was not reached in committee.)

USE OF THE POLICE POWER

2. DIFFERENTIATED ZONES OF HEIGHT LIMITATION

A most important question to the city planner is to what extent American municipalities may, in the exercise of the police power, copy regulations common in German cities and prescribe different building regulations for different districts of a city. The principle is not new in the United States. Many cities have at least two building districts from one of which non-fireproof buildings are excluded. The constitutionality of fire zone ordinances is universally upheld.

The building regulations in the city of Köln are taken as illustrating the German system, because they are simple compared with the regulations in some other German cities. The city is divided into four building districts, the first of which comprises the area inside the old city walls and contains the central business district. In this district buildings may have four stories and a height of 66½ feet, and may occupy 75 per cent of an inner lot and 80 per cent of a corner lot. The second district is made up of the more closely built suburbs of urban character, and here buildings may have not more than three stories, a height of not more than 52½ feet, and may occupy 75 per cent of the lot if the building does not exceed 26 feet in height, but only 65 per cent otherwise. In the third district the buildings are limited to two stories, a height of 38 feet, and may occupy 65 per cent of the lot if they do not exceed 20 feet in height, and only 50 per cent otherwise. The fourth district is devoted to detached buildings or villas of two stories and 52½ feet in height. Only 40 per cent of the site may be covered by buildings, or 50 per cent if the site is a corner lot. In this district also there must be at least 33 feet between buildings and 16½ feet from the boundary of the lots to the buildings. Reference to the map of Köln will show that the districts have been so located that just outside the old walls of the city is a broad band of open villa buildings, and that the more closely built suburban districts are also separated by the same open style of construction.

An approach to the German system is found in Boston and in Washington. The Massachusetts commission on height of buildings authorized under chapter 333 of the statutes of 1904, was empowered merely to divide the city of Boston into districts of two classes in such manner that the parts of the city in which the greater part of the buildings were used for business or commercial purposes should be included in District A and the rest of the city in District B. The statute itself prescribed the limit of 125 feet for buildings in District A and further provided that in District B no buildings should be over 80 feet. Under a later act, chapter 383 of the statutes of 1905, the commission was empowered to designate that part of District B where buildings exceeding 80 feet and not exceeding 100 feet could be erected; and there was a further provision in this act which limited the height of buildings in certain designated districts to 70 feet. The commission's first report fixed the boundaries of District A, and the second report regulated the height of buildings in District B in accordance with the width of the street and the width of the building. On all streets over 64 feet wide the buildings could be erected to one and one-half times the width of the street up to 100 feet, provided that their height did not exceed twice their narrowest width.

Boston's several zones are more highly differentiated than even those of Köln, but the Köln regulations are much more severe than the most drastic of the Boston provisions. Thus Boston has a narrowly limited business zone and several other zones differing, not in accordance with the distance from the business center, but in accordance with the width of the street and width of the buildings. The commission's report and the decisions of both the state and federal courts sustaining it are unique in the United States. The court held that in the exercise of the police power the legislature could determine an absolute height limitation for all buildings in the city, and could delegate to a commission the right to fix the boundaries of building districts and to establish varying height limitations in one of these districts.*

* For text of the acts, see Appendix, pp. 221, 223.
For text of the decisions, see Appendix, pp. 219, 226 ff.

CARRYING OUT THE CITY PLAN

This decision has been generally accepted as of great importance in working out some of the details of city planning. There is not involved in it the question of the amount of space which can be occupied by buildings in the different building districts, and for this reason the decision is not a complete precedent for the introduction of the zoning system of Germany in the United States, but it is likely that the Massachusetts court would uphold an ordinance framed to include all the details of the Köln system.

If the legislature can establish two building districts it certainly can establish three or even four. If its authority to delegate to a commission power to regulate the height of buildings in each district is sustained by the courts on the ground that it is a reasonable way of securing an adequate amount of light and air, it should follow that the power to regulate the amount of space that each building may occupy in a horizontal direction can also be delegated. Building codes prescribe the distance between buildings or the open space which must attach to each building, and this regulation is sanctioned by the decisions. It is as logical to provide a larger proportion of open space in districts where the demand for land is less as it is to provide less height for buildings in such districts. An ordinance which prescribes for different building districts varying amounts of land which may be occupied, as well as varying heights of buildings, is much more calculated to lessen the fire risk and to safeguard the health of the community than one which is operative only in the area of greatest land values and most congested occupancy. The burden is on the private owner to show that the legislative act is unreasonable. That the courts will be slow to declare unreasonable the legislative finding has been established in numerous decisions, and applying this test of reasonableness to an ordinance which would include the principle of the zone system of Köln it is difficult to see how it could be successfully questioned.

It is quite another question whether it would be expedient to introduce such an ordinance. Local conditions might be such that property owners would be right in refusing to entrust so important a question to a municipal administration or to a commission appointed by that administration. In purchasing lots they may cheerfully submit to the restrictions imposed by a land company, no matter how much their rights are curtailed. They may agree to set back their buildings 20 feet from the line of their property; they may agree to build nothing on the land except a dwelling house of certain value and to have the rest of it set out in gardens, and even to submit the position and design of their houses, hedges, fences, and gates for approval to a small committee representing the vendors of the tract. Such restrictions, when drawn to meet the conditions of the real estate market, attract buyers rather than repel them, because these restrictions upon the liberty of individual lot owners protect each against the danger of certain injurious actions by any neighbors. Yet a suggestion of control from municipal authorities might raise a strong protest. It is an interesting speculation whether some form of district building regulations subject to a referendum within each district will not meet American conditions successfully.

LIMITATIONS ON THE DEGREE TO WHICH THE OFFENSIVE USE OF LAND MAY BE CARRIED

The right of the municipality in any given case to suppress uses of land depends on the language of its charter, but under a universal charter provision a municipality may protect the general welfare of its people, and many uses of land are enjoined under this general power.

1. USES OF LAND WHICH IMPAIR THE FREE USE OF A PUBLIC HIGHWAY

Encroachments on the highway of signs, awnings, posts, porches, stoops, stands, and so forth, are generally included among those offensive uses of land which are prohibited in the exercise of the police power. If their use obstructs the street or diminishes the space available for walking, or impedes traffic, they may be abated or indicted as nuisances, and it is not necessary that the comfort of the public should be interfered with materially.*

* State vs. Berdetta, 73 Ind. 185.

But the right of suppression is as well put on other grounds. The municipality either owns the land in the highway or possesses an easement in the land for highway purposes, and can prohibit by virtue of this ownership any use inconsistent with those purposes. The case of the Fifth Avenue Coach Co. *vs.* City of New York, 111 N. Y. Supp. 759, is in point.* The action was brought by the plaintiff coach company to enjoin New York City from interfering with advertising signs displayed on the outside of their auto stages which travel on Fifth Avenue. The court denied the injunction on the ground that the plaintiff did not show a clear right to warrant the interference of the court, since the ordinance of the city under which the advertising of the plaintiff company was prohibited was a reasonable regulation of the use of the street and did not operate to impair the plaintiff's franchise. In discussing the nature of the plaintiff's advertising business, however, the court said:

"It is along the entrance to parks and along the parks themselves preserved to attract lovers of nature and the beautiful that these unnatural and inartistic moving picture signs are displayed. But out of place, disagreeable and offensive though they are both to the civic pride and esthetic taste, and although the tendency of equitable jurisprudence is to extend its jurisdiction to include this situation, the fact remains that no authority now exists which will justify the legal con-

* Affirmed in 194 N. Y. 19.

clusion that the plaintiff's signs now constitute a nuisance."

The decision shows a tendency to give increasing regard to esthetic considerations, since it holds the ordinance a reasonable street regulation. In the same way, without resorting to the police power, the municipality may regulate the use of streets for poles and wires, and may compel the placing of wires underground as a condition of the franchise.

2. USES OF LAND WHICH CONSTITUTE A NUISANCE

A use of land which is inherently unlawful and unprofitable and dangerous to the safety and health or offensive to the morals of a community may be treated as a nuisance, *per se*. Rotten or decayed food or meat, infected bedding or clothing, mad dogs, animals affected with contagious diseases, and imminently dangerous structures, are conspicuous instances of nuisances *per se*. Such conditions may be summarily abated without previous notice. A use of land which does not in itself constitute a nuisance, but may become so by reason of its locality or the conditions surrounding its maintenance, may be prohibited altogether or confined to certain parts of a municipality.

Certain occupations are so generally recognized as belonging to the objectionable class, either because of the odors or noises which are inseparable from them, although conducted in the most care-

USE OF THE POLICE POWER

ful manner, that they are specifically named in municipal charters as nuisances which the municipality may abate. Thus, slaughter houses, glue factories, soap factories, canning factories, smelting works, rendering establishments, stables, and fertilizer factories are generally included in this class.* Some of these ordinances have been tested by the courts and found to be a reasonable exercise of the police power:

Rendering establishments:	Grand Rapids *vs.* Weiden, 97 Mich. 82
	Meigs *vs.* Lister, 23 N. J. Eq. 199
Slaughter houses:	Harmison *et al. vs.* City of Lewiston, 46 Ill. App. 164
	Ex parte Heilbron, 65 Cal. 609
	Beiling *vs.* City of Evanston, 144 Ind. 644
Smelting works:	Appeal of Pa. Lead Co., 96 Pa. 116
Stables:	Shiras *vs.* Olinger, 50 Ia. 571
Fertilizer factories:	Evans *vs.* Fertilizer Co., 160 Pa. 209
The emission of dense smoke:	People *vs.* Lewis, 86 Mich. 273
	Atlantic City *vs.* France, 74 N. J. Law 389
	Harmon *vs.* Chicago, 110 Ill. 400

* Charter of City of Dallas, Sect. 5, Par. 12. Charter of Detroit, Chap. 7, Sect. 44. Charter of Portland, Ore., Art. 4, Sect. 73, Par. 27.

Other courts have come to different conclusions with the same or very similar ordinances applied under different conditions, the courts holding that a declaration by municipal authorities that an occupation is a nuisance does not make it so in fact:

Slaughter houses:	Wreford *vs.* People, 14 Mich. 41
Stables:	Phillips *vs.* City of Denver, 19 Col. 179
The emission of dense smoke:	St. Louis *vs.* Heitzeberg Packing Co., 141 Mo. 375
	St. Paul *vs.* Gilfillan, 36 Minn. 298

3. DIFFERENTIATED DISTRICT REGULATIONS

Legislation in Massachusetts gives a further right by authorizing boards of health of cities or towns "to assign certain places for the exercise of any trade or employment which is a nuisance or hurtful to the inhabitants, injurious to their estates, dangerous to the public health, or is attended by noisome and injurious odors." They may also prohibit "the exercise thereof with the limits of the city or town or in places not so assigned."*

It does not seem to have been the practice of Massachusetts boards of health to exercise the right of assigning offensive occupations to certain parts of the city, and therefore the question of the

* Massachusetts Revised Laws, Chapter 75, Section 91.

right of the community to impair the value of private property by assigning objectionable occupations to certain districts has not been tested. The practical answer to this objection to segregating offensive occupations within defined limits is that they would be located only in those portions of the city where the value of the land or the character of occupation showed that legal actions by property owners included in the district would be unlikely, and, if brought, would be either dismissed or a nominal amount of damages be awarded.

Los Angeles has largely applied the principle of separating industrial districts from residential districts. By an ordinance adopted in 1909 seven industrial districts were established in the city, and by an ordinance of the next year all the rest of the city, with unimportant exceptions, was declared to be a residential district. The ordinance further provides that industrial occupations may be permitted in certain excepted portions of the residence district, and the right is reserved to except other portions as conditions warrant. It is made unlawful for any person, firm, or corporation "to erect, establish, maintain or carry on within the residential district described in section 1 of the ordinance any stone crusher, rolling mill, carpet beating establishment, fireworks factory, soap factory, or any other works or factory where power other than animal power is used to operate, or in the operation of the same, or any hay barn, wood yard, lumber yard, public laundry or wash house."

The ordinance was tested in the case of Ex Parte Quong Wo.* The petitioner, Quong Wo, who had been convicted and imprisoned for carrying on a public laundry and wash house in a residence district, sought to be discharged from custody. The court dismissed the application for a writ of habeas corpus, finding that it was within the lawful exercise of the police power to confine the business of operating a public laundry or wash house within defined limits. The following language of the decision is particularly in point:

"There can be no question that the power to regulate the carrying on of certain lawful occupations in a city includes the power to confine the carrying on of the same to certain limits whenever such restriction may reasonably be found necessary to subserve the ends for which the police power exists. . . . It is primarily for the legislative body clothed with this power to determine when such regulations are essential, and its determination in this regard, in view of its better knowledge of all the circumstances and the presumption that it is acting with a due regard for the rights of all parties will not be disturbed in the courts, unless it can plainly be seen that the regulation has no relation to the ends above stated, but is a clear invasion of personal or property rights under the guise of police regulation."

This decision was reviewed and upheld in the

* 161 Cal. 220.

case of Montgomery's application for a writ of habeas corpus, the only difference in the cases being that the petitioner in the latter case was imprisoned for carrying on or maintaining a lumber yard within the residence district.* The contention was made by Montgomery that a lumber yard was not one of those specific occupations which could be regulated under the exercise of the police power since it was not enumerated in the charter of the city. The court found specifically that if the ordinance could be upheld under the general police power of the city, it would not fall merely because the city had specific authority under its charter to suppress certain other kinds of business.

A similar ordinance has been proposed for the city of St. Paul:†

Section 2. It shall be unlawful to establish or maintain within said district any carpet beating establishment, stone crusher, rolling or planing mill, public laundry, fireworks, soap or cigar factory, machine shop, slaughter house or rendering works, brewery, distillery, tanning, furrier or canning plants, or any hospital or sanitarium, or asylum for defectives, or any establishment, works or factory which by reason of noise, offensive smell or vapor, or unsanitary effect, may be unhealthy or disturbing or injurious to persons or property within said district.

Section 3. Any person violating this ordinance shall be deemed guilty of misdemeanor and punished by

* 163 Cal. 457.
† Also see Acts of Minnesota, 1913, Chaps. 98 and 420; Acts of New York, 1913, Chap. 774; Acts of Wisconsin, 1913, Chap. 743.

a fine of not less than twenty-five, or more than one hundred dollars, or by imprisonment of not more than ninety days, or both fine and imprisonment. Each day of the violation of the prohibition herein contained shall be construed as a separate offense.*

4. OFFENSIVE USES OF LAND NOT SUBJECT TO MUNICIPAL REGULATION

There remains a class of occupation which imperils neither the safety nor health of the community and yet is very damaging to the value of land as a place of residence. A business that produces little or no smoke or noise and no odors that are unhealthful may, because of the appearance of the buildings which it occupies or the class of persons which it attracts, be an undesirable neighbor. This is the sort of occupation that the developers of a high class residential district exclude by restrictions in the deed, but the police power has never been extended to preventing or removing structures or occupations which merely disfigure the city's physical aspect or which bring together people who may be socially uncongenial. It is not held to be within the scope of the police power to guard the amenities of life.

The Missouri legislature of 1891 gave authority to municipalities to exclude by ordinance "the institution and maintenance of any business avocation on the property fronting on boulevards . . . and to establish a building line to which all build-

---

* For further references see Veiller, Lawrence: A Model Housing Law, pp. 62 ff. See also "Protecting Residential Districts," a paper read by Lawrence Veiller at the Sixth National Conference on City Planning, Toronto, 1914.

ings and structures shall conform." Ordinances based on this legislation were tested in several cases in the supreme court and in each case declared unconstitutional on the ground that the legislation deprived owners of property without due process of law and made no provision for compensation. The theory was advanced by attorneys for the city that the ordinance was passed in pursuance of the police power, but this suggestion was held thoroughly untenable by the court.*

An ordinance of the city of Baltimore prohibited the erection of new buildings without a permit, and directed that the permit should not be granted unless in the judgment of the appellate tax court "the size, general character, and appearance of the building will conform to the general character of the buildings previously erected in the locality and will not tend to depreciate the value of the surrounding improved and unimproved property." In a well considered decision this ordinance was held *ultra vires*.†

An ordinance of Bay St. Louis, Mississippi, prohibited the building of houses, shanties, huts, or tents between the road and sea without a special permit, except such as are known as summer houses for shade only, and "all houses built without a permit shall be nuisances." The road mentioned in the ordinance was much used by pleasure vehicles, and on the land side were many expensive

* For cases see St. Louis *vs.* Hill, 116 Mo. 527. St. Louis *vs.* Dorr, 145 Mo. 466.

† Bostock *vs.* Sams, 95 Md. 400.

houses. The ordinance was obviously designed to preserve the view of the gulf from the road and prevent the obstruction of the cool winds from the water. The court found the ordinance unconstitutional, and in discussing the theory that it could be defended in the exercise of the police power, said, "There is scarcely a suggestion that the object of the ordinance is other than to enhance the beauty of the street."*

Offenses to the sense of smell and to the sense of hearing are enjoined on the ground of health, but the medical fraternity has not convinced the legal fraternity that offenses to the sense of sight are damaging to the health. It should be a very interesting task to frame a medico-legal brief which would convince a reputable tribunal of the necessity to give a broader meaning to the phrase "public welfare," and we should have a decision which would be as influential as the case of Welch vs. Swasey in Massachusetts. One of the greatest authorities on police power says: "It is conceded that the police power is adequate to restrain offensive noises and odors. A similar protection to the eye, it is conceived, would not establish a new principle but carry a recognized principle to further application."† The same authority recognized the difficulty of administering such an extension of the power as applied to the elimination

---

* Questini vs. Bay St. Louis, 64 Miss. 483.
† Freund, Ernst: The Police Power, p. 166. Chicago, Callaghan and Co., 1904.

of objectionable signs: "Such regulation would have to define what signs are prohibited and some test would have to be discovered by which to discriminate that which is merely unesthetic from that which is so offensive as to fall under the police power, since the prohibition of all advertising signs would be out of the question."

Some forms of advertising which are now allowed in practically every city in the United States could be enjoined on the ground of endangering public health. The custom, for instance, of covering the whole side or front of a building with advertisements pictured or lettered in electric lights might be enjoined as an injury to health, since at least the glare interferes with the sleep of occupants of buildings facing such a sign. But, generally speaking, the decisions on this phase of the general subject of the police power as illustrated by the bill-board cases which we are about to discuss are conclusive that whatever may be the effect on the judiciary from the increase in esthetic sentiment, the great consensus of opinion is at present against the exercise of the police power to restrain that form of use of land which is merely offensive to the sense of sight.

BILL-BOARDS. The bill-board evil is the classic illustration of offensiveness to even the most poorly nourished artistic sense. Several ordinances of one kind or another have been attempted to legislate it

CARRYING OUT THE CITY PLAN

out of existence. Park commissions have attempted to protect the neighborhood of parks and parkways by an ordinance of exclusion. But every drastic measure has been successfully thwarted by repeated court decisions.*

A very recent Missouri case† has been generally understood to announce a different rule and to uphold the prohibition of bill-boards as an exercise of the police power. The case arose under an ordinance of the city of St. Louis of which the following are the essential provisions:

1. No bill-board hereafter erected shall exceed fourteen feet in height above the ground.

2. All bill-boards shall have an open space at the bottom of at least four feet.

3. No bill-board shall exceed five hundred feet in area.

4. No bill-board shall approach the street line nearer than fifteen feet or the side line of the lot on which it stands nearer than six feet.

Besides these structural requirements there seems to be a discrimination in the matter of license fees against structures used as bill-boards; for although no fees are charged for fences which may be used for bill posting, a fee is imposed for the erection of bill-boards; and although a fee of only $1.00 is charged for the alteration or erection of buildings costing less than $1,000, a fee of $100 is charged for a bill-board 50 feet long, the total

* Appendix, p. 246.
† St. Louis Gunning Advertising Co. vs. St. Louis.

cost of which may not exceed $100. The same disproportionate charges are made for the erection or alteration of signs on the top of buildings.

The ordinance was attacked on every possible ground: First, as a taking of property without due process of law; second, as denying the equal protection of the laws by prescribing restrictions against structures on which advertising is displayed, but not against similar ones structurally as objectionable,—in other words, discriminating against the *kind of use* to which a structure is put; third, as taking property without compensation and without public necessity. The case was first heard before a justice of the supreme court, and his finding that the ordinance was a reasonable exercise of the police power was upheld by the full bench with two judges dissenting. To the contention raised by counsel for the bill-board company that the statute discriminates, the court replied that there can be no discrimination, since bill-boards are of necessity in a class by themselves because of their temporary character and consequent cheap and insecure structure. In distinguishing them from other structures on the top of buildings, like tanks, chimneys, towers, poles, and so forth, the court says: "Should they (bill-boards) be required to be constructed with the same permanency (as tanks, towers, and so forth), that fact alone would destroy their commercial value and put them out of business, for the cost of construction would greatly exceed the amount of income that would be derived therefrom." It is the finding that bill-boards are "nuisances in character" distinguished from all other apparently similar structures by their cheapness and insecurity that distinguishes the Missouri decision from those which have held similar ordinances invalid as an unwarranted exercise of the police power.

The Missouri case finds something more dangerous in bill-boards than the paper on them containing the advertisement. The decision amounts to this: All bill-boards are likely to fall; to construct them safely would involve a cost which would prohibit their erection; all bill-boards are likely to harbor nuisances; all bill-boards increase the fire hazard. One form of regulation would be to require construction specifications, but it is just as reasonable to move them back from the lot line and so limit their height that the danger from them is removed. It is also reasonable to require an open space at the bottom and at the sides of the lot so as to check nuisances that tend to grow up behind the barrier and to decrease the risk of fire.

This St. Louis case has been taken to the supreme court of the United States on a writ of error, but it goes up with the advantage to the city that the highest state court has found it a valid exercise of the police power. The supreme court is slow to overthrow such a finding and the chance is good for establishing a precedent irrespective of the

USE OF THE POLICE POWER

reasoning of the court. The decision can not be cited as sustaining the exercise of the police power for esthetic purposes, but the charge is well founded that esthetic considerations are poorly concealed behind the pretext of guarding the safety, morals, and health of the people.

As a method of largely suppressing the billboard evil it is believed that the drastic St. Louis ordinance will be effective, since the burden put upon the maintenance of such structures will be likely to take away much of the profit that they bring. But it is very doubtful whether the St. Louis method will be generally followed as a method of suppressing the evil. Certainly in those jurisdictions where a careful consideration has been given to ordinances of like character, it is not to be expected that there will be different findings than heretofore. In cities where the question is new, it is not likely that the courts will follow the Missouri court in saying that billboards can not be safely erected because of their temporary character. Until the public's good taste, its sense of orderliness, harmony, and beauty, are ranked more nearly on the same plane as its health, safety, and morals, or until the doctors have established a positive injury to health through the sense of vision, we may expect no protection against unsightly structures through the exercise of the police power.

CARRYING OUT THE CITY PLAN

OTHER METHODS OF CONTROL

Although the degree of control over intensive and offensive uses of land which is desirable in the development of a city plan can not be attained under the exercise of the police power, the municipality may accomplish some of the same purposes by purchasing or taking under eminent domain an easement in the land which it is desired to control. If the decision in the Copley Square case, as usually interpreted, discussed in Chapter I, is good law and is generally followed, it would support the recent legislation in Missouri, in Indiana and Colorado, which excludes objectionable occupations from land fronting on parks and boulevards by purchasing or condemning the right of the owners to use their land for such purposes.* The constitutionality of the acts of Massachusetts authorizing the establishment of building lines beyond which no building can be constructed has never been questioned; but in all such legislation provision is made for compensating land owners for damages. An ordinance has been introduced in Denver to provide for taking such easements in land adjacent to parks and parkways by condemnation and for assessing the cost of the taking upon the district benefited. This idea is suggestive of large possibilities but has not as yet been tested.

* For text see Appendix, p. 219.

CONCLUSION

In conclusion, the police power is constantly being held to justify interference with the use of private property. The only limit to such interference is a judicial determination that a specific ordinance is not a reasonable means of protecting the safety, health, and morals of the community. It is for the legislative body to determine in the first instance the reasonableness of the means. It is a sound judicial principle, carried exceptionally far in the Missouri case cited on page 162, that courts will be slow to overthrow the determination of the legislature.

CHAPTER VI

THE WORK OF ADMINISTRATIVE AGENCIES IN THE EXECUTION OF A CITY PLAN

WE have thus far considered how the municipal authorities may execute a plan by enforcing those rights which the legislature has delegated to them as the representatives of the people. Through the ownership of land and by the exercise of the police power the city may absolutely control the working out of many details of a plan. But a city is seriously handicapped in the use of both of these methods of control. The acquisition of land by any method is expensive, and by the condemnation method is both expensive and slow. To enforce a police ordinance requires an injunction after a court hearing, and the usual administrative agency is slow to ask for an injunction and the usual court is slow to grant it. Some details, at least, of a city plan will be executed, in the future as in the past, by the mere guidance of developments undertaken on private initiative without resort to legal compulsion.

A plan for a city's growth generally approved by the business interests, by public service corporations, and by the public, and administered by a tactful agency which advocates the execution of the proper features of the plan at the right time carries with it the persuasion of good business policy. It becomes the thing to do to fall in line with such a plan.

THE CONTROL OF STREET LAY-OUT BY ADMINISTRATIVE PRESSURE

In a growing community, even if the public authorities are utterly supine in the matter, private initiative will constantly increase the number of house lots and bring about the creation of streets necessary to give access to them. These streets may promptly become public ways or they may remain private ways for a long time; but in the aggregate they form the most important single element in the city plan, largely controlling every other feature. The most obvious and perhaps the most important step in the wise guidance of a city's growth is the endeavor to make the streets thus brought into existence through private initiative serve not merely the immediate selfish purpose of the dealer in real estate but the permanent interests of the whole community. The attempt to control private development is made through the supervision of all plans offered for record, supplemented in a few cities by the establishment of an official street plan to which all private plattings are expected to conform.

CARRYING OUT THE CITY PLAN

The right in a municipality to supervise all plans of subdivisions is well recognized in the United States, but the exercise of the right is by no means general. It varies from a purely formal supervision, to a real attempt to control private development. A street which is to be a public highway is frequently required to conform to standard specifications as to width, sidewalk space, surfacing, and so forth. In some cities a considerable measure of co-operation is secured and owners of property are induced to change even the number and direction of proposed streets at the suggestion of the municipal authorities.

The method of enforcing the right of supervision in most general use is to refuse for record any plan of proposed streets and lots which has not been approved by the proper municipal authorities. Owners who persist in their plan are prevented from describing lots by a short reference to a recorded plan and must in each transfer describe by metes and bounds. The inconvenience is considerable, although the burden of this falls rather on the title examiner who is paid for his labor and on the purchaser than on the vendor. In cities where the custom of dealing in lots by reference to a recorded plat instead of by metes and bounds is nearly universal, a prospective purchaser may balk at buying a lot that fails to conform to the customary standard in this respect.

Another method of control, also in pretty general use, is the refusal to accept a non-conforming street as a public highway. Instead of having the benefit of the co-operation of the municipality in the construction of water mains, sewer pipes, and other municipal services, and instead of being entirely relieved of their upkeep, the cost of both construction and maintenance of the highway and of the various conduits for public service falls on the owners of lots abutting on the private street. Unfortunately, these owners are rarely the offending developers of the property; they usually are innocent purchasers who have bought lots, relying on the supposition that they were on an accepted or acceptable street. Rather than pursue their rights against the land company which made the sale, they are more likely to prevail on the municipal authorities to waive the requirements and accept the street as a public highway.

The experience of at least one town has worked out a variation of these methods of pressure. Massachusetts towns, by the acceptance of Chapter 191 of the acts of 1907, may authorize the board of selectmen to act as a board of survey with power to compel the submission of all plans for the location of streets or highways for their approval.* It was found that while development companies were usually quite willing to submit plans and accept suggestions, when the land was cut up into streets and lots the plans which had

* For text of act see Appendix, p. 280.

been accepted by the board of survey frequently had not been followed. Consequently the town adopted the following regulation:

Whenever application is made to the selectmen acting as the board of survey, by the owner or owners of a parcel of land for the approval of a plan showing the layout of streets in said land, such owner or owners shall furnish a bond conditioned for the prompt construction of said street or streets in accordance with the grades and layout approved by the board of survey. . . .

This practice seems effective at least in cases where the developer desires the approval of the board of survey, but the situation is still left without remedy where the developer is willing to subdivide his land without submitting his plans to the municipal authorities and to construct and maintain streets at his own expense.

The possibilities of official supervision have not been fully realized, partly because of the too frequent use of political influence and partly because of an adherence to old methods, and of an utter lack of scientific handling of the problem and the absence of a well considered city plan. The property owner often objects with justice to the arbitrary specifications required both for the width of a street and the allotments of space for sidewalk and parking strips. Even in cities where most has been accomplished in the planning of a street system there has not been a sufficient regard for the difference in the use of streets as affecting their width and cross section. Many cities require all streets to have a certain minimum width, either 40, 50, or 60 feet between property lines, whereas in some cases a width less than this standard minimum would be much more suitable. Often a street is made 70 feet wide because it is the extension of a street 70 feet wide, although this width both for the old street and the new may be too great or too little. Sidewalks in many cities are given a fixed width in proportion to the width of the entire street, although that width may be excessive or inadequate for sidewalk purposes in special cases.

But at best, supervision by these means will fail of great effectiveness because too much depends on persuasion and there is too little opportunity for legal pressure. The property owner can block the best laid plans of the municipality. To obtain positive control of property development land or rights in land must be taken, and for this the city must pay.

With the purpose of forestalling private development several cities have established bureaus to prepare an official plan of streets to which private platting is expected to conform. A device included in the legislation creating some of these street planning bureaus, which aims to place the location and design of streets absolutely in the control of the municipality, is contained in the provision that owners who erect buildings within the limits of a proposed street as laid down on the official plan will receive no compensation for damage to their buildings when the street is constructed.*

But in every state which has enacted this provision except Pennsylvania this interference with private property is regarded as a taking of property without compensation, therefore unconstitutional, or has been expressly so held by the supreme court.† From early times Pennsylvania statutes have given the properly constituted municipal authorities power to determine in advance the location of all streets without compensation for the interference with the rights of property owners. By act of June, 1836, commissioners were authorized to set off a certain tract of land and plot it with streets and squares. Notice was then given to property owners concerned, and after a hearing of objections the plan with or without amendments was recorded and became official "and the streets, lanes, and alleys so approved shall forever after be deemed, adjudged and taken to be public highways." In 1841 the court of general sessions refused to grant a petition establishing this plan on the ground of the unconstitutionality of the statute. The case on a writ of certiorari went to the supreme court which reversed the decision of the lower court and found that

The mere laying out of the streets can not be said of itself to be the taking of the property of individuals

---

* See Appendix for text of legislation, pp. 243 ff., 282.

† Forster vs. Scott, 136 N. Y. App. 577. See Appendix, p. 244.
Edwards vs. Bruorton, 184 Mass. 529. See Appendix, p. 245.

WORK OF ADMINISTRATIVE AGENCIES

upon which they are laid out for public use at some future day, but rather a designation of what may be required for that purpose thereafter, so that the owners of the property may in due time be fully apprised of what is anticipated and regulate the subsequent improvements which they shall make thereon accordingly. . . . Until the actual opening the owners thereof continue not only to hold the same interest in them but likewise to have the right to enjoy them and in the same manner as they did previously.*

Thirty years later, in 1871, the supreme court further extended the principle by holding that if buildings were erected within the line of the street after notice of the plan was given to the owners, the damage to such building on the opening of such street could not be paid for, "otherwise the map or plan would be entirely nugatory.† The same question was considered in 1893 and the principle was held well established.‡ Curiously enough, the first Pennsylvania case was decided on the reasoning in a New York case decided in 1836, Furman St., 17 Wend. 649,§ but this New York decision was reversed in 1892 by the case of Forster *vs.* Scott, 136 N. Y. App. 577,‖ the court holding that

Whenever a law deprives the owner of the benefit, use and free enjoyment of his property or imposes restraint upon such use or enjoyment that materially

* In re District of Pittsburgh, 2 W. and S. 320.
† Forbes St., 70 Pa. 125.
‡ Bush *vs.* McKeesport, 166 Pa. 57. See Appendix, p. 244.
§ See Appendix, p. 243. ‖ See Appendix, p. 244.

affects its value without legal process or compensation, it deprives him of the property within the meaning of the constitution.

This power of determining the lines of a street without immediate construction of the street has allowed a widening of some of Philadelphia's narrow business streets in a way impossible in a city of any other state. In 1870 it was determined to increase the width of Chestnut Street from 40 to 50 feet by an addition of five feet on either side. Land abutting on this street has great value and was occupied by costly buildings, and if condemnation proceedings had been instituted for acquiring the additional 10 feet the expense of the improvement would have been perhaps prohibitive. But the act of 1870 provided that compensation should not be paid till a building was reconstructed and set back to the new building line, and thus the expense for getting a 50-foot street was distributed over many years and nothing was paid for buildings. The same process has been adopted for at least two other downtown streets of Philadelphia, but this power has not been employed to increase the width of streets in built-up areas in any other city of Pennsylvania.

PLATTING BOARDS IN VARIOUS CITIES

PHILADELPHIA. Official planning in Philadelphia is done by the bureau of surveys. The board is composed of fourteen district surveyors presided over by the chief engineer and surveyor of the city. Each district surveyor has charge of a particular section of the city, with a corps of engineers and assistants under his immediate direction. He is the only person having the authority to make an official survey of public or private property in his district. All fees for work done for private parties are paid into the city treasury by the individual for whom the work is done. Such a system gives each district surveyor a practical knowledge of the land and of the land owners, and the confidence which is had in the district surveyor has done more to prevent violations of the street plan than the penalties contained in the legislation. The city has a plan of streets ready for each district before the land owners are ready to subdivide their land. When any one or more of the land owners begin to consider platting their land the district surveyor must be consulted, and the city is in a strategic position to carry through its own officially adopted plan.

BOSTON. The board of survey in Boston was created in 1891* with power to make plans of such territory "as the board may deem advisable, showing thereon the location of such streets or ways, whether already laid out or not as the board shall be of opinion that the present or future interests of the public require or will require." For five years the activity of the board resulted in

---

* The act does not differ in principle from that creating a Town Board of Survey. See Appendix, p. 280.

planning 6,000 acres of comparatively unoccupied territory. The board of survey was succeeded and its duties were taken over by the long established and conservative board of street commissioners in 1896. Since this time there has been much less activity, if the amount of territory covered by a street plan is an accurate measure. The fifteen years of the work of the street commission resulted in the platting of about the same amount of territory as was covered by the board of survey in five years. The difference may be due to a lack of sufficient appropriation. The act of 1891 carried with it a special appropriation for the work of platting new streets, and the city council during the life of the board of survey was very liberal with appropriations for this purpose. During the subsequent history of the street commissioners the only amount available for purposes of platting was what could be spared out of the total appropriation for street work. It is also a fair conclusion that there was less enthusiasm for platting under the board of street commissioners than under the board of survey, which was created for that specific purpose.

A provision in the board of survey act, like those in the Pennsylvania acts, withholds compensation to property owners who erect structures in the streets proposed for new areas, but the supreme court held that this no-damage provision was an interference with the use of property and that since no compensation was given the owner it was an unconstitutional interference.* Although

* Edwards *vs.* Bruorton, 184 Mass. 529. See Appendix, p. 245.

this opinion was not necessary for a decision of the case there is little question that the dictum would be followed in Massachusetts, and in accordance with this dictum the street commissioners have been advised by the city of Boston law department that building lines can not been forced without payment of compensation.

It is conjectural just how much this decision has weakened the effectiveness of the board of survey acts as instruments for building up an adequate street system, since no record is kept of the violation of the lines which the board of survey has laid down. The official plan has standing among respectable property owners who recognize a real economy in a planned street system. Conservative banks in Boston refuse to loan on property subject to a board of survey line unless the building plans show the observance of these lines. Careful conveyancers in examining a Boston title inquire whether there is a board of survey line on the property. The practice in Boston is to issue from the city hall a certificate showing all municipal claims against any given parcel of property, and the existence of a board of survey line is noted on this certificate. Pressure can still be brought to bear on non-conforming owners by refusal on the part of the city to co-operate with them in the construction and maintenance of the water, sewer, and lighting systems. It is the general impression among those who are most closely acquainted with the work of the laying-out of the streets that violations of the street lines are of infrequent occurrence.

Under Chapter 191 of the acts of 1907, Massachusetts towns may authorize their selectmen to act as a board of survey with the same power to lay out official streets as the Boston street commissioners. Several towns of the state have accepted the act and in a very few cases survey lines have been imposed on particular streets, but there has been no general extension of the street plan into unoccupied areas.

NEW YORK. New York had a topographical bureau for four years, dating from the first Greater New York charter, January 1, 1898, but during these formative years there was little or no progress with official plans. On January 1, 1902, the amended charter placed the topographical work in each of the five boroughs under the control of the borough president, and since then five separate bureaus have had charge of the completion of the map of the city and the drainage plan. The disadvantage of separate planning bureaus, particularly where the territory of two boroughs is contiguous, is obvious. There is, however, one opportunity for securing co-ordination in street planning. All plans must be submitted by the presidents of the boroughs to the board of estimate and apportionment, and they do not become official without the approval of that board. In Manhattan and Brooklyn the plans submitted consist almost entirely in changes in the official map which

WORK OF ADMINISTRATIVE AGENCIES

is practically complete for both boroughs. The following table shows the work of the topographical bureaus in the other boroughs since 1902:

TABLE 7.—PROGRESS MADE IN MAPPING THE BOROUGHS OF THE BRONX, QUEENS, AND RICHMOND, NEW YORK CITY, TO JANUARY 1, 1913[a]

	BOROUGH		
	The Bronx	Queens	Richmond
Total area in acres	26,523	75,111	36,600
Acres approved for mapping prior to Jan. 1, 1902			
Tentative	..	..	..
Final	14,430	5,402	60
Total	14,430	5,402	60
Between Jan. 1, 1902, and Jan. 1, 1912			
Tentative[b]	956	3,416	7,940
Final	10,004	14,476	964
Total	10,960	17,892	8,904
During 1912			
Tentative	..	12,984	2,540
Final	234	3,070	..
Total	234	16,054	2,540
Total area in acres mapped to Jan. 1, 1913			
Tentative[b]	956	16,168	10,480
Final	24,668	22,948	1,024
Total	25,624	39,116	11,504
Per cent of borough area in acres mapped to Jan. 1, 1913			
Tentative[b]	3.6	21.5	28.6
Final	93.0	30.6	2.8
Total	96.6	52.1	31.4

[a] Report of Chief Engineer, Board of Estimate and Apportionment, 1912, page 66.

[b] Excludes areas for which final maps have been adopted.

CARRYING OUT THE CITY PLAN

BALTIMORE. The Baltimore topographical survey commission was created by ordinance in 1893 for the purpose of making a complete survey of the city, including about seventeen square miles of undeveloped territory, rural in character, which had become a part of the city in 1888. With the completion of the survey an official plan was adopted for the annexed territory in 1893 by the mayor and city council, and subsequently by act of the general assembly of Maryland, Baltimore was prohibited from accepting a deed of dedication or the opening in any manner of a street which did not conform to the general plan or the plan duly amended. Amendments of the official plan must be approved by the topographical survey commission and adopted by the city council before they can be incorporated.

In spite of the legislation in Maryland which seems to put the control of city planning in the hands of the city, and in spite of the activity of topographical bureaus of New York City, the limitations on municipal control of street planning in both Baltimore and New York are the same as in Boston. Official streets in both cities have been blocked by the owners of the land or speculative builders, and cases of successive house planting in New York City are notorious. And yet, the advantages of official street plans are considered to offset these limitations and street planning bureaus have passed the experimental stage.

WORK OF ADMINISTRATIVE AGENCIES

Their success furnishes a precedent for many cities in the United States which still exercise little or no control over a phase of planning where the interest of the private owner is so often opposed to the public good. The possibilities of administrative pressure in the solution of other city planning problems now determined on the initiative of private or corporate interests suggest themselves. The development of the water front, the location of railroad terminals, the transit problem, have all been distinctly recognized as requiring the permanent attention of a special planning board representing the public interest. But in those fields where the public interest is apt to conflict with the advantage of private or corporate owners, the value of expert suggestion and study can never be as fully realized as where the execution of a plan is entirely in the control of the municipality.

PLANNING OF PUBLIC WORK OTHER THAN STREETS

In the location and design of public parks and in the location and design of public buildings, including bridges, the administrative agency of the municipality or other governmental unit has a free hand. The establishment and development of a system of parks and parkways are now entrusted very generally to an administrative board which employs expert advice and considers the park problems of the entire city as a unit. The location and design of public structures are, however, in most cases left to the judgment of the several departments which will use or maintain them; but occasionally the function of a municipal art commission is enlarged so that its approval is necessary to the selection of the site and design for public structures as well as for the location and design of "works of art."

In New York City the art commission must approve the location and design of all structures for which the contract price exceeds $250,000; but in the case of other public structures the approval of the commission need not be required if the mayor or the board of aldermen request the commission not to act.*

The Philadelphia art jury created in 1912 was given this additional power by the legislature of 1913.

No construction or erection in a city of the first class of any building, bridge or its approaches, arch, gate, fence, or other structure or fixture which is to be paid for wholly or in part by appropriation from the city treasury or other public funds, or for which the city or any other public authority is to furnish a site, shall be begun until the approval of the jury shall have been given to the design and proposed location thereof. The approval of the jury shall also be required in respect to all structures or fixtures belonging to any person or corporation which shall be erected upon or extend over any highway, stream, lake, square,

* Charter of New York City as amended by Chapter 675 of the laws of 1907, Section 637.

park or public place within the city. . . . In deeds for land made by any city of the first class restrictions may be imposed requiring that the design and location of structures to be altered or erected thereon shall be first approved by the art jury of each city. Nothing requiring the approval of the jury shall be erected or changed in design or location without its approval. If the jury fails to act upon any matter submitted to it within 60 days after such submission, its approval of the matter submitted shall be presumed.*

In spite of the complete control which a municipality has over the location and design of public structures and the creation and extension of its park system, the obstacles to the formulation of and adherence to a consistent plan are as persistent and often as effective as those which prevent the control of street development.

Expert suggestions have too frequently been disregarded by a purely political city council whose power of appropriation is a most effective check on the execution of city plans. One of the chief objections to the usual form of city government with a mayor and a large elected council of one or two chambers, aside from incompetence and wastefulness and, at the worst, dishonesty, arises from this power of obstruction. Neither the people's representatives in council nor the engineers and architects in the employ of the city departments have been educated to the idea of a unified city. The department system emphasizes a city's subdivisions; the political system emphasizes still different subdivisions; and neither group of subdivisions logically fits into a city plan. There may be interesting historical reasons for the combination of certain areas into this or that group; politicians may have had shrewd reasons for establishing certain political boundaries; but the topographical conditions of the site often prove the strangeness of the compound. Several sections contained in a political subdivision may be separated by considerable water-ways or difficult grades so that transit between parts of the same political district is almost prohibitively expensive; and yet that district must be treated as a unit when appropriations for public improvements are considered. The ward or district method of electing city councilmen does not produce a body interested in the best development of the city as a unit, the best transit system for the whole city, the best park system for the whole people, the most complete playground system for all the children. Instead, forty units, more or less, with selfish ideas fostered by local business men and property owners, are represented each by a councilman whose best equipment is his ability to get things for his own ward, and the city plan develops like a crazy quilt.

The last few years have seen considerable development of the unit idea. One interesting step is the correlation of all the departments of a city administration. This is done, first, by the crea-

WORK OF ADMINISTRATIVE AGENCIES

tion of a new administrative board in which are united for purposes of efficiency and economy the various departments. Thus under a board of public works or of public improvement are united the maintenance work of the city, and the construction of streets, water mains, sewers, and so forth, each of which municipal services was formerly in charge of a separate department.

The mayor's cabinet in Kansas City, Missouri, is an interesting experiment in correlation. A weekly conference of the heads of all city departments is held at which questions from each department which affect the development of the entire city are discussed, and the policy of each department is influenced by its effect on other departments. For nine months the experiment was tried only in connection with the city administration. It succeeded so well that to the members of the city administration were added representatives from several organizations and industrial bodies. These conferences are said to have resulted in an improvement in the city's management by the securing of a most desirable measure of co-operation between the administration and the tax payers. Kansas City was a most advantageous field for an experiment of this kind. The creation of the park and boulevard system of the city had already produced the finest kind of co-operation between property owners and the park commission, and an eager willingness on the part of the citizenship to contribute to the carrying

CARRYING OUT THE CITY PLAN

out of the unit idea as expressed in plans of the commission.

The elimination of ward representation in city government is a recent advance toward the unit idea. It is sometimes expressed in the commission form of government, sometimes in a single city council elected at large. From the viewpoint of city planning the most notable advantage of this simplified form of government is that the administration represents the entire city and is not a collection of representatives from the several parts of the city. Other advantages due to a saving in time and money caused by a smaller body with a businesslike procedure, are no doubt real. It is more satisfactory in urging the need of planning measures to deal with a few men, whether bad or good, efficient or stupid. It is also wholesome to fix the responsibility of a policy on an administration consisting of a few men rather than to trace the responsibility through a maze of committees and motions to an irresponsible clerk. City planning legislation may chance to succeed in two chambers of a city council in spite of numbers, because of the domination of one or two individuals; but when responsibility for success or failure must be fixed, it will not be placed on those individuals but ingeniously distributed over various committees. If the single council of limited number is likely to produce better councilors, just so far city planning measures may be benefited; but there is no guaranty of this result. However constituted, the smaller body does represent the entire city; and though each individual member will have by natural and political inheritance a desire for the advancement of his own locality, he may be controlled by the greater fact that he is chosen by all the citizens of the city.

Boston is the largest city with sufficient experience to test this theory. Certain critics of the charter of 1909 tried to strike a locally popular note by alleging that wards without representation in the council did not get their share of the annual appropriations for local improvements. This statement is not borne out by the facts. The figures for the years 1910 and 1911 show a total appropriation of $2,132,881 for local improvements excluding appropriations for highways, sewers, bridges, and other improvements in which the city as a whole is interested. Of this sum, $795,163 was used in four districts which had no representative, as the term was formerly used in the council. The entire membership in the council came from six districts of the city, or seventeen wards. Distributing the amount spent on these districts among the seventeen wards would result in an average of $78,689 each, with which an average of $90,395 for each of the eight wards in unrepresented districts compares very favorably. Five members of the council of nine live in three wards whose appropriations for the last two years for local improvements make a total of $133,000. This is only one-sixteenth of the total appropriated, and the remaining fifteen-sixteenths is for districts which all together had only a minority in the council. Such evidence is an interesting corroboration of the sound conclusion that the elimination of sectional representation is an important step toward the carrying out of the unit idea in comprehensive city planning.

PLANNING COMMISSIONS
1. HISTORY

The appointment of planning commissions is the most recent step in the development of the unit idea in city planning. In theory, the function of this new agency is to correlate the official plans prepared in the various municipal departments, to pass upon unofficial plans or suggestions for improvement, and to make plans of its own in all cases where no existing agency has jurisdiction. Hartford, Connecticut, was the first to establish such a commission under a resolution of the Connecticut Legislature of 1907.* The Chicago plan commission dates from 1909; the Baltimore and Detroit commissions from the following year.

In 1911 Pennsylvania and New Jersey passed general acts enabling cities of the second class (Pittsburgh and Scranton) in Pennsylvania and cities of the first class in New Jersey, to create an additional executive department to be known as the department of city planning. In 1913, by

* See Appendix, p. 296.

general law, New York state authorized the appointment of planning commissions in all cities and incorporated villages; Pennsylvania extended the act of 1911 with important amendments to cities of the third class, and Massachusetts made planning commissions mandatory in all cities and towns of over 10,000. In the same year by special act of the Connecticut Assembly plan commissions were authorized for the cities of New Haven and West Hartford, following the precedent of Hartford; in Ohio, Cleveland* and Dayton included city planning commissions in their new city charters.

The following list of active plan commissions does not include temporary commissions appointed merely to make a report or prepare a city plan.

TABLE 8.—YEARS IN WHICH PLANNING COMMISSIONS WERE AUTHORIZED, AND SOURCE OF AUTHORIZATION, FOR THE 54 CITIES OR TOWNS HAVING PLANNING COMMISSIONS IN APRIL, 1914

City	Year	Authorized by
Hartford, Conn.	1907	Act
Chicago, Ill.	1909	Ordinance
Baltimore, Md.	1910	Act
Detroit, Mich.	1910	Ordinance
Jersey City, N. J.	1911	Act
Newark, N. J.	1911	Act
St. Louis, Mo.	1911	Ordinance
Pittsburgh, Pa.	1911	Act
Philadelphia, Pa.	1911	Ordinance
Salem, Mass.	1911	Ordinance
Lincoln, Neb.	1911	Ordinance

TABLE 8.—(CONTINUED)

City	Year	Authorized by
Trenton, N. J.	1912	Ordinance
Cincinnati, Ohio	1913	Ordinance
Scranton, Pa.	1913	Act
Schenectady, N. Y.	1913	Ordinance
Pittsfield, Mass.	1913	Act
Fitchburg, Mass.	1913	Act
Waltham, Mass.	1913	Act
Lawrence, Mass.	1913	Act
Lowell, Mass.	1913	Act
Springfield, Mass.	1913	Act
Northampton, Mass.	1913	Act
Holyoke, Mass.	1913	Act
Malden, Mass.	1913	Act
Louisville, Ky.	1913	Ordinance
New Haven, Ct.	1913	Act
New London, Ct.	1913	Ordinance
Bridgeport, Ct.	1913	Ordinance
Erie, Pa.	1913	Act
Providence, R. I.	1913	Ordinance
Adams, Mass. (town)	1913	Act
Chelsea, Mass.	1913	Act
Chicopee, Mass.	1913	Act
Cambridge, Mass.	1913	Act
Chester, Pa.	1913	Act
Easton, Pa.	1913	Act
Syracuse, N. Y.	1914	Act
Meadeville, Pa.	1914	Act
Reading, Pa.	1914	Act
Scranton, Pa.	1914	Act
Harrisburg, Pa.	1914	Act
Oil City, Pa.	1914	Act
Boston, Mass.	1914	Act
Gloucester, Mass.	1914	Act
Haverhill, Mass.	1914	Act
Melrose, Mass.	1914	Act
Medford, Mass.	1914	Act
Newton, Mass.	1914	Act
Newburyport, Mass.	1914	Act
Somerville, Mass.	1914	Act
Taunton, Mass.	1914	Act
Watertown, Mass. (town)	1914	Act
Framingham, Mass. (town)	1914	Act
Binghamton, N. Y.	1914	Act

A suburban metropolitan plan commission was also created in 1913 for Pennsylvania cities of the first class (Philadelphia), to have jurisdiction over a district comprising the cities within 25 miles of Philadelphia. This commission is to be composed of fifteen members appointed by the governor of the state. Its aim is to secure "coordinating comprehensive plans of highways and roads, parks and parkways, and all other means of intercommunication; water supply, sewerage and sewage disposal, collection and disposal of garbage, housing, sanitation and health, playgrounds, civic centers, and other public improvements that will affect the character of the district as a whole or more than one political unit within the district."* The aims of the commission can be realized only by recommendation to the several governmental units contained in the district. This legislation is particularly interesting since it is the first successful attempt to create a metropolitan planning commission.

The commission of inquiry appointed by the governor of Massachusetts in 1911 presented to the legislature of 1912 a draft for just such a planning commission, which contained a novel feature for getting its plans carried out. Massachusetts is well supplied with executive commissions with some planning functions. It has a highway board, a grade crossing commission, a transit commission, a gas and electric light com-

* Act No. 226 of 1913.

mission, a railroad commission, a metropolitan park commission, and a metropolitan water and sewer board, all with jurisdiction in the metropolitan district. The commission of inquiry wisely recommended the necessity of keeping these existing commissions in office. Their tasks were large enough.

The new commission was to be distinctly a planning and not an executing body. Its province was to be suggestion, advice, supervision, and correlation. The cities and towns of the metropolitan district were to be offered, for the consummation of improvements classed as metropolitan by the planning commission, the credit of the state and a direct contribution toward the cost of improvements by the state and by the metropolitan district at large, if the local unit accepted in its development the plan of the commission. The device thus incorporated in the bill recognized two strongly rooted attributes in municipal character—jealousy of local self-government and openness to persuasion when the persuasion is golden. It distinctly kept hands off of metropolitan commissions, county commissions, and local governments, by the provision that all improvements should be executed by the body that would have executed them before the passage of the bill. It offered merely to provide a plan for the whole district and help on the financial burden. All improvements in the metropolitan district submitted to the proposed planning commission were to be classified as local improvements, as ordinary metropolitan improvements, or as extraordinary improvements. In the case of purely local improvements the locality stood the entire financial burden; in the case of ordinary metropolitan improvements the localities in which the improvement was located paid 65 per cent of the entire cost, the metropolitan district 20 per cent and the state 10 per cent; in the case of an extraordinary metropolitan improvement the distribution of the expense was to be determined by a commission appointed by the supreme court of the state.

A feature of very real financial assistance was offered by the provision that towns or cities of the district might borrow money to meet the expense of metropolitan improvements, and this loan would not be considered in reckoning the debt limit. The weakness of the device is in the provision that 20 per cent of the cost of metropolitan improvements should be paid by the entire district. It is very questionable whether there is unity enough in any metropolitan district to allow a fixed assessment over the whole district for an improvement where the most direct benefit is to only two or three towns. But this interesting experiment did not survive the legislative hearing. It was defeated not so much because of opposition to the principle of the bill as out of real or imaginary fear in the minds of the political leaders in the towns and cities about Boston, who see in any plan for a more unified development of the metropolitan district the domination of Boston.

Another legislative experiment in city planning which did not come to maturity should also be mentioned. In 1910 the city of Seattle adopted an amendment to the city charter by the addition of a new article which created a municipal plans commission. Seattle was just then finishing some costly reconstruction, washing away grades and widening important thoroughfares, and the wisdom of avoiding such an experience again appealed to the city with peculiar emphasis. The amendment put on the commission the duty of procuring plans for the arrangement of the city with a view to such expansion as would meet probable future demands. Of the twenty-one members of the commission seven represented the city or county government, and fourteen were appointed by the mayor from nominations of fourteen groups representing architects, engineers, business, real estate, the water front owners, and the public service corporations. The commission served without compensation but was authorized to employ experts, not exceeding three, to prepare a comprehensive plan.

So far there is nothing new in the legislation, but the next provisions are unique. The report was to be presented to the mayor and council not later than December 30, 1911, and

They shall cause the recommendations of the commissions to be submitted to the people at the next general or special election. If a majority of the voters shall favor the adoption of said plan so reported it shall be adopted and shall be the plan to be followed by the city executive departments in the growth, evolution, and development of the city of Seattle until modified or amended at some subsequent election.

After a most thoroughgoing study by an expert, the commission presented an excellent plan and went out of existence September 30, 1911. There was no provision in the legislation for educating the people sufficiently to enable them to cast an intelligent vote. The Seattle experiment is interesting in being the first attempt to make the whole electorate directly responsible for the direction of the city's growth. It is in accordance with the democratic ideas of legislation which have come out of the west. The people were not ready for so big a program and defeated the project at the polls in the spring of 1912.

No one of these commissions has had a history long enough to be judged by its accomplishments. The Hartford commission, which is the oldest, has fulfilled one of its duties by the publication of a preliminary report embodying the recommendations of the advisory architects for a plan of the city. Its chief activity outside of this has been along lines similar to these employed by the Baltimore topographical survey commission. Detroit's commission, after working without adequate appropriation for two years, has started the preparation of a plan. The Newark commission under expert advice has prepared two reports; one preliminary in character reviewing the general problem and making some recommendations in regard to the improvement of street lines and grades and street car operations; the other, a special study of a most congested point in Newark at the junction of Broad and Market streets. Other commissions have outlined plans of activity.

2. THE FUNCTIONS OF A CITY PLANNING COMMISSION

The effectiveness of any city planning commission is bound to be dependent on the attitude of other existing administrative agencies which have as a part of their function the planning and execution of public improvements. This attitude does not spring merely from self-interest of the older agencies. If, for instance, the street commission or the bureau of survey is doing its work of planning a street system well and seeing that parts of it get constructed at the proper time, there would seem to be little in this line for a planning commission. The same may be said of the park commission, the school board, and others. The city, in other words, may have administrative agencies which are covering practically the entire field of municipal effort in planning the streets, the parks, the public buildings, and other works.

The legislation under which city plan commissions are established recognizes the difficulty in the creation of a new administrative body whose powers may overlap those of existing agencies. This is evidenced particularly in the provision covering membership and scope of powers. Co-operation with existing administrative agencies and with law making bodies is aimed at in Hartford, in St. Louis, and in Salem, Massachusetts, by having both the administrative and legislative side of the government represented on the commission. In each of these cities the mayor is ex-officio chairman of the city plan commission. In Hartford seven of the nine city plan commissioners are members of the city administration. Besides the mayor, the official members are the city engineer, president of the street commissioners, president of the park commissioners, the superintendent of parks, and a member from both branches of the city council. In St. Louis seven of the fifteen members are from official life, the mayor, the president of the board of public improvement, the street commissioner, the park commissioner, the building commissioner, the president of the city council, and the speaker of the house of delegates. In Salem, Massachusetts, the city government is represented in the commission by the mayor, the president of the board of aldermen, and the president of the common council. Detroit's commissioner of public works, commissioner of parks and boulevards, and city engineer are ex-officio members of the plan commission, but without power to vote.

CARRYING OUT THE CITY PLAN

Further to avoid conflict with existing agencies, commissions are given very limited powers which make them hardly more than advisory bodies. That of Baltimore, for instance, has merely the duty of investigating all plans proposed for the extension of highways and the establishment of a civic center and other public improvements in connection therewith, and reporting the results of its investigations to the city council. Several commissions are charged with the constructive duty of preparing a systematic plan, and in connection therewith are given more or less control over private platting in order to compel conformity with the plan. The Detroit commission has an additional power similar to that given to a municipal art commission. Section 6 provides:

No work of art shall be removed, relegated or altered in any way, nor shall any property be acquired for park or boulevard purposes, nor playground, nor shall any property be condemned for the widening or extension of any park, boulevard or public playground unless the project has been submitted to and approved by the city plan commission; nor shall any gift to the city of a monumental character be accepted until the sketch, plan and location of the same has been approved by the city commission.

FIRST FUNCTION: TO SECURE CORRELATION OF EFFORTS. But assuming existing agencies which plan adequately for each class of the physical elements of a city and which carry out satisfactorily these several plans, there is still needed a permanent body, non-partisan in character, whose primary function shall be to harmonize the plans of existing agencies and to bring forward for execution those plans which are most demanded. This new agency should be the constant guardian of the city plan to which every question of planning policy should be referred, just as questions of financial policy are now referred to a finance commission in several cities of the United States.

That the lack of correlation is a serious problem is proved in the experience of many cities. There is no guarantee of co-operation between the several administrative departments with planning functions. There is, of course, some co-operation, but the maximum or minimum depends on nothing except the good sense and friendly feeling of bureau heads. It is not an unusual thing for the street department to spend some time and some money on resurfacing, only to have the street opened within a month by the water or sewer department for the installation of new water pipes or drains. And what is true of streets and highways can be illustrated in other departments of planning activity.

An improvement is now too seldom considered in its relation to the whole plan. Alternative schemes for a subway are discussed and determined in the interest of those whose property is affected, and the effect of either scheme on the relief of congestion or the opening of new territory to residence gets scant consideration. Street car companies and representatives of the city and property owners fasten on the city a transit system approaching a maze in intricacy and leaving focal points without connection. The transportation problem alone needs a trained agency constantly studying tendencies of retail trade, of the drift of waterfront activities, and constantly suggesting the need for new connecting links either for highways or transit lines.

However desirable in theory may be this vesting of control over physical development of the city in a new agency, there is little or no provision for it in the procedure of existing plan commissions. They are for the most part frankly advisory boards, and in some cases have no power even of suggestion unless called upon by the mayor and council. If the plan commission is to be an intelligent correlating agency, there must be provision for constant reference to it of new construction work of all municipal departments even at the risk of swamping the clerical force of the city planning commission by a mass of detail with little bearing on the city plan. And if any department proposes a serious violation of the plan for the whole city, the plan commission should have the opportunity to arrest the proposed violation long enough to get the point at issue before the public and their representatives in city council and thus fix the responsibility for whatever action is taken after careful consideration.

There are, of course, objections to this modified

veto power. It tends to undo an excellent municipal reform by which has been achieved the concentration of responsibility for a public action, and it tends also to produce delay in the execution of public work. But with such a power a judicious and tactful commission would settle most differences in conference, and without it even an ideally constituted commission might be helpless. Just what form this veto shall take and how it shall affect the relations between existing administrative departments and the new agency will depend largely on local conditions, and this question with many others of organization and procedure must wait for more than a theoretical answer until existing commissions have had a longer history. Interesting in this connection is section 3 of the recent Pennsylvania act authorizing plan commissions in third class cities, which provides that all bills and ordinances must, upon introduction in the city council, be referred to the plan commission. The proposed measures may be disapproved by the plan commission but disapproval shall not operate as a veto.*

SECOND FUNCTION: TO FACILITATE FUTURE IMPROVEMENTS. The second function of the city planning commission is to suggest changes in the way of doing things calculated to facilitate the execution of a plan. The city planning field is peculiarly one for investigation and experimentation, and the city planning agency is as necessary

* For text of the act, see Appendix, p. 290.

in it as an experiment station in the fields of forestry and agriculture.

It took but little experimenting to prove the economic value of a flexible street which may be stretched to meet future demands. The flexibility is produced sometimes by imposing a building line set back from the street line varying distances,— even the minimum distance of 10 feet on either side providing an inexpensive increase in the street's width of 20 feet. The same result is accomplished by the city's acquiring a greater width than is at present necessary for the use of the street and allowing a certain portion of this width on either side to be used by the owners for garden purposes, but not for buildings of any kind.

Boston's experiments with her narrow streets in congested retail districts have brought about the use of one-way streets and the regulations against standing vehicles. Other cities have taken a census of traffic conditions along important traffic ways and, in New York City at least, there have been attempts made to direct the lines of traffic particularly at congested centers.

It is possible to have a degree of flexibility even in an area closely built up with expensive buildings, such as downtown districts of any large city, if the planning board is given the right to modify the provisions of the building code in return for concessions from property owners, and a very necessary widening of streets is made possible which otherwise would be prohibitively expensive.

WORK OF ADMINISTRATIVE AGENCIES

In cities, for instance, which have established a height limitation for buildings, even in the central business district, owners fronting on narrow streets might grant to the city land enough to give the street adequate width if their loss in floor space was compensated, not in money but by allowing them to exceed the height limitation by the addition of other stories to their buildings. A building with a 100-foot frontage and 100-foot depth, 10 stories in height, would lose in actual floor area 10,000 feet by a grant to the city of 10 feet for sidewalk purposes along its entire frontage. By adding another story 10 to 15 feet in height, 9,000 feet of this loss would be returned. To determine the feasibility of such suggestions as this would be particularly the province of the city planning board.

Parks and playgrounds now purchased or appropriated at great expense and even then but meagerly supplied in many cities, should be reserved in advance of actual need. Where the problem has best been solved, as in the small parks and playgrounds of Chicago, the commissioners are able to locate wisely new parks and playgrounds in accordance with the density of population, as shown on maps of the city, which are kept up to date. The suggestion is that this can be done with sufficient accuracy before prices rise, and that a planning board is best qualified to make such a reservation because of its intimate knowledge of the trend of industry and other factors which determine the density of population.

The plan commission should be concerned not only with the original planning of the streets but with the changes of the street system made necessary by the location of new industries, the location of new terminal stations either for steam lines or rapid-transit lines, or the appearance of any new element which will create a focal center and attract a stream of travel. There is not a city of 100,000 in the United States which ought not today to widen streets or open new ones in order to give an adequate approach to travel centers. If this widening or opening were done at the time when it could be done most economically and when a planning board would advise it, if the problem were constantly studied by such a board, cities would be saved great outlays for reconstruction and great losses through failure to reconstruct.

3. BROAD OPPORTUNITIES OF THE PLANNING COMMISSION

The city planning board would be quick to discover desirable changes in legislation. The activity in city planning legislation of the 1913 Pennsylvania Legislature shows what may be accomplished by a commission intimately acquainted with the local difficulties which prevent satisfactory execution of plans. It passed a city planning act for the cities and towns within 25 miles of

Philadelphia. It authorized the appointment of city planning commissions for cities of the third class. It increased the power of the Philadelphia art jury so that its approval is made necessary for the selection of the site as well as the design of public structures.* It granted to all the cities of the state the power to indicate on the official plan, reservations of parks and playgrounds in the same way as they now are allowed to establish an official plan for streets.

Various phases of the planning problem are from time to time made the subject of investigation by special commissions, as for instance, the Massachusetts commission appointed to consider the methods of land acquisition which have been described on page 106. Such studies might be better conducted by the plan commissions whose experience with other planning problems would be of great value.

Finally, the commission should at all times be a propagandist body educating the citizens to see the economy of planning in general and to decide every specific question of the city's physical growth from the standpoint of city planning. The thoroughgoing work of the Chicago plan commission in this field is an example of what can be accomplished.

The creation of a city plan commission would be justified if it did nothing but safeguard the unit idea by correlating the work of other municipal

* For text of legislation see Appendix, p. 305.

departments in accordance with the city plan. If it is also to make clear to the citizens the value of city planning and to be a bureau of city planning research, its task will be so consuming that it need not take over any of the functions of existing agencies.

APPENDIX A

LEGISLATION AND DECISIONS

I. RESTRICTIONS ON THE USE OF LAND

A. BUILDING LINES

1

CHARTER OF THE CITY OF ST. LOUIS. Article VI, Sect. 1. Boulevards, Conditions for the establishment.

The Municipal Assembly may by ordinance, recommended by the Board of Public Improvements, establish and open boulevards or change existing streets into boulevards . . . and may regulate the traffic thereon, and may exclude heavy driving thereon, or any kind of vehicle therefrom, and may exclude and prohibit the erection or establishment or maintenance of any business houses, or the carrying on of any business vocation on the property fronting on such boulevard, and may establish a building line to which all buildings, fences or other structures thereon shall conform. . . . Adequate compensation shall be allowed the owners of property fronting or bordering thereon for damages occasioned by the establishment of a building line on such boulevard, and by limiting the use to which such property may be put by the owners thereof.

2

ACTS OF INDIANA, 1909. Chap. 89, Sect. 7.
Building lines—Cities of 100,000 or over.

The Board of Public Works may establish a line determining the distance at which all structures to be erected upon any premises fronting any park, parkway, park boulevard or boulevard shall be erected, and may, in the name of the city acquire by condemnation the right to prevent the erection of, and to require the removal of, all structures outside of such lines. . . .
The establishing of any building line outside of any park, parkway, or boulevard, as herein provided, in connection with the condemnation of the land for the same, shall be understood to be condemnation and the perpetual annihilation of all rights of the owners of property which shall front on such park, parkway or boulevard, or across which such building line shall run, to erect any building or structure whatever or any part thereof between such building line and such boulevard, park or parkway; or such result may be accomplished by absolute condemnation of the land, with perpetual and irrevocable free license to use and occupy such land between any building line established and the outside line of such park, parkway, park boulevard or boulevard for all purposes except the erection of buildings or other structures. No subdivision into lots of any lands lying within five hundred feet of such boulevards, parks or parkways shall be valid without the approval of such board of park commissioners.

3

REVISED LAWS OF MASSACHUSETTS. Chap. 48, Sect. 103, as amended by Chap. 572 of Acts of 1913.

Building lines in cities and towns.

If the city council of a city or if a town accepts the provisions of this section or has accepted the corresponding provisions of earlier laws, a building line not more than 40 feet distant from the exterior line of a highway or town way may be established in the manner provided for laying out ways, and thereafter no structures shall be erected or maintained between such building line and such way, except steps, windows, porticos and other usual projections appurtenant to the front wall of a building to the extent prescribed in the vote establishing such building line, and except that buildings or parts of buildings existing at the time of the establishment of the building line may be permitted to remain and to be maintained to such extent and under such conditions as may be prescribed in the vote establishing such building line. Whoever sustains damage thereby shall have the same remedies therefor as for damages sustained by the laying out of a town way.

4

HOUSE OF REPRESENTATIVES, JANUARY 24, 1910.
61st Congress, 2d Session. H. R. 19069. (Identical with S. 5715)

A BILL providing for the establishment of building lines and special building restrictions in the District of Columbia.

Be it enacted by the Senate and House of Representa-

tives of the United States of America in Congress assembled, That the Commissioners of the District of Columbia are hereby authorized and empowered from time to time and at all times hereafter by public notice by advertisement published in some newspaper or newspapers of general circulation in the said District at least once a week for three successive weeks prior to the expiration of said notice, to designate any highway or highways, street or streets, or avenue or avenues in the District of Columbia now existing or which may hereafter be created or dedicated or condemned or purchased, or any part or parts thereof, the land fronting upon which shall thereafter be subject to certain building restrictions (which restrictions said commissioners may impose, alter, amend, or modify at the time such designation is made, or at any time or times thereafter), and the said highways, streets, or avenues, or part or parts thereof so designated shall be classed as Class A streets, and all other highways, streets, and avenues, or part or parts thereof shall be classed as Class B streets, and it shall be the duty of the said commissioners, and especially of the engineer commissioner, to give preference, in their discretion, to Class A streets in all recommendations and estimates for street improvements, and in all matters of sidewalk construction, laying of curbs, and the maintenance of the surface of the streets. And said commissioners are hereby further authorized and empowered in making, altering, amending, or modifying said special restrictions to include in whole or in part the *establishment of building lines, prohibitions as to the erection or alteration of buildings designed or proposed to be used for business purposes, prohibitions as to the establishment of any place of business, and such requirements as to height of buildings, materials of construction, and architectural design as shall secure, in the judgment of said commissioners, the beautiful and harmonious appearance, as viewed from the public streets, of all structures to be erected or altered on the land to which said restrictions shall apply: Provided, That no such designation shall be made unless the owners of ninety per centum, or more, measured by the front foot, of the property fronting upon the street, avenue, or part or parts thereof under consideration shall in due form have dedicated, or granted, or conveyed, or assigned to the District of Columbia, in consideration of benefits received or to be received, easements in, to, and upon their property by virtue of which said special restrictions may be established:* Provided further, That the Commissioners of the District of Columbia may exercise their judgment as to whether such special restrictions shall cover only the ninety per centum or more of frontage, the owners of which have conveyed easements as above provided, or, in addition to such frontage, any portion of the remaining property fronting on the highway, street, or avenue, or part or parts thereof under consideration.

SECT. 2. That if said commissioners in the exercise of their judgment shall designate highways, streets, or avenues, or any part or parts thereof, and shall impose any special restrictions authorized by this Act so as to include property fronting on any such highway, street, or avenue which has not been dedicated or granted or conveyed or assigned to the District of Columbia, then, at any time within one year from the date of any such designation, and not thereafter, the owner or owners thereof, or any person having an interest therein, may recover as damages just compensation from the District of Columbia for the taking, if any, of the easements involved in said designation, subject to deduction for benefits; and said damages and benefits and all benefits herein mentioned shall be appraised by a commission composed of three capable and disinterested persons, to be appointed by the supreme court of the District of Columbia, holding a district court of the United States for said District, upon application, in writing, made within said year and not thereafter by such owner or owners or person having an interest against the District of Columbia; and upon failure of any such owner or owners or person having said interest to thus present such claim within said period, said right shall cease and determine.

SECT. 3. That the Commissioners of the District of Columbia be, and they are hereby, authorized and directed, as soon as practicable after every recovery of damages as just compensation as in this Act provided, to institute proceedings in said court to *assess the amount of said damages, the interest thereon,* and *all costs* whatsoever of *the proceeding wherein the said damages have been ascertained against and upon all property covered by said designation, pro rata in proportion as said property may be found to be benefited, omitting from consideration all property found by the court in the proceeding to recover said damages as just compensation to have been damaged than more benefited.*

Sections 4–7 inclusive relate to the procedure in assessing benefits.

SECT. 8. That the Commissioners of the District of Columbia are hereby authorized to appoint an advisory commission to consist of the inspector of buildings of the District of Columbia, the municipal architect of said

District, two architects to be nominated by the Washington Chapter of the American Institute of Architects, and a landscape gardener, the two first named officials to serve without compensation and the other members of said commission to receive such compensation as may be fixed, from time to time, by said commissioners. The duties of said commission shall be to advise said commissioners in all matters connected with the purposes of this Act, and to perform such other duties as may be assigned to it by said commissioners.

SECT. 9. That the sum of fifteen thousand dollars, or so much thereof as may be necessary, is hereby appropriated, one half out of the revenues of the District of Columbia, and the other half out of any moneys in the United States Treasury not otherwise appropriated, to carry out the provisions of this Act.

SECT. 10. That it shall be the duty of all owners of, and persons and corporations interested in, any property fronting upon any highway, street, avenue, or part or parts thereof, designated or made subject to any special restriction, or on which any easement or right is taken or imposed by virtue of this Act, to comply, in every case, with such designation and restriction, and in event any such owner, person, or corporation, after notice from the Commissioners of the District of Columbia so to do, shall fail, neglect, or refuse to comply as aforesaid, the said commissioners are hereby authorized and empowered, in the name of the District of Columbia, by proceedings in equity in the supreme court of the District of Columbia, to obtain, without giving any bond or security whatsoever in such case at any time or in any court, an injunction or other proper process, mandatory or otherwise, to compel such compliance; and in the enforcement of such process the court shall have those powers ordinarily exercised by it in compelling obedience to its writs of injunction or mandamus; and the issuance of any notice as aforesaid by said commissioners shall be prima facie evidence of the right of the District of Columbia to a preliminary injunction on the filing of any bill, petition, or other proceeding; and the said court shall give precedence to every such case and shall adjudge and decide the same within thirty days after said case shall have been submitted; and the opinion of said court in every such case shall be rendered in writing and shall be filed in such case as a part of the record thereof.

B. BUILDING HEIGHTS

1

ACTS OF MASSACHUSETTS, 1898. (Chap. 452)

AN ACT relative to the height of buildings on and near Copley Square in the city of Boston.

Section 1. Any building now being built or hereafter to be built, rebuilt, or altered in the city of Boston upon any land abutting on St. James Avenue between Clarendon Street and Dartmouth Street, or upon land at the corner of Dartmouth Street and Huntington Avenue, now occupied by the Pierce Building, so called, or upon land abutting on Dartmouth Street now occupied by the Boston Public Library building, or upon land at the corner of Dartmouth Street and Boylston Street now occupied by the New Old South Church building, may be completed, built, rebuilt, or altered to the height of ninety feet and no more; and upon any land or lands abutting on Boylston Street between

Dartmouth Street and Clarendon Street may be completed, built, rebuilt, or altered to the height of one hundred feet and no more; provided, however, that there may be erected on any such building above the limits hereinbefore prescribed, such steeples, towers, domes, sculptured ornaments, and chimneys as the board of park commissioners of said city may approve. *Section 2* repeals St. 1896, c. 313, and St. 1897, c. 379, so far as they limit the height of buildings erected along the line of streets, parkways, or boulevards bordering on public parks. *Section 3* provides for the payment of damages to any person owning or having an interest in an uncompleted building begun before the fourteenth day of January, 1898, which is affected by the act, and *Section 4* provides for compensation to all persons sustaining damages to their property by reason of the limitation of the height of buildings prescribed by the act.

2

ATTORNEY GENERAL *vs*. HENRY B. WILLIAMS et als.
174 Mass. 476. 1899.

Information in equity by the attorney general to restrain the erection and maintenance of a building on Copley Square in Boston above the height of ninety feet prescribed by statute 1898, c. 452, entitled "An act relative to the height of buildings on and near Copley Square in the city of Boston."

Knowlton, J. . . . The first question raised by the report is whether the statute is constitutional. The streets mentioned in the statute are adjacent to Copley Square. On the case as now presented we must assume that Copley Square, in the language of the information, "is an open square and a public park intended for the use, benefit and health of the public, and is surrounded by buildings devoted to religious, charitable, and educational purposes, some of which contain books, manuscripts and works of art of great value, many of which are in their nature irreplaceable."

. . . It adds to the public park rights in light and air and in the view over adjacent land above the line to which buildings may be erected. These rights are in the nature of an easement created by the statute and annexed to the park. Ample provision is made for compensation to the owners of the servient estates. In all respects the statute is in accordance with the laws regulating the taking of property by right of eminent domain, if the Legislature properly could determine that the preservation or improvement of the park in this particular was for a public use. The uses which should be deemed public in reference to the right of the Legislature to compel an individual to part with his property for a compensation, and to authorize or direct taxation to pay for it, are being enlarged and extended with the progress of the people in education and refinement. Many things which a century ago were luxuries or were altogether unknown, have now become necessaries. It is only within a few years that lands have been taken in this country for public parks. Now the right to take land for this purpose is generally recognized and frequently exercised. . . . It hardly would be contended that the same reasons which justify the taking of land for a public park do not also justify the expenditure of money to make the park attractive and educational to those whose tastes are being formed and whose love of beauty is being cultivated. . . . It is argued by the defendants that the Legislature, in passing this statute, was seeking to preserve the architectural symmetry of Copley Square. If this is a fact, and if the statute is merely for the benefit of individual property owners, the purpose does not justify the taking of a right in land against the will of the owner. But if the Legislature, for the benefit of the public, was seeking to promote the beauty and attractiveness of a public park in the capital of the Commonwealth and to prevent unreasonable encroachments upon the light and air which it had previously received, we cannot say that the law-making power might not determine that this was a matter of such public interest as to call for an expenditure of public money, and to justify the taking of private property. While such a determination should not be made without careful consideration, and while the governing tendency towards an enlargement of the field of public expenditure should be jealously watched and carefully held in check, a determination of this kind once made by the Legislature cannot be lightly set aside.

3

ACTS OF MASSACHUSETTS, 1904. Chap. 333.

AN ACT relative to the height of buildings in the city of Boston

Section 1. The city of Boston shall be divided into districts of two classes, to be designated districts A and B. The boundaries of the said districts, established as hereinafter provided, shall continue for a period of fifteen years, and shall be determined in such manner that those parts of the city in which all or the greater part of the buildings situate therein are at the time of such determination used for business or commercial purposes shall be included in the district or districts designated A, and those parts of the city in which all or the greater part of the buildings situate therein are at the said time used for residential purposes or for other purposes not business or commercial shall be in the district or districts designated B.

Section 2. Upon the passage of this act the mayor of the city shall appoint a commission of three members, to be called "Commission on Height of Buildings in the City of Boston." The commission shall immediately upon its appointment give notice and public hearings, and shall make an order establishing the boundaries of the districts aforesaid, and, within one month after its appointment, shall cause the same to be recorded in the registry of deeds for the county of Suffolk. The boundaries so established shall continue for a period of fifteen years from the date of the said recording. Any person who is aggrieved by the said order may, within thirty days after the recording thereof, appeal to the commission for a revision; and the commission may, within six months after its appointment, revise such order, and the revision shall be recorded in the registry of deeds for the county of Suffolk, and shall date back to the original date of recording. The members of the commission shall serve until the districts have been established as aforesaid; and any vacancy in the commission caused by resignation, death or inability to act shall be filled by the mayor, on written application by the remaining members of the commission or of ten inhabitants of the city. The members of the commission shall receive such compensation as the mayor shall determine.

Section 3. In the city of Boston no building shall

be erected to a height of more than one hundred and twenty-five feet above the grade of the street in any district designated A, and no building shall be erected to a height of more than eighty feet above the grade of the street in any district designated B. These restrictions shall not apply to grain or coal elevators or sugar refineries in any district designated A, nor to steeples, domes, towers or cupolas erected for strictly ornamental purposes, of fireproof material, on buildings of the above height or less in any district.

The supreme judicial court and the superior court shall each have jurisdiction in equity to enforce the provisions of this act, and to restrain the violation thereof.

Section 4. This act shall take effect upon its passage.

Approved May 13, 1904.

4

ACTS OF MASSACHUSETTS, 1905. Chap. 363.

AN ACT relative to the height of buildings in the city of Boston

Section 1. Within thirty days after the passage of this act the mayor of the city of Boston shall appoint a commission of three members to determine, in accordance with the conditions hereinafter provided, the height of buildings within the district designated by the commission on height of buildings in the city of Boston as district B, in accordance with chapter three hundred and thirty-three of the acts of the year nineteen hundred and four.

Section 2. Said commission shall immediately upon its appointment give notice and public hearings, and shall make an order establishing the boundaries of or otherwise pointing out such parts, if any, of said district B as it may designate in which buildings may be erected to a height exceeding eighty feet but not exceeding one hundred feet, and the height between eighty feet and one hundred feet to which buildings may so be erected, and the conditions under which buildings may be erected to said height, except that such order may provide for the erection of buildings as aforesaid to a height not exceeding one hundred and twenty-five feet in that portion of said district B which lies within fifty feet from the boundary line separating said district B from the district designated by the commission on height of buildings in the city of Boston as district A in accordance with said chapter three hundred and thirty-three, provided said boundary line divides the premises affected by such order from other adjoining premises both owned by the same person or persons, and within sixty days after its appointment shall cause the same to be recorded in the registry of deeds for the county of Suffolk. Any person who is aggrieved by such order may, within sixty days after the recording thereof, appeal to the commission for a revision; and the commission may, previous to the first day of January in the year nineteen hundred and six, revise such order, and the revision shall be recorded in the registry of deeds for the county of Suffolk and shall date back to the original date of recording. The boundaries so established shall continue for a period of fifteen years from the date of the recording of the order made by the commission on height of buildings in the city of Boston under chapter three hundred and thirty-three of the acts of the year nineteen hundred and four. The members of the commission shall receive such compensation as the mayor shall determine.

LEGISLATION AND DECISIONS

Section 3. Within such parts of district B as may be designated by the commission as aforesaid (which may, except as hereinafter provided, include any parts of said district B affected by prior acts limiting the height of buildings) buildings may be erected to the height fixed by the commission as aforesaid, exceeding eighty feet but not exceeding one hundred feet, or one hundred and twenty-five feet as hereinbefore provided, and subject to such conditions as may be fixed as aforesaid by the commission; but within the following described territory, to wit:—Beginning at the corner of Beacon street and Hancock avenue, thence continuing westerly on Beacon street to Joy street, thence continuing northerly on Joy street to Myrtle street, thence continuing easterly on Myrtle street to Hancock street, thence continuing southerly on Hancock street and Hancock avenue to the point of beginning, no building shall be erected to a height greater than seventy feet, measured on its principal front, and no building shall be erected on a parkway, boulevard or public way on which a building line has been established by the board of park commissioners or by the board of street commissioners, acting under any general or special statute, to a greater height than that allowed by the order of said boards; and no building upon land any owner of which has received and retained compensation in damages for any limitation of height or who retains any claim for such damages shall be erected to a height greater than that fixed by the limitation for which such damages were received or claimed.

Section 4. No limitations of the height of buildings in the city of Boston shall apply to churches, steeples. towers, domes, cupolas, belfries or statuary not used for purposes of habitation, nor to chimneys, gas holders, coal or grain elevators, open balustrades, skylights, ventilators, flagstaffs, railings, weather vanes, soil pipes, steam exhausts, signs, roof houses not exceeding twelve feet square and twelve feet high, nor to other similar constructions such as are usually erected above the roof line of buildings.

Section 5. This act shall take effect upon its passage.

Approved May 8, 1905.

5

WELCH vs. SWASEY. 193 Mass. 364

This was a petition for a writ of mandamus addressed to members of the board of appeal from the building commissioner of the city of Boston, ordering the respondents to direct the building commissioner to grant to the petitioners a permit to erect a building to the height of 120 feet, 6 inches. The permit had been refused by the building commissioner on the ground that the proposed structure would exceed the height limit provided by acts 1904, chapter 333, and acts 1905, chapter 383. The petitioners appealed on the ground that the statutes were unconstitutional and void.

The commission appointed by the mayor under chapter 383 of the acts of 1905, made the following orders: (1) In district B buildings may be erected on streets exceeding 64 feet in width to a height equal to one and a quarter times the width of the street on which the building stands, and if situated on more than one street the widest street should be taken, and the height of the building is to be made from the mean grade of the curbs of all streets upon which the building is situated, and not exceeding one hundred feet in any of them. (2) If the street is of uneven width, its width will be considered as the average width opposite the building to be erected. (3) The width of a street shall be held to include the width of any space on the same side of the street upon which a building stands, upon or within which space no building can be lawfully erected by virtue of any building line established by the board of street commissioners, or the board of park commissioners, acting under general or special laws. (4) All streets or portions of streets upon which buildings may be erected on one side only shall be considered as of a width of 80 feet as to that portion upon which building may be erected on one side only. (5) In the case of irregular or triangular open spaces formed by the intersection of streets, the width of the street shall be taken as the width of the widest street entering said space at the point of entrance. (6) No building shall be erected on a parkway, boulevard or public way on which a building line has been established by either of said boards acting under general or special laws to a height greater than allowed by said general or special law nor otherwise in violation of section 3 of said chapter 383, acts of 1905. (7) No building shall be erected to a height greater than eighty feet unless its width on each and every public street on which it stands will be at least one half its height. (8) Nothing in the order shall be construed as affecting any condition or restriction imposed by deed, agreement or by operation of law on any property in said district B.

The said commission further provides that buildings may be erected to a height not exceeding 120 feet in that portion of district B as established by the commission on the height of buildings in its order dated Dec. 3, 1904, which lies 50 feet westerly from the boundary line running from Columbus Av. to the center of Boylston St. separating district B from district A provided that said portion of district B is owned by same persons who own adjoining premises in district A.

KNOWLTON, C. J.: The principal question presented by this case is whether St. 1904, p. 283, c. 333, and St. 1905, p. 309, c. 383, and the orders of the commissioners appointed under them, relative to the height of buildings in Boston, are constitutional. A jurisdictional question, if the petitioner is entitled to relief, is whether a remedy can be given him by a writ of mandamus.

The principal question may be subdivided as follows: First, can the Legislature, in the exercise of the police power, limit the height of buildings in cities so that none can be erected above a prescribed number of feet; second, can it classify parts of a city so that in some parts one height is prescribed and in others a different height; third, if so, can it delegate to a commission the determination of the boundaries of these different parts, so as to conform to the general provisions of the statute; fourth, can it delegate to a commission the making of rules and regulations such as to permit different heights in different places, according to the different conditions in different parts of one of the general classes of territory, made in the original statute; fifth, if it can, are the rules and regulations made by the commissioners within the statute, and within the constitutional authority of the Legislature and its agents?

In the exercise of the police power the Legislature may regulate and limit personal rights and rights of property in the interest of the public health, public morals and public safety. Com. *vs.* Pear, 153 Mass. 242, 63 N. E. 719; Com. *vs.* Strauss, 191 Mass. 545, 78 N. E. 136; California Reduction Co. *vs.* Sanitary Works, 199 U. S. 306–318, 26 Sup. Ct. 100, 50 L. Ed. 204. With considerable strictness of definition, the general welfare may be made a ground, with others, for interference with rights of property, in the exercise of the police power. Com. *vs.* Strauss, *ubi supra*.

The erection of very high buildings in cities, especially upon narrow streets, may be carried so far as materially to exclude sunshine, light and air, and thus to affect the public health. It may also increase the danger to persons and property from fire, and be a subject for legislation on that ground. These are proper subjects for consideration in determining whether in a given case, rights of property in the use of land should be interfered with for the public good. . . . . In People *vs.* D'Oench, 111 N. Y. 359, 18 N. E. 562, a statute limiting the height of dwelling houses to be erected in the city of New York, was treated as unquestionably constitutional. See 1 Abbott, Mun. Corp. 237, 2 Tiedeman on State and Federal Control, 754. .

. . . It is for the Legislature to determine whether the public health or public safety requires such a limitation of the rights of land owners in a given case. Upon a determination in the affirmative, they may legislate accordingly.

The next question is whether the General Court may establish different heights for different neighborhoods, according to their conditions and the uses to which the property in them is put. The statute should be adapted to the accomplishment of the purposes in which it finds its constitutional justification. It should be reasonable, not only in reference to the interests of the public, but also in reference to the rights of land owners. If these rights and interests are in conflict in any degree, the opposing considerations should be balanced against each other, and each should be made to yield reasonably to those upon the other side. The value of land and the demand for space, in those parts of Boston where the greater part of the buildings are used for purposes of business or commerce, is such as to call for buildings of greater height than are needed in those parts of the city where the greater part of the buildings are used for residential purposes. It was, therefore, reasonable to provide in the statute that buildings might be erected to a greater height in the former parts of the city than in the latter, even if some of the streets in the former are narrower than those in the latter.

The general subject is one that calls for a careful consideration of conditions existing in different places. In many cities there would be no danger of the erection of high buildings in such locations and of such a number as to affect materially the public health or safety, and no statutory restrictions are necessary. Such restrictions in this country are of very recent origin, and they are still uncommon. Unless they place the limited height at an extreme point, beyond which hardly any one would ever wish to go, they should be imposed only in reference to the uses for which the real estate probably will be needed, and the manner in which the land is laid out, and the nature of the approaches to it.

It was decided in Com. *vs.* Boston Advertising Company, 188 Mass. 348, 74 N. E. 601, 69 L. R. A. 817, 103

Am. St. Rep. 494, that a statute of this kind cannot constitutionally be passed for a mere esthetic object. It was said in Attorney General *vs.* Williams, 174 Mass. 476-480, 55 N. E. 77, that the statute then before the court, enacted under the right of eminent domain, with compensation for landowners, would have been unconstitutional if it had been passed "to preserve the architectural symmetry of Copley Square," or "merely for the benefit of individual landowners." The inhabitants of a city or town cannot be compelled to give up rights in property, or to pay taxes, for purely æsthetic objects; but if the primary and substantive purpose of the legislation is such as justifies the act, considerations of taste and beauty may enter in, as auxiliary. We are of opinion that the provision of St. 1904, p. 283, c. 333, for dividing parts of the city into two classes, in each of which there is a prescribed limit for the height of buildings, was within the power of the Legislature, and in accordance with the constitutional principle applicable to the enactment.

The delegation to a commission of the determination of the boundaries of these parts of the two classes was within the constitutional power of the General Court. The work of the commissioners under the first act was not legislation, but the ascertainment of facts, and the application of the statute to them for purposes of administration. Such subsidiary work by a commission is justified in many cases.

. . . .

The delegation to a commission of the power to fix different heights in different places in the parts included in class B, under St. 1905, p. 309, c. 363, goes further, and allows the commissioners to make rules and regulations which are in the nature of subsidiary legislation. This is within the principle referred to in Brodbine *vs.* Revere, *ubi supra,* and in some of the other cases above cited. It is that under our system in Massachusetts, matters of local self-government might always be intrusted to the inhabitants of towns. On the establishment of cities this power is exercised by the city council, or by some board or commission representing the inhabitants. Even in towns such powers have long been exercised by local boards, for example,— by the board of health. Originally such representatives of the local authority were elected by the people; but for many years local boards, appointed by the governor or other executive authority, have sometimes been entrusted with the exercise of this legislative authority. It is true that they are further from the people than the members of a city council, for whom the people vote, but in a true sense they represent the inhabitants in matters of this kind. Our decisions cover this point also. Com. *vs.* Plaisted and Brodbine *vs.* Revere, *ubi supra.* It does not follow that all rules and regulations made under such a delegation of authority would be constitutional, merely because the original statute is unobjectionable. Such rules may be tested by the courts to see whether they are reasonably directed to the accomplishment of the purpose on which the constitutional authority rests, and whether they have a real, substantial relation to the public objects which the government can accomplish. A statute, ordinance or regulation will not be held void merely because the judges differ from the legislators as to the expediency of its provisions. But if it is arbitrary and unreasonable, so as unnecessarily to be subversive of rights of property, it will be set aside by the courts. . . . .

We do not see that the action of the commissioners, under St. 1905, was beyond their power under the Constitution. It was seemingly in accordance with the general purpose of the Legislature, and was directed to considerations which they deemed proper in adjusting the rights and interests of property owners and the public. The question is not whether the court deems all the provisions wise; but whether they appear to be outside of the constitutional power of the commission. In prescribing heights in the district, the commissioners might make the width of the streets on which a building was to be erected one factor to be considered. Their action in this particular relates wholly to buildings in class B, which includes only the residential parts of the city.

We cannot say that the prohibition of the erection of a building of a greater height than 80 feet in class B, unless its width "on each and every public street on which it stands will be at least one-half its height," was entirely for æsthetic reasons. We conceive that the safety of adjoining buildings, in view of the risk of the falling of walls after a fire, may have entered into the purpose of the commissioners. We are of opinion that the statutes and the orders of the commissioners are constitutional.

We think that the court has jurisdiction to dispose of the case in the merits, under this petition for a writ of mandamus. The wrong alleged is that the building commissioner, and afterwards the board of appeal, refused to give the petitioner a permit to erect a building. It is conceded that he was not entitled to a permit if the statutes and orders referred to are constitutional. The petitioner alleges that the board of appeal refused to do their duty, and that his only effectual remedy is by a writ of mandamus, ordering them to grant a permit. The case comes within the general rule giving jurisdiction to issue such writs. Farmington River Water Power v. County Commissioners, 112 Mass. 206-212; Carpenter *vs.* County Commissioners, 21 Pick. 258-259; Attorney General *vs.* Boston, 123 Mass. 460. See Locke *vs.* Selectmen of Lexington, 122 Mass. 290; Attorney General *vs.* Northampton, 143 Mass. 589, 10 N. E. 450.

The building commissioner and the board of appeals are not judicial officers. St. 1892, p. 471, c. 419; St. 1894, p. 494, c. 443. The fact that a refusal to act is founded on a mistake of law does not preclude a remedy by a writ of mandamus. In cases where the duty to perform an act depends solely on the question whether a statute or ordinance is constitutional and valid, the question may sometimes be determined on a petition for a writ of mandamus. Attorney General *vs.* Boston, 123 Mass. 450; Warren *vs.* Charlestown, 2 Gray, 84; Larcom *vs.* Olin, 160 Mass. 102-110, 35 N. E. 113.

Petition dismissed.

6

WELCH, TRUSTEE, *vs.* SWASEY, et al.   29 U. S. Supreme Court Reporter. 567, Oct., 1908

In error to the Supreme Judicial Court of the State of Massachusetts to review a judgment denying a mandamus to compel the board of appeal from the building commissioner of the city of Boston to issue a building permit. Affirmed.

LEGISLATION AND DECISIONS

Statement by Mr. Justice Peckham:

The plaintiff in error duly applied to the justices of the supreme judicial court of the state of Massachusetts for a mandamus against the defendants, who constitute a board of appeal from the building commissioner of the city of Boston, to compel the defendants to issue a permit to him to build on his lot on the corner of Arlington and Marlborough streets, in that city. The application was referred by the justice presiding to the full court, and was by it denied (193 Mass. 364, 118 Am. St. Rep. 523, 79 N. E. 745), and the plaintiff has brought the case here by writ of error.

The action of defendants in refusing the permit was based on the statutes of Massachusetts, chap. 333 of the Acts of 1904, and chap. 383 of the Acts of 1905. The reason for the refusal to grant the building permit was because the building site for the proposed building was situated in one of the districts B, as created under the provisions of the acts mentioned, in which districts the height of the buildings is limited to 80, or, in some cases, to 100 feet, while the height of buildings in districts A is limited to 125 feet. The height of the building which plaintiff in error proposed to build and for which he asked the building permit was stated by him in his application therefor to be 124 feet, 6 inches.

The designation of what parts in districts B and upon what conditions a building could be therein erected more than 80 while not more than 100 feet high was to be made by a commission, as provided for in the act of 1905, and the commission duly carried out the provisions of the act in that respect. The sole reason for refusing the permit was on account of the proposed height of the building being greater than the law allowed.

CARRYING OUT THE CITY PLAN

The plaintiff in error contended that the defendants were not justified in their refusal to grant the permit, because the statutes upon which their refusal was based were unconstitutional and void; but he contended that, if they were valid, the defendants were justified in their refusal.

The court, while deciding that mandamus was a proper remedy, held that the statutes and the reports of the commissions thereunder were constitutional.

Mr. Justice Peckham delivered the opinion of the court:

The ground of objection of plaintiff in error to this legislation is that the statutes unduly and unreasonably infringe upon his constitutional rights (a) as to taking of property without compensation; (b) as to denial of equal protection of the laws.

Plaintiff in error refers to the existence of a general law in Massachusetts, applicable to every city therein, limiting the height of all buildings to 125 feet above the grade of the street (Acts of 1891, Chap. 355), and states that he does not attack the validity of that act in any respect, but concedes that it is constitutional and valid. See also on same subject, Acts of 1892, Chap. 419, Par. 25, making such limitation as to the city of Boston. His objection is directed to the particular statutes because they provide for a much lower limit in certain parts of the city of Boston, to be designated by a commission, and because a general restriction of height as low as 80 or 100 feet over any substantial portion of the city is, as he contends, an unreasonable infringement upon his rights of property; also that the application of those limits to districts B, which comprise the greater part of the city of Boston, leaving the general 125-feet limit in force in those portions of the city which the commission should designate (being the commercial districts), is an unreasonable and arbitrary denial of equal rights to the plaintiff in error and others in like situation.

Stating his objections more in detail, the plaintiff in error contends that the purposes of the acts are not such as justify the exercise of what is termed the police power, because, in fact, their real purpose was of an esthetic nature, designed purely to preserve architectural symmetry and regular sky lines, and that such power cannot be exercised for such a purpose. It is further objected that the infringement upon property rights by these acts is unreasonable and disproportioned to any public necessity, and also that the distinction between 125 feet for the height of buildings in the commercial districts described in the acts, and 80 to 100 feet in certain other or so-called residential districts, is wholly unjustifiable and arbitrary, having no well-founded reason for such distinction, and is without the least reference to the public safety, as from fire, and inefficient as means to any appropriate end to be attained by such laws.

In relation to these objections the counsel for the plaintiff in error, in presenting his case at bar, made a very clear and able argument.

Under the concession of counsel, that the law limiting the height of building to 125 feet is valid, we have to deal only with the question of the validity of the provisions stated in these statutes and in the conditions provided for by the commissions, limiting the height in districts B between 80 and 100 feet.

We do not understand that the plaintiff in error makes the objection of illegality arising from an alleged delegation of legislative power to the commissions provided for by the statutes. At all events, it does not raise a Federal question. The state court holds that kind of legislation to be valid under the state Constitution, and this court will follow its determination upon that question.

We come, then, to an examination of the question whether these statutes with reference to limitations on height between 80 and 100 feet, and in no case greater than 100 feet, are valid. There is here a discrimination of classification between sections of the city, one of which, the business or commercial part, has a limitation of 125 feet, and the other, used for residential purposes, has a permitted height of buildings from 80 to 100 feet.

The statutes have been passed under the exercise of so-called police power, and they must have some fair tendency to accomplish, or aid in the accomplishment of, some purpose for which the legislature may use the power. If the statutes are not of that kind, then their passage cannot be justified under that power. These principles have been so frequently decided as not to require the citation of many authorities. If the means employed, pursuant to the statute, have no real, substantial relation to a public object which government can accomplish, if the statutes are arbitrary and unreasonable, and beyond the necessities of the case, the courts will declare their invalidity.

In passing upon questions of this character as to the validity and reasonableness of a discrimination or classification in relation to limitations as to height of buildings in a large city, the matter of locality assumes an important aspect. The particular circumstances prevailing at the place or in the state where the law is to become operative,—whether the statute is really adapted, regard being had to all the different and material facts, to bring about the results desired from its passage; whether it is well calculated to promote the general and public welfare,—are all matters which the state court is familiar with; but a like familiarity cannot be ascribed to this court, assuming judicial notice may be taken of what is or ought to be generally known. For such reason this court, in cases of this kind, feels the greatest reluctance in interfering with the well-considered judgments of the courts of a state whose people are to be affected by the operation of the law. The highest court of the state in which statutes of the kind under consideration are passed is more familiar with the particular causes which led to their passage (although they may be of a public nature) and with the general situation surrounding the subject-matter of the legislation than this court can possibly be. We do not, of course, intend to say that, under such circumstances, the judgment of the state court upon the question will be regarded as conclusive, but simply that it is entitled to the very greatest respect, and will only be interfered with, in cases of this kind, where the decision is, in our judgment, plainly wrong. In this case the supreme judicial court of the state holds the legislation valid, and that there is a fair reason for the discrimination between the height of buildings in the residential as compared with the commercial districts. That court has also held that regulations in regard to the height of buildings, and in regard to their mode of construction in cities, made by legislative enactments for the safety, comfort, or convenience of the people, and for the benefit of property owners generally, are valid. Atty. Gen. *vs.* Williams (Knowlton *vs.* Williams) 174 Mass. 476, 47 L. R. A. 314, 55, N. E. 77. We concur in that view, assuming, of course, that the height and conditions provided for can be plainly seen to be not unreasonable or inappropriate.

In relation to the discrimination or classification made between the commercial and the residential portion of the city, the state court holds in this case that there is reasonable ground therefor, in the very great value of the land and the demand for space in those parts of Boston where a greater number of buildings are used for the purposes of business or commercially than where the buildings are situated in the residential portion of the city, and where no such reasons exist for high buildings. While so deciding, the court cited, with approval, Com. *vs.* Boston Advertising Co. 188 Mass. 348, 69 L. R. A. 517, 108 Am. St. Rep. 494, 74 N. E. 601; which holds that the police power cannot be exercised for a merely esthetic purpose. The court distinguishes between the two cases, and sustains the present statutes. As to the condition adopted by the commission for permitting the erection, in either of the districts B, that is, the residential portion, of buildings of over 80 feet, but never more than 100, that the width on each and every public street on which the building stands shall be at least one half its height, the court refuses to hold that such condition was entirely for esthetic reasons. The chief justice said: "We conceive that the safety of adjoining buildings, in view of the risk of the falling of walls after a fire, may have entered into the purpose of the commissioners. We are of opinion that the statutes and the orders of the commissioners are constitutional."

We are not prepared to hold that this limitation of 80 to 100 feet, while in fact a discrimination or classification, is so unreasonable that it deprives the owner of the property of its profitable use without justification, and that he is therefore entitled under the Constitution to compensation for such invasion of his rights. The discrimination thus made is, as we think, reasonable, and is justified by the police power.

It might well be supposed that taller buildings in the commercial section of the city might be less dangerous in case of fire than in the residential portion. This court is not familiar with the actual facts, but it may be that, in this limited commercial area, the high buildings are generally of fireproof construction; that the fire engines are more numerous and much closer together than in the residential portion, and that an unlimited supply of salt water can be more readily introduced from the harbor into the pipes, and that few women or children are found there in the daytime, and very few people sleep there at night. And there may, in the residential part, be more wooden buildings, the fire apparatus may be more widely scattered, and so situated that it would be more difficult to obtain the necessary amount of water, as the residence quarters are more remote from the water front, and that many women and children spend the day in that section, and the opinion is not strained that an undiscovered fire at night might cause great loss of life in a very high apartment house in that district. These are matters which, it must be presumed, were known by the legislature, and whether or not such were the facts was a question, among others, for the legislature to determine. They are asserted as facts in the brief of the counsel for the city of Boston. If they are, it would seem that ample justification is therein found for the passage of the statutes, and that the plaintiff in error is not entitled to compensation for the reasonable interference with his property rights by the statutes. That, in addition to these sufficient facts, considerations of an esthetic nature also entered into the reasons for their passage, would not invalidate them. Under these circumstances there is no unreasonable interference with the rights of property of the plaintiff in error, nor do the statutes deprive him of the equal protection of the laws. The reasons contained in the opinion of the state court are, in our view, sufficient to justify their enactment. The judgment is therefore affirmed.

7

Absolute Height Limitations

Baltimore, Md.	175 feet.
Boston	125 ft. or 2½ times width of widest street on which building fronts in business section.
	80 ft. in residence section.
Charleston, S. C.	125 ft. or 2½ times width of widest street, as in Boston.
Chicago	200 ft.
Cleveland	200 ft. or 2½ times width of widest street, as in Boston.
Erie, Pa.	200 ft. or 2½ times width of widest street, as in Boston.

LEGISLATION AND DECISIONS

Los Angeles	150 ft.
Manchester, N. H.	125 ft.
Newark, N. J.	200 ft.
Portland, Oregon	160 ft.
Scranton, Pa.	125 ft.
Worcester, Mass.	125 ft.
Denver, Colo.	12 stories.
Providence, R. I.	120 ft.

C. "SURVEY LINES"

FURMAN ST. 17 WENDELL (N. Y.) 649. 1836

By a law of April 12, 1816, section 18, a survey of the village of Brooklyn was to be made and the resulting map was to constitute a permanent plan for laying out the streets of Brooklyn. The act provided that owners who violated the plan were not to receive damages.

The court, in upholding this provision, found that unless damages were withheld from owners building in designated lines of streets, section 18 of the act would be nugatory. The legislation clearly intended that improvements within the street lines should not be paid for. "By expensive erections an owner otherwise might bring an enormous burden upon others for opening the street."

This decision was cited with approval and followed in the case of Re Dist. of City of Pittsburgh, decided in 1841, 2 W. & S. 320. This language is found in the opinion: "The mere laying out of streets cannot be said of itself to be a taking of the property of individuals, upon which they are laid out, for public use at some future day, but rather a designation of what may be required for that purpose thereafter, so that the owners

CARRYING OUT THE CITY PLAN

of the property may in due time be fully apprised of what is anticipated and regulate the subsequent improvements, which they shall make thereon accordingly.

. . . Until the actual opening "the owners thereof continue not only to hold the same interest in them, but likewise to have the right to enjoy and in the same manner as they did previously."

In the case of Bush *vs.* McKeesport, City, 166 Pa. 57, the court upheld the validity of the following clause: "No person shall hereafter be entitled to recover any damages for any buildings or the improvements of any kind which shall or may be placed or constructed upon or within the lines of any located street or alley, after the same shall have been located or ordered by counsel."

But the New York court has since come to a different conclusion in the case of Forster *vs.* Scott, 136 App. Div. 577, and the Massachusetts court has also found against the constitutionality of such a provision. In Forster *vs.* Scott, the plaintiff had given a deed to the defendant warranting against incumbrances. A proposed street was located on the plaintiff's land. The court held that this was not an incumbrance since the act of 1882, chapter 419 was unconstitutional in providing that "No compensation shall be allowed for any building, erection or construction which at any time, subsequent to the filing of the maps, plans, etc., may be built in part or in whole upon or through any street, avenue, road, public square, or place."

"Whenever a law deprives the owner of the beneficial use and free enjoyment of his property, or imposes restraints upon such use and enjoyment that materially affect its value without legal process or compensation it deprives him of his property within the meaning of the constitution."

LEGISLATION AND DECISIONS

EDWARDS *vs.* BRUORTON, 184 Mass. 529
KNOWLTON, C. J.

"This is an action for breach of a covenant in a deed. A public street called Jersey Street was laid out by the street commissioners of Boston over a part of the premises under authority of statute 1891, c. 323, and the existence of this street constitutes a breach of the covenant in the deed if the statute gave the board authority to lay it out. It is contended that the statute is unconstitutional . . . because in section 9 it provides that no compensation shall be given for land taken for a street, if the owner, after the filing of a plan in accordance with the statute, shall erect any building within the boundaries of any way and not remove it when required by the street commissioners."

. . . .

"This was intended to prevent any use of property inconsistent with the plan after the filing of a plan and before the laying out of a way. If it could have that effect, it might materially interfere with the use which an owner might desire to make of his estate for many years after the filing of the plan and before the laying out of a way. The statute provides no compensation for this interference with private property. The legislation can not constitutionally so interfere with the use of property without giving compensation to the owner." . . .

"In the act before us, there is no express prohibition of the owner's use of his property, but it is declared that if he uses it otherwise than in accordance with the plans of the street commissioners it may be taken from him for a way without giving him compensation. This attempt to except him from the general rule in regard to the taking of property under the right of eminent domain is unconstitutional and ineffectual."

The court then finds that the unconstitutional parts of the statute are not so connected with the rest of the statute as to invalidate it, and that the street laid out under the provisions of the statute became a legally located public way, and that its existence constituted a breach of the covenant in the deed.

D. BILL-BOARDS

Bill board decisions may be thus classified:

1. Where the ordinance has been held invalid on the ground that its purpose was the removal of the bill-boards for æsthetic reasons and where the character of the bill-boards as nuisances was not raised, the decisions are uniformly against the reasonableness of the ordinance.

People *vs.* Green, 85 N. Y. App. 400.—The ordinance prohibited the posting of any advertisement whatever upon fences enclosing private property fronting on or adjacent to any public park. There was no claim that the posting of advertisements in any such places was an injury to the morals, health or safety of the city. The ruling was merely against the extension of the police power for æsthetic purposes.

Commonwealth *vs.* Boston Advertising Co. 188 Mass. 348.—The ordinance prohibited all signs so near a parkway as to be visible to the naked eye and was clearly intended to accomplish æsthetic purposes.

Varney *vs.* Williams, 100 Pac. Rep. 867.—The ordinance absolutely prohibited maintenance and erection of all bill-boards for advertising purposes. There was no attempt to restrict its operation to bill-boards that were insecure or otherwise dangerous or to advertising that might be indecent. "Bearing in mind that the ordinance does not purport to have any relation to the protection of passers by from injury by reason of unsafe structures, to the diminution of hazard of fire, or to the prevention of immoral displays we find that the one ground upon which the town council may be thought to have acted is that the appearance of bill-boards is or may be offensive to the sight of persons of refined tastes." The promotion of æsthetic or artistic consideration has never been held to justify an exercise of the police power.

II. Where the court considers the ordinance as an attempt to protect either the health, safety or morals of the community and finds that it is an unreasonable regulation.

State *vs.* Whitlock, 149 N. C. 542.—The ordinance prohibited the erection of bill-boards on the lot line. The court found that this was an invasion of private rights, since such structures might be built with absolute safety.

Crawford *vs.* City of Topeka, 51 Kas. 761.—The court, in holding the ordinance unreasonable, said: "In what way can the erection of a safe structure for advertising purposes near the front of a lot endanger public safety any more than a like structure for some other lawful purpose. Perhaps regulations might be made with reference to the manner of construction so as to insure safety but the absolute prohibition would be an unwarranted invasion of private rights." The unreasonableness of the ordinance is seen when it is considered that the posting of a harmless paper upon a structure changes it from a lawful to an unlawful one. To the same effect are the following cases: Bryan *vs.* City of Chester, 212 Pa. St. 259; Bill Posting Sign Co., *vs.* Atlantic City, 71 N. J. Law, 72; Chicago *vs.* Gunning System, 214 Ill. 628; Passaic *vs.* Patterson Bill Posting Co., 72 N. J. Law, 285.

II. PROCEDURE IN ACQUIRING LAND BY CONDEMNATION AND IN ASSESSING BENEFITS

1

AMENDMENT TO CONSTITUTION OF NEW YORK, Art. 1, Sec. 7. Adopted Nov. 4, 1913

When private property shall be taken for any public use, the compensation to be made therefor, when such compensation is not made by the State, shall be ascertained by a jury, *by the supreme court, with or without a jury but not with a referee,* or by not less than three commissioners, appointed by a court of record, as shall be prescribed by law. Private roads may be opened in the manner to be prescribed by law; but in every case the necessity of the road and the amount of all damage to be sustained by the opening thereof shall be first determined by a jury of free-holders, and such amount, together with the expenses of the proceeding, shall be paid by the person to be benefited. General laws may be passed permitting the owners or occupants of agricultural lands to construct and maintain for the drainage thereof, necessary drains, ditches and dykes upon the lands of others, under proper restrictions and with just compensation, but no special laws shall be enacted for such purposes.

The legislature may authorize cities to take more land and property than is needed for actual construction in the laying out, widening, extending, or re-locating parks, public places, highways or streets, provided, however, that the additional land and property so authorized to be taken shall be no more than sufficient to form suitable building sites abutting on such park, public place, highway or street. After so much of the land and property has been appropriated for such park, public place, highway or street as is needed therefor, the remainder may be sold or leased.

Words in italics are new.

2

ACTS OF NEW YORK, 1911. Chap. 679

AN ACT to amend the Greater New York charter, in relation to the payment of the cost of certain public improvements.

The People of the State of New York, represented in Senate and Assembly, do enact as follows:

Section 1. Chapter six of the Greater New York charter, as re-enacted by chapter four hundred and sixty-six of the laws of nineteen hundred and one, is hereby amended by adding thereto a new section, to be known as section two hundred and forty-seven, to read as follows:

§ 247. Before a public improvement of any kind (except an improvement to be made pursuant to the rapid transit act) involving the acquisition or the physical improvement of property for streets, public places, parks, bridges, approaches to bridges, for the disposal and treatment of sewage or the improvement of the waterfront, or involving both such acquisition and physical improvement of property, which acquisition or physical improvement, or both, is estimated to cost the sum of fifty thousand dollars or more, shall be authorized, the board of estimate and apportionment may determine in what manner and in what shares and proportions the cost and expense of the acquisition or physical improvement, or both, shall be paid by the city of New York, by one or more boroughs thereof, by a part or portion of one or more boroughs thereof, or by the respective owners, lessees, parties and persons respectively entitled unto or interested in the lands, tenements, hereditaments and premises not required for the said improvement, which said board shall deem peculiarly benefited thereby.

If said board shall determine that the cost of such acquisition or physical improvement, or both, shall be apportioned between or among the city of New York, one or more boroughs thereof, a part or portion of one or more boroughs thereof, or the respective owners, lessees, parties and persons respectively entitled unto or interested in the lands, tenements, hereditaments and premises not required for the said improvement, which said board shall deem peculiarly benefited thereby, the said board may also determine in what manner and in what proportion the cost and expense of such acquisition or physical improvement, or both, shall be borne either by the city of New York, by one or more boroughs thereof, by a part or portion of one or more boroughs thereof, or by the respective owners, lessees, parties and persons respectively entitled unto or interested in the lands, tenements, hereditaments and premises not required for the said improvement, which said board shall deem peculiarly benefited thereby.

3

KANSAS CITY *vs.* BACON et al. 157 Mo. 450

VALLIANT, J. Appeal from a judgment of the circuit court of Jackson county assessing benefits against property of the defendants in the proceedings to establish Penn Valley park in Kansas City.

For the establishing of the park 134 acres of land were condemned and the total amount assessed as the value thereof to be paid the owners was $870,759.60, and for the payment of that amount assessments as of benefits were made on a large number of lots included in what is known as West Park district, among which were lots owned severally by defendants Bacon and Monroe. The assessments on the lots of Mrs. Bacon aggregated $3,252.49; those on the lots of Monroe, $991.17. The amount assessed against the city as general benefits was $1.

. . . .

The point against which the main force of appellants' argument is directed is instruction 11 given at the request of the city, and which is:

"11. By your verdict you shall show a correct description of each piece or parcel of property taken and the value thereof, and of each piece or parcel of private property damaged and the amount of injury thereto. You shall also show by your verdict the amount, if any, assessed against the city, and shall show the amount of benefits assessed against each piece or parcel of private property found benefited within the benefit district.

In estimating the benefits that may accrue to the city and to the public generally, or to any property in the benefit district by reason of the proposed improvement, you shall consider only such benefits as are direct, certain and proximate."

. . . .

The law contemplates that a public improvement

may bring a benefit to the property of individuals separate from that which it brings to the city in general, and that it may bring a benefit to the city in general separate from that which it brings to the property of the individuals, and that when it comes to apportioning the cost, the individuals and the city should each bear the burden in proportion to the respective benefit, but the benefit in the one case must be as "direct, certain and proximate" as in the other.

. . . .

Conceding all that the learned counsel say concerning the difference between general and special taxation, we do not see how it affects the question relating to the character of the benefits the city is required to pay for in a case like this. And if it is lawful for the jury to estimate the benefit to the city at large with a view to charging a proper share of the cost of the improvement to the city and thereby to that extent relieve the burden of the property owners; that is to say, if that feature of the law which contemplates laying a portion of the burden on the city at large is not in violation of the fourteenth amendment to the Constitution of the United States, then there must be some rule to guide the jury in assessing those benefits, and if it is not proper to instruct the jury that the only benefits to the city at large which they are to consider are such "as are direct, certain and proximate," then the contrary is true, and they should be instructed to consider benefits that are indirect, uncertain and remote. We recognize that the task of assessing benefits either to private property or to the city at large is a very difficult one, and that the temptation to the jury to indulge in conjecture is great, but still they ought to be admonished that the law requires them to use their reason and judgment, and not their imagination. The provision of the law requiring the benefits to the city at large to be estimated by the jury should either be eliminated entirely or else the jury should be instructed as to what the law means by such benefits, and if it does not mean such "as are direct, certain and proximate," it is meaningless.

. . . .

The specific charge of inequality before the law that these appellants make is that the city has been relieved of its just proportion of the cost of the park, and that portion has been laid, together with their own burden, on these appellants. In their brief they say that the jury should first have estimated the benefit to the city at large and should have charged only the balance of the cost as benefits against the private property, that the assessment of one dollar against the city was no assessment at all.

If the case was given to the jury under proper instructions, whatever opinion we may have as to the fact, we can not say as a matter of law that an assessment of merely nominal benefit was unlawful.

. . . .

See also Kansas City *vs.* Bacon 147 Mo. 259, in which this language is found:

"In the absence of misleading instructions or evidence of misconduct a verdict of one dollar against the city at large is not as a matter of law ground to disturb a verdict."

In this case there was an assessment on property holders of $600,000, and of $1.00 against the city.

And:

Kansas City *vs.* Smart, 128 Mo. 272, where there was an assessment of $140,000 against the benefit district and $1.00 against the city.

4

PARK LAW OF INDIANAPOLIS. Chap. 231. Acts of Indiana, 1911

AN ACT concerning the "department of public parks" in cities of the first and second classes, defining it's powers and duties, conferring certain powers upon the common council and mayor of such cities in relation to said park department, legalizing appointments of boards of park commissioners in such cities, and acts done by such boards, repealing conflicting laws, and declaring an emergency.

[S. 378. Approved March 6, 1911.]

SECTION 1. CITIES—FIRST AND SECOND CLASS—DEPARTMENT OF PARKS.

SECTION 2. PARK COMMISSIONERS—TERMS.

SECTION 3. ORGANIZATION—REPORTS—MEETINGS—FUNDS.

SECTION 4. CONTROL OF PARKS AND BOULEVARDS—POWERS.

SECTION 5. LETTING OF CONTRACTS.

SECTION 6. BREACH OF AGREEMENT—SUIT—RULES—TAXATION.

SECTION 7. SALE OF PARK LANDS—PARK LINE—AMUSEMENT PLACES.

SECTION 8. BEQUESTS OF PROPERTY—USE AND CONTROL—GARDENS, ETC.

SECTION 9. POWER OVER WATERWAYS, ETC.

SECTION 10. CONDEMNATION—EMINENT DOMAIN. The said board of park commissioners are authorized to exercise the power of eminent domain within such city, for the purpose of carrying out any of the provisions of this act, and outside of such city within five miles of the limits of such city. And in case such board of park commissioners cannot agree with the owners, lessees or occupants of any real estate selected by them for the purposes herein set forth, they may proceed to procure the condemnation of the same as hereinafter provided, and in addition thereto, when not in conflict nor inconsistent with the express provisions of this act, may proceed under the general laws of the State of Indiana governing the condemnation of the right of way for the purposes of internal improvement which may be in force at the time, and the provisions of such laws are hereby extended to parks, parkways, park boulevards and pleasure driveways, or parts thereof, so far as the same are not in conflict or inconsistent with the terms of this act.

SECTION 11. COMMON COUNCIL—PARK DISTRICTS. The common council of any such city shall have power, by ordinance upon and in accordance with the recommendation of the board of park commissioners, to lay off and divide the territory thereof into any number of park districts that the conveniences of the citizens of such city and of administration of the department of public parks may require; and, after such districts are established, may from time to time, in like manner, add new territory to any established district, or create new districts from territory which may be annexed to any such city. When such division is thus made of the territory of any such city into districts, or when alterations are thus made in the districts, the boundaries thereof shall be accurately defined, and the descriptions of boundaries shall be entered by such board at full length in the records of such board and shall be recorded in the office of the recorder of the county in which such city is situated; and a duly authenticated copy thereof shall be filed with the comptroller of such city.

SECTION 12. BOULEVARD—PROCEEDINGS TO IMPROVE. The board of park commissioners of any such city shall have the power to order the improvement of any boulevard or any pleasure driveway or part thereof, under the control of such board, by paving the same, curbing and constructing sidewalks thereon, or either paving, curbing and constructing sidewalks thereon in the same manner and subject to the same limitation as to form and procedure, and to the same extent as is or may be in the future conferred upon the board of public works of any such city to improve any street, alley or sidewalk within such city; the cost of such improvement of such boulevard or pleasure driveway shall become a lien upon property to the same extent, enforceable in the same manner, with the same rights as to payments by installments and appeal as are or may be provided for in the case of street and sidewalk improvements ordered by the board of public works; and the provisions of said laws applicable to street and sidewalk improvements ordered by the board of public works of any such city are hereby extended to the improvement of any such boulevard, or pleasure driveway: *Provided,* That said board shall have exclusive authority to determine the kind of pavement to be used. And said park board shall have the power to change and fix the grade of any boulevard, park boulevard, or public driveway, or public ground under its control, to the same extent as such power is now or may be in the future conferred upon the board of public works of any such city to change and fix the grade of any street, alley or public place within any such city: *Provided*, That whenever the land along one side of a boulevard or pleasure driveway is owned by the city or used by the city for park purposes, one-half the cost of such improvement may be assessed against the property benefited in such park district, or districts, to the extent and in the proportion the same shall be benefited as hereinafter provided; and in case it should be determined by said board that no part of the cost of such improvement is properly assessable against the property of a district, or districts, in which the improvement is made, the same may be paid by such city out of any funds available for such purposes.

SECTION 13. APPROPRIATION OF PROPERTY—IMPROVEMENTS. The board of park commissioners of such cities of the first and second classes, as supplemental to other powers conferred by this act, shall have the power, whenever in their discretion such course is advisable, to appropriate property in the manner hereinafter provided for the purpose of: (a) establishing a park, parkway, pleasure driveway or boulevard, or (b) widening or extending any park, parkway, pleasure driveway or boulevard, or (c) opening, widening, or extending any route or right of way for a sewer or channel of any water course connected with or necessary for the protection of any park, parkway, pleasure driveway or boulevard, or (d) constructing any embankment or levee along such water course for the protection of any such park, parkway, pleasure driveway or boulevard, or (e) constructing any bridge or viaduct upon or connected with any such park, parkway, pleasure driveway or boulevard, or (f) converting any street or alley connecting any parks, parkways and boulevards in any such city into a boulevard or pleasure driveway; and also said board shall have power, in the same proceedings, to provide for the construction of improvements of such property for a park, parkway, pleasure driveway or boulevard, in case such property is appropriated or to be appropriated for such purpose; or to provide for the construction necessary for the widening or extending of the same, in case such be the purpose for which the land is appropriated or to be appropriated; or to provide for the construction necessary for the opening, widening or extending of any such route or right of way for a sewer or channel of any such water course, in case such property is appropriated or to be appropriated for such purpose; or to provide for the construction of any such embankment or levee along any such water course as aforesaid, in case such property is appropriated or to be appropriated for such purpose; or to provide for the construction of any such bridge or viaduct, in case such be the purpose for which such property is appropriated or to be appropriated; or to provide for the converting of any such street or alley into a pleasure driveway or boulevard, in case such be the purpose of the appropriation; furthermore, such board may provide for the construction of any of the foregoing work or improvements when the property or part thereof necessary for the same has been secured by contract or otherwise as hereinafter provided.

SECTION 14. PROCEEDINGS IN APPROPRIATING PROPERTY. Whenever, as provided in the foregoing section, said board shall deem it advisable to appropriate property and in conjunction proceed with the work of construction, or to appropriate property, or to proceed

LEGISLATION AND DECISIONS

with such construction when the property necessary, or part thereof, has been secured by contract or otherwise, it shall adopt a resolution declaring such purpose, describing the lands to be appropriated or used therefor, and such other lands as may be injuriously or beneficially affected by said proceedings, and in case improvement of [or] construction is provided for in said resolution, shall cause proper plans and specifications and an estimate of the cost of the proposed work to be prepared by its engineer selected to do such work, which shall be open to inspection by all persons interested in or affected by the appropriation of such lands and the construction of such work, and cause notice of the passage and purport of such resolution and, in case of improvement or construction is provided for in said resolution, of the fact that such plans and specifications have been prepared and can thus be inspected, to be published in some daily newspaper of general circulation in such city once each week for two consecutive weeks. Such notice shall name a time, not less than ten days after the date of publication at which such board shall receive or hear remonstrances from persons interested in or affected by such proceeding. At the time so fixed therefor said board shall hear remonstrances, if any are presented, and after considering the same, take final action, confirming, modifying or rescinding their original resolution. Such action shall be final and conclusive upon all persons. In said resolution and notice separate description of each piece or parcel of property shall not be required, but it shall be sufficient description of the property purchased, or to be purchased, appropriated or damaged to give a description of the entire tract by metes and bounds, whether the same shall

CARRYING OUT THE CITY PLAN

be composed of one or more pieces or parcels, and whether owned by one or more person or persons; also, it shall be sufficient, in said resolution and notice, to prescribe the limits within which private property shall be deemed benefited by the proposed improvement, which benefit districts may include one or more park districts, part or parts of such district or districts and lands benefited outside of said city: *Provided, however,* That at the time before the final adoption of said resolution the resident property-holders in any benefit district, as thus defined, shall have the right to remonstrate against any undertaking by said park board, the cost of which may in whole or in part be assessed against their property. In the event that a majority of such resident property-holders shall remonstrate in writing before the date set for such final adoption of such resolution, no assessment shall be made in such district for such purpose for a period of one year thereafter and then only upon a new resolution duly adopted.

SECTION 15. IMPROVEMENT BIDS—DEPOSIT.

SECTION 16. LIST OF PROPERTY—DAMAGES—BENEFITS. Upon such final order being made, as above provided, said board shall cause to be prepared a list or roll of all the owners or holders of property sought to be taken, if any, or which will be either injuriously or beneficially affected by the appropriation of such land and the construction of such work, or by either such appropriation or construction. Such list shall not be confined to the owners of property adjacent to the line of the proposed work, but shall extend to and include all property taken or injuriously affected thereby, and also shall include all lands benefited by the location, establishment, construction or improvement of any such park, parkway, pleasure driveway, boulevard, improvement or structure provided for in the foregoing sections, whether within or without the limits of said city, not more than five miles from the limits thereof. In addition to such list of names, the same shall show with reasonable certainty a description of such properties to be appropriated or affected, either injuriously or beneficially, belonging to such persons, and no greater certainty in names and descriptions shall be necessary to the validity of any assessment than is required in the assessment of taxes.

SECTION 17. ASSESSMENT—DAMAGES—BENEFITS. Upon the coming in of such list such board shall proceed to consider, determine and award, first, the amount of damages sustained by the owners of the several parcels of land required to be taken and appropriated, if any, as is provided for in the above sections of this act, or which will be injuriously affected thereby; second, to consider, determine and assess the amount of benefits accruing to the several tracts or parcels of property benefited by reason of the location, establishment and construction of any such park, parkway, pleasure driveway, boulevard, or other work or improvement provided for in the above sections of this act. No assessments of benefits shall be made in excess of fifteen per cent of the value of the land so assessed exclusive of the improvement upon the land so assessed; and the total of such assessment against any part or parcel of land assessed, during the ten year period of existence of powers herein conferred shall not exceed fifteen per cent of the value of the land so assessed. The damages awarded and the benefits assessed shall be severally shown as against each parcel of land shown on said list: *Provided*, That the board of park commissioners of any such city shall in any event direct the payment of the cost of any park, parkway, pleasure driveway, boulevard or construction of any improvement provided for in the above sections of this act, over and above the total amount of all assessments of benefits, or to the extent of the benefits to the city as a whole, as determined by said board, to be made out of the general park fund of any such city available for such purpose: *Provided further*, That in the event the total cost of any such park improvement, including cost of lands, construction, shaping of soil, planting of trees and shrubbery and other work and improvements called for in such resolution, and including costs of making assessments and collections, should exceed the total of benefits to such lands assessed plus the amount available from the general park fund or other sources for any such park improvement, then said board shall proceed no further under said resolution, but shall rescind all action therefrom taken. In case said board shall have ordered the cost of the construction of pavements, curbing and gutters, separately, under the provisions of section 12 hereof, to be paid by abutting property owners, as in said section provided, and it shall appear that the entire cost of the same can not be met by assessments against abutting property owners, not including such city, then such board shall have power to assess the remainder of the cost of such pavement, curbing and sidewalks against the lands of the district or districts wherein such proposed improvement is situate to the extent and in the proportion that the same shall be benefited, in the manner as provided for assessing the cost of other structures and improvements named in sections 13 and 14 of this act: *Provided*, That the resolution of such board shall in each instance state the method of proposed assessment to be adopted.

When said list shall have been thus completed said board shall cause to be published in some daily newspaper of general circulation in said city, once each week for two successive weeks, a notice describing the location of the lands appropriated, if any, or of the lands on which such improvement is to be made, and the general character of the improvement and the boundaries of the area or district to be assessed; said notice shall also state that the assessment roll, with the names of the owners in favor of whom damages have been awarded and against whom assessments have been made, and descriptions of property affected, with the amounts of preliminary assessments or awards as to each piece or parcel of property affected, is on file and can be seen in the office of said board. Said notice shall also name a day not earlier than ten days after the date of the last publication on which said board shall receive and hear remonstrances from persons with regard to the amount of their respective awards or assessments. Furthermore, said board shall cause a written notice to be served upon the owner of each piece or parcel taken or injuriously affected, showing separately each item of such determination as to lands or parts of lands so owned by him, by leaving a copy at his last and usual place of residence in such city, or by delivering a copy to such owner personally; and said board shall also cause to be mailed by United States mail a notice to the place of residence, if known, of persons owning lands or parts of lands against which special assessments have been made, showing each item of such determination as to such persons. In case any person affected be a non-resident, or his residence shall be unknown, then he shall be notified by publication in some daily newspaper of general circulation once each week for three successive weeks. Said notices shall name a day not earlier than ten days after service of such notice, or after the last date of publication, or after the date of mailing as above provided, on which said board shall receive and hear remonstrances from persons with regard to the amount of their respective awards or assessments. Persons not included in such lists of assessments or awards and claiming to be entitled to the same shall be deemed to have been notified of the pendency of the proceeding by the original notice of the resolution of the board and by the first publication as in this section provided.

SECTION 18. PROPERTY OF INSANE OR INFANTS.

SECTION 19. REMONSTRANCE HEARING. Any person notified or deemed to be notified under the preceding sections may appear before such board on the day fixed for hearing such remonstrances with regard to awards and assessments, and remonstrate against the same. All persons appearing before said board having an interest in said proceedings shall be given a hearing. After such remonstrances shall have been received and said hearings had, said board shall thereupon either sustain or modify, by increasing or decreasing the awards or assessments. Any person thus remonstrating, who is aggrieved by the decision of the board, may, within fifteen days thereafter, take an appeal to the circuit or superior court in the county in which such city is located. Such appeal shall only affect the amount of the assessment or award of the person appealing.

SECTION 20. APPEAL. Such appeal may be taken by filing an original complaint in such court against such city within the time named, setting forth the action of such board in respect to such assessment or award and stating the facts relied upon as showing an error on the part of such board. Such court shall rehear the matter of such assessment or award de novo, and confirm, lower or increase the same, as may seem just. In case such court shall reduce the amount of benefit assessed against the land of such propertyholder ten per cent. of the assessment by said board, or increase the amount of damages awarded in his favor ten per cent. of the amount awarded by such board, the plaintiff in such suit shall recover costs, otherwise not. The amount of the judgment in such court shall be final, and no appeal shall lie therefrom.

SECTION 21. LOCAL ASSESSMENT DUPLICATE—LIENS.

SECTION 22. PAYMENT OF DAMAGES—TENDER.

SECTION 23. PAYMENT TO OWNERS—TITLE TO LANDS.

SECTION 24. RECORDING LAND DESCRIPTIONS.

SECTION 25. APPOINTMENTS VALID.

SECTION 26. TEN-YEAR LIMIT—ASSESSMENT. The power herein granted for the assessments of benefits shall expire ten years from the date at which this act shall take effect: *Provided*, That after the expiration of said ten year period, said board of park commissioners shall have and exercise powers therein granted in respect to the opening and improvement of streets, ways and boulevards, of which they have control, similar to powers of the board of public works of such cities in respect to streets and highways.

SECTION 27. AGGREGATE BENEFITS. The powers

CARRYING OUT THE CITY PLAN

herein granted for the assessment of benefits against property, except as to powers similar to those of the board of public works of such cities, are hereby further limited as follows: The aggregate amount of benefits which may be assessed against property by such park board in cities of the first class during said ten year period, from and after the taking effect of this act, shall not exceed one million, two hundred and fifty thousand dollars. The total amount of such local benefits which may be assessed by such board of park commissioners in cities of the first class during any one year after the taking effect of this act, shall not exceed two hundred thousand dollars. The aggregate amount of benefits which may be assessed against property by such board of park commissioners in cities of the second class during said ten year period, from and after the taking effect of this act, shall not exceed five hundred thousand dollars. The total amount of such local benefits which may be assessed by any such board of park commissioners in cities of the second class during any one year after the taking effect of this act shall not exceed fifty thousand dollars: *Provided*, That if in any one year such board of park commissioners in any city of the first or second class should assess an amount less than the annual limitation herein contained, then and in that event any such board may, in the following or any subsequent year, make such assessments in excess of said annual limitation to the amount of such difference between such annual limitation and the amount assessed in any previous year. The limits herein fixed shall not be deemed to apply to any sum which may be raised from a general tax levy, and appropriated by the council of such city for the use of such park board, or received from any source other than through benefit assessments, but the limiting amounts herein named shall apply only to such benefit assessments, not including those ordered by powers similar to those of the board of public works.

SECTION 28. REPEAL.

SECTION 29. EMERGENCY.

5

ACTS OF MASSACHUSETTS, 1912. Chap. 339

AN ACT to authorize the City of Boston to abate a portion of the betterment assessments made on account of the laying out and construction of Columbia Road.

Section 1. The board of street commissioners of the city of Boston *may* at any time within two years after the passage of this act abate such proportion of any assessment for a betterment made on account of the laying out and construction of Columbia Road from Franklin Park, in Dorchester, to Marine Park, in South Boston, not exceeding in the case of lots unimproved at the time of the passage of the order for the said laying out and construction twenty per cent, and in the case of lots improved at the time of the passage of said order and lots bordering on the parts of the said road formerly known as the Strandway and Dorchesterway thirty-three and one-third per cent, as said board shall deem just and expedient.

Section 2. Said board may by its certificate authorize the treasurer of the city to repay the excess of any amount paid on account of said assessments over the amounts determined as the revised assessments in accordance with the provisions of this act, and said excess shall be repaid by the treasurer from the appropriation from which the improvement was paid for to the person for whom payment was made, or to his legal representatives.

6
ACTS OF MASSACHUSETTS, 1912. Chap. 537

AN ACT to provide for reducing the betterments charged for the improvement of Bennington Boulevard in East Boston.

Section 1. The city of Boston is hereby *required* to reduce the betterments charged for the improvement of Bennington Boulevard in the East Boston district of the said city in such manner and to such extent as shall be agreed upon by the city and the owners of the lands concerned. In case of their failure to agree, the amount of the reduction to be made under the provisions of this act shall be determined by the superior court for the county of Suffolk, if a petition therefor is filed in the office of the clerk of the court by the owners of the land within two years after the passage of this act. The case shall be heard by a single judge, if the parties so agree, or by a jury if either party requests a trial by jury; and the jury shall view the premises if either party so requests.

III. EXCESS CONDEMNATION
1
ACTS OF OHIO, 1904. Found in the Annotated Statutes
C. 2, P. 755

All municipal corporations shall have power to appropriate, enter upon and hold, real estate within their corporate limits for the following purposes: . . . .

12th: For establishing esplanades, boulevards, parkways, park grounds, and public reservations in, around and leading to public buildings, and for the purpose of reselling such land with reservations in the deeds of such resale as to the future use of said lands so as to protect public buildings and their environs, and to preserve the view, appearance, light, air, and usefulness of public grounds occupied by public buildings and esplanades, and parkways leading thereto.

2

LAWS OF MARYLAND, 1908. Chap. 166
Condemnation of Property. Baltimore

To acquire by purchase or condemnation any land or any interest therein which it may require for schoolhouses, engine-houses, court-houses, markets, streets, bridges and their approaches, the establishment or enlargement of parks, squares, gardens or other public places, the establishment of esplanades, boulevards, parkways, park grounds or public reservations around, adjacent, opposite or in proximity or leading to any public building or buildings, or which it may require for any other public or municipal purpose; and also any and all land and property or interest in land and property adjoining and extending such distance as may be adjudged necessary from any property in use or about to be acquired for such esplanade, boulevard, parkway, park grounds or public reservation, as aforesaid, the use of which said adjacent property it may be deemed necessary or beneficial to subject to lawful restrictions or control, in order to better protect or enhance the usefulness of such public building or buildings or in any manner to promote the interests of the public therein, or to more fully effectuate the purpose of the establishment of such esplanade, boulevard,

CARRYING OUT THE CITY PLAN

parkway, park grounds or public reservations, and to sell thereafter such adjacent lands or property subject to such reservations or restrictions as to the subsequent use thereof, as may appear advisable for the protection of such public building or buildings, or for enhancing the usefulness thereof, or in any manner to promote the interests of the public therein, or for better insuring the protection or usefulness of such esplanade, boulevard, parkway, park grounds or public reservations, or in any manner to better accomplish the purposes and serve the public interests for which they shall have been or shall be established. The Mayor and City Council of Baltimore may prescribe the procedure for condemnation of any land or property situated wholly within the City of Baltimore, which under the foregoing provisions it is authorized to condemn, but such procedure as the said Mayor and City Council of Baltimore may adopt shall include provision for reasonable notice to the owner or owners, and for appeals to the Baltimore City Court by any person interested, including the Mayor and City Council of Baltimore from the decision of any commissioners or other persons appointed to value such land or property, or interest therein. Nothing herein shall be construed as depriving the city of any power of condemnation for any purpose already vested in it. The Mayor and City Council of Baltimore shall have full power and authority to provide by ordinance for ascertaining whether any and what amount of benefits will accrue to the owner or possessor of any ground or improvements within the City of Baltimore by reason of the establishment or enlargement of any park, squares, gardens, esplanades, boulevards, parkways, park grounds, public reservations or other public places, for which said owner or possessor ought to pay compensation, and to provide by ordinance for assessing or levying the amount of such benefits on the property of persons so benefited; provided, that provision is made therein for reasonable notice to the person or persons against whom such benefits are to be assessed, and provided that provision be made for appeals to the Baltimore City Court by any person or persons interested, including the Mayor and City Council of Baltimore, from the decision of any board, commissioners, or other persons appointed or authorized to assess such benefits.

3

VIRGINIA ACTS OF ASSEMBLY, 1906. Chap. 194

Approved March 14, 1906

1. Be it enacted by the general assembly of Virginia, That any city or town of this Commonwealth may acquire by purchase, gift or condemnation property adjoining its parks or plats on which its monuments are located, or other property used for public purposes or in the vicinity of such parks, plats or property which is used and maintained in such a manner as to impair the beauty, usefulness or efficiency of such parks, plats or public property, and may likewise acquire property adjacent to any street the topography of which, from its proximity thereof, impairs the convenient use of such street, or renders impracticable, without extraordinary expense, the improvements of the same, and the city or town so acquiring any such property may subsequently dispose of the property so acquired, making limitations as to the use thereof, which will protect the beauty, usefulness, efficiency or convenience of such parks, plats or property.

2. This act shall be in force on and after ninety days from the adjournment of the general assembly of Virginia.

4

ACTS OF PENNSYLVANIA, 8 June, 1907. No. 315

AN ACT authorizing cities of this Commonwealth to purchase, acquire, take, use, and appropriate private property, for the purposes of making, enlarging, extending, and maintaining public parks, parkways, and playgrounds; authorizing the said cities to purchase, acquire, take, use, and appropriate neighboring private property, within two hundred feet of the boundary lines of such public parks, parkways and playgrounds, in order to protect the same by resale, with restrictions; authorizing the resale of such neighboring property, with such restrictions in the deeds of resale in regard to the use thereof as will protect such public park, parkways, and playgrounds; and providing for the manner of ascertaining, determining, awarding, and paying compensation and damages in all cases where property is taken, used, and appropriated for the said purposes.

Section 1. Be it enacted &c., That it shall be lawful for, and the right is hereby conferred upon, the cities of this Commonwealth to purchase, acquire, enter upon, take, use, and appropriate private property, for the purpose of making, enlarging, extending, and maintaining public parks, parkways, and play grounds within the corporate limits of such cities, whenever the councils thereof shall, by ordinance or joint resolution, determine thereon; That where such private property is outside of the city, it may be annexed thereto by ordinance of said city: And provided, That where any poorhouse properties are taken, and such cities shall have made adequate provisions for thereafter accommodating and supporting the poor of the districts, wards, and townships within such cities, wherein such poorhouses are located, nominal damages only shall be allowed for such taking, and the land shall be held on condition that such city shall continue to make adequate provisions for the poor of such districts, wards or townships.

Section 2. It shall be lawful for, and the right is hereby conferred upon, cities of this Commonwealth to purchase, acquire, enter upon, take, use, and appropriate neighboring private property, within two hundred feet of the boundary lines of such property so taken, used, and appropriated for public parks, parkways, and playgrounds, in order to protect the same by the resale of such neighboring property with restrictions, whenever the councils thereof shall, by ordinance or joint resolution, determine thereon: Provided, That in the said ordinance or joint resolution, the councils thereof shall declare that the control of such neighboring property, within two hundred feet of the boundary lines of such public parks, parkways, or playgrounds, is reasonably necessary, in order to protect such public parks, parkways, or playgrounds, their environs, the preservation of the view, appearance, light, air, health, or usefulness thereof.

Section 3. That it shall be lawful for, and the right is hereby conferred upon, the cities of this Commonwealth to resell such neighboring property, with such restrictions in the deeds of resale in regard to the use thereof as will fully insure the protection of such public parks, parkways, and playgrounds, their environs, the preservation of the view, appearance, light, air, health and usefulness thereof, whenever the councils thereof shall, by ordinance or joint resolution, determine thereon.

CARRYING OUT THE CITY PLAN

Section 4. The taking, using, and appropriating, by the right of eminent domain as herein provided, of private property for the purpose of making, enlarging, extending, and maintaining public parks, parkways, and playgrounds, and of neighboring property, within two hundred feet of the boundary lines of such public parks, parkways, and playgrounds, in order to protect such public parks, parkways, and playgrounds, their environs, the preservation of the view, appearance, light, air, health, and usefulness thereof, by reselling such neighboring property, with such restrictions in the deeds of resale as will protect said property, so taken for the aforesaid purpose, is hereby declared to be taking, using, and appropriating of such private property for public use: Provided, however, That the proceeds arising from the resale of any such property so taken, shall be deposited in the treasury of said cities, and be subject to general appropriation by the councils of said city.

Section 5. In all cases wherein cities of this Commonwealth shall hereafter take, use, and appropriate private property for the aforesaid purposes, by ordinance or joint resolution, if the compensation and damages arising therefrom cannot be agreed upon by the owners thereof and such cities, such compensation and damages shall be considered, ascertained, determined, awarded, and paid in the manner provided in an act entitled "An act providing for the manner of ascertaining, determining, awarding, and paying compensation and damages in all cases where municipalities of this Commonwealth may hereafter be authorized by law to take, use, and appropriate private property for the purpose of making, enlarging, and maintaining public parks, within the corporate limits of such municipality," approved the eighth day of June, Anno Domini one thousand eight hundred and ninety-five.

Section 6. All acts or parts of acts inconsistent herewith are hereby repealed.

Approved the eighth day of June, A.D. 1907.

Edwin S. Stuart.

5
Pennsylvania Mutual Life Ins. Co. vs. Philadelphia

Pa. Supreme Court. April 15, 1913.

Bill in equity for an injunction to restrain the city of Philadelphia from appropriating certain land under the provisions of the Act of June 8, 1907 (text is given on page 272), and that the ordinance of Jan. 16, 1913, be declared unconstitutional.

From the record it appeared that by ordinance, councils of Philadelphia undertook to appropriate certain land within 200 feet of a proposed parkway.

By ordinance of Jan. 16, 1913, the mayor was authorized to enter into an agreement on behalf of the city with the Bell Telephone Co., whereby the land so appropriated should be conveyed to the telephone company in fee, subject to certain building restrictions. The purpose of the transaction was admittedly to protect the parkway from the construction of an unsightly building in the vicinity.

The lower court held the act constitutional but awarded the injunction on the ground that the ordinance of Jan. 16, 1913, was defective in that it was not preceded by an ordinance prescribing general restrictions for the protection of the parkway. Plaintiff and defendant appealed.

CARRYING OUT THE CITY PLAN

Opinion:

"The view we take of the case requires us to determine the single question whether the purpose or use for which the city intends to take the plaintiff's land is a public use within the constitutional provision permitting its appropriation under the power of eminent domain. . . . . Primarily the question is for the legislative department of the government, but ultimately for the courts. . . . .
There is no constitutional or statutory definition of the words 'public use,' and none of the adjudicated cases has given a definition of the words which can have universal application. It has been held that the words are equivalent to public benefit or advantage, while numerous other cases hold that to constitute a public use the property must be taken into direct control of the public or of public agencies, or the public must have the right to use in some way the property appropriated.

We think this (latter) interpretation of the words 'public use' is in accord with their plain and natural signification, and with the weight of the best considered authorities. It furnishes a certain guide to the legislature as well as to the courts in appropriating private property for public use. It enables the state and the owner to determine directly their respective rights in the latter's property. If, however, public benefit, utility or advantage is to be the test of a public use, then, as suggested by the authorities, the right to condemn the property will not depend on a fixed standard by which the legislative and judicial departments of the government are to be guided, but upon the views of those who at the time are to determine the question. There will be no limit to the power of either the legislature or the courts to appropriate private property to public use except their individual opinions as to what is and what is not for the public advantage and utility. If such considerations are to prevail, the constitutional guarantees as to private property will be of small moment. . . . .

We think that the sections of the Act of 1907, authorizing the acquisition of private property outside a public park, parkway and playground, are not a constitutional exercise of legislative authority. It will be observed that these sections confer authority to appropriate and resell with such restrictions as may be prescribed property outside the line of the parkway, and it is justified by declaring that it is done to protect the parkway and for the preservation of the view, appearance, light, air, healthfulness or usefulness thereof. The protection of the highway is the only 'public use' to which the land is to be applied. The property is not to be taken and held by the city for any use for which a statute confers on the city the right to appropriate it. . . . . . Prior to this legislation, the state had not authorized the taking of private property by the exercise of the power of eminent domain for such purpose. It is a step far in advance of the policy of the state as heretofore declared in her organic law, and is a liberal construction of a power which we have uniformly held must be strictly construed.

. . . .

Holding as we do that the use to be made of property located outside a public highway is not a public use for which private property may be taken by the city against the consent of the owners, the effect of the act of 1907 is to permit the taking of the property of one citizen without his consent and vesting the title thereto in another. . . . . . . One may be deprived of his home for the benefit of another. In view of its provisions conferring almost unlimited discretion on cities or their officials in exercising the powers granted, it is idle to say that the statute furnished no opportunity to produce such results or to promote a private purpose. . . . .

The court below is directed to enter a decree declaring unconstitutional so much of the Act of June 8, 1907, as authorizes cities to take and appropriate neighboring private property within 200 feet of the boundary line of property appropriated for public parks, parkways and playgrounds, ... and enjoining perpetually the city from appropriating plaintiff's property outside of and adjacent to the parkway."

6

CONSTITUTION OF MASSACHUSETTS. Article 10, Part 1

Amended, Nov., 1911

The legislature may by special acts for the purpose of laying out, widening or relocating highways or streets, authorize the taking in fee by the commonwealth, or by a county, city or town, of more land and property than are needed for the actual construction of such highway or street: *provided, however,* that the land and property authorized to be taken are specified in the act and are no more in extent than would be sufficient for suitable building lots on both sides of such highway or street, and after so much of the land or property has been appropriated for such highway or street as is needed therefor, may authorize the sale of the remainder for value with or without suitable restrictions.

7

PROPOSED AMENDMENT TO CONSTITUTION OF NEW YORK. Article I, Section 6

Defeated, 1911

"When private property shall be taken for public use by a municipal corporation, additional adjoining and neighboring property may be taken under conditions to be prescribed by the legislature by general laws; property thus taken shall be deemed to be taken for public use."*

8

AMENDMENT TO CONSTITUTION OF WISCONSIN, Article XI

Adopted Nov. 4, 1912

Section 3a. The state or any of its cities may acquire by gift, purchase or condemnation lands for establishing, laying out, widening, enlarging, extending, and maintaining memorial grounds, streets, squares, parkways, boulevards, parks, playgrounds, sites for public buildings, and reservations in and about and along and leading to any or all of the same; and after the establishment, lay-out, and completion of such improvements, may convey any such real estate thus acquired and not necessary for such improvements, with reservations concerning the future use and occupation of such real estate, so as to protect such public works and improvements, and their environs, and to preserve the

---

*See page 248 of this Appendix for the amendment which passed in 1913.

view, appearance, light, air, and usefulness of such public works.

9
AMENDMENT TO CONSTITUTION OF OHIO, Article XVIII

Adopted 1912

Section 10. A municipality appropriating or otherwise acquiring property for public use may in furtherance of such public use appropriate or acquire an excess over that actually to be occupied by the improvement, and may sell such excess with such restrictions as shall be appropriate to preserve the improvement made. Bonds may be issued to supply the funds in whole or in part to pay for the excess property so appropriated or otherwise acquired, but said bonds shall be a lien only against the property so acquired for the improvement and excess, and they shall not be a liability of the municipality nor be included in any limitation of the bonded indebtedness of such municipality prescribed by law.

IV. LEGISLATION CREATING PLANNING AGENCIES

A. BOARDS OF SURVEY

ACTS OF MASSACHUSETTS, 1907, Chap. 191

AN ACT to authorize the Establishment of Boards of Survey in Towns.

Section 1. The selectmen of any town which accepts the provisions of this act shall constitute a board of survey for that town.

Section 2. Any person or corporation desiring to lay out, locate or construct any street or way in any town which accepts the provisions of this act, after the date of such acceptance, shall, before the beginning of such construction, submit to said board of survey suitable plans of such street or way, to be prepared in accordance with such rules and regulations as the board may prescribe. Upon the receipt of such plans, with a petition for their approval, the board shall give a public hearing thereon, after giving notice of such hearing by publication once a week for two successive weeks in a newspaper published in the town, the last publication to be at least two days before the hearing; and after such hearing the board may alter such plans and may determine where such street or way shall be located, and the width and grades thereof, and shall so designate on said plans. The plans shall then be approved and signed by the board and filed in the office of the clerk of the town, who shall attest thereon the date of the filing.

Section 3. The board of survey shall from time to time cause to be made under its direction plans of such territory or sections of land in any town which accepts the provisions of this act, as the board may deem advisable, showing thereon the location of such street or ways, whether already laid out or not, as the board shall be of opinion that the present or future interests of the public require or will require in such territory, showing clearly the direction, width and grades of each street or way; and the board may employ such assistants and incur such expenses in regard to said plans as it may deem necessary, not exceeding the amount of money appropriated by the town for the purpose. Before making any such plan the board shall give a public hearing as to the location, direction, width and

CARRYING OUT THE CITY PLAN

grades of streets or ways in the territory to be shown on the plan, after giving notice of such hearing by publication once a week for two successive weeks in a newspaper published in the town, the last publication to be at least two weeks before the hearing, and shall, after making any such plan, give a like notice of hearing, and a hearing thereon, and shall keep the plan open to public inspection for one month after the first publication of notice of such hearing. After such hearing and after the alterations deemed necessary by the board have been made in such plan, the plan shall be marked as made under the provisions of this act, shall be signed by the board, and shall then be filed in the office of the clerk of said town, who shall attest thereon the date of such filing.

Section 5. If any building shall hereafter be placed or erected in any town which accepts the provisions of this act within the boundaries of any street or way shown on any plan filed with the town clerk as herein provided, or on land adjacent to any such street or way the grade of which at the time of placing or erecting such building is other than the grade shown on said plan, or on land adjacent to any street or way the plan and profile of which have not been approved by said board of survey, no damages caused to any building so placed or erected, by the construction of such street or way as shown on said plan, or caused to any building so placed or erected, or to the land upon which such building is placed or erected, by the subsequent change of grade of any street or way the plan of which has not been approved by said board of survey, shall be recovered by or paid to the owner of the whole or any part of the estate of which the land upon which said building so placed or erected formed a part at the date of the first publication of notice of hearing as aforesaid.

B. PLANNING COMMISSIONS

1

ACTS OF MASSACHUSETTS, 1913.   Chap. 494

AN ACT to provide for the establishment of local planning boards by cities and towns.

SECTION 1. Every city of the commonwealth, and every town having a population of more than ten thousand at the last preceding national or state census, is hereby authorized and directed to create a board to be known as the planning board, whose duty it shall be to make careful studies of the resources, possibilities and needs of the city or town, particularly with respect to conditions which may be injurious to the public health or otherwise injurious in and about rented dwellings, and to make plans for the development of the municipality with special reference to the proper housing of its people. In cities, the said board shall be appointed by the mayor, subject to confirmation by the council, and in cities under a commission form of government, so called, the members of the board shall be appointed by the governing body of the city. In towns, the members of the board shall be elected by the voters at the annual town meeting.

SECTION 2. Every planning board established hereunder shall make a report annually to the city council or governing body in cities and to the annual town meeting in towns, giving information regarding the condition of the city or town and any plans or proposals for the development of the city or town and estimates of the cost thereof; and it shall be the duty of every such local planning board to file a copy of all reports made by it with the homestead commission.

SECTION 3. The homestead commission, created by chapter six hundred and seven of the acts of the year nineteen hundred and eleven, is hereby directed to call the attention of the mayor and city governments in cities and the selectmen in each town having a population of more than ten thousand at the last preceding national or state census to the provisions of this act in such form as may seem proper; and said commission is furthermore authorized and directed to furnish information and suggestions from time to time to city governments and to the selectmen of towns and to local planning boards, when the same shall have been created, such as may, in its judgment, tend to promote the purposes of this act and of those for which the said commission was established.

SECTION 4. The city council or other governing body in cities is authorized to make suitable ordinances, and towns are authorized to make suitable by-laws, for carrying out the purposes of this act, and they may appropriate money therefor.

SECTION 5. This act shall take effect upon its passage. [*Approved April 16, 1913.*

2

LAWS OF NEW YORK, 1913. Chap. 699

AN ACT to amend the general municipal law by adding thereto a provision authorizing cities and incorporated villages to appoint planning commissions, and to appropriate money for the same.

The People of the State of New York, represented in Senate and Assembly, do enact as follows:

SECTION 1. The general municipal law is hereby

amended by adding thereto a new article to be numbered twelve-a, to be entitled city and village planning commissions, and to read as follows:

ARTICLE 12-a

CITY AND VILLAGE PLANNING COMMISSIONS

Section 234. CREATION, APPOINTMENT AND QUALIFICATIONS.
    235. OFFICERS, EXPENSES AND ASSISTANCE.
    236. GENERAL POWERS.
    237. MAPS AND RECOMMENDATIONS.
    238. PRIVATE STREETS.
    239. RULES.
    239-a. CONSTRUCTION OF ARTICLE.

Section 234. CREATION, APPOINTMENT AND QUALIFICATIONS. Each city and incorporated village is hereby authorized and empowered to create a commission to be known as the city or village planning commission. Such commission shall be so created in incorporated villages by resolution of the trustees, in cities by ordinance of the common council, except that in cities of the first class, having more than a million inhabitants, it shall be by resolution of the board of estimate and apportionment or other similar local authority. In cities of the first class such commission shall consist of not more than eleven, in cities of the second class of not more than nine, in cities of the third class and incorporated villages of not more than seven members. Such ordinance or resolution shall specify the public officer or body of said municipality, that shall appoint such commissioners, and shall provide that the appointment of as nearly as possible one third of them shall be for a term of one year, one third for a term of two years, and one third for a term of three years; and that at the expiration of such terms, the terms of office of their successors shall be three years; so that the term of office of one third of such commissioners, as nearly as possible, shall expire each year. All appointments to fill vacancies shall be for the unexpired term. Not more than one third of the members of said commission shall hold any other public office in said city or village.

Section 235. OFFICERS, EXPENSES AND ASSISTANCE. The commission shall elect annually a chairman from its own members. It shall have the power and authority to employ experts, clerks, and a secretary, and to pay for their services and such other expenses as may be necessary and proper, not exceeding, in all, the annual appropriation that may be made by said city or village for said commission. The body creating the commission shall by ordinance or resolution provide what compensation if any, each of such commissioners shall receive for his services as such commissioner. Each city and incorporated village is hereby authorized and empowered to make such appropriation as it may see fit for such expenses and compensation, such appropriations to be made by those officers or bodies in such city or village having charge of the appropriation of the public funds.

Section 236. GENERAL POWERS. The body creating such planning commission may, at any time, by ordinance or resolution, provide that the following matters, or any one or more of them, shall be referred for report thereon, to such commission by the board, commission, commissioner or other public officer or officers of said city or village which is the final authority thereon before final action thereon by such authority: the adoption of any map or plan of said city or incorporated village, or part thereof, including drainage and sewer or water system plans or maps, and plans or maps for any public water front, or marginal street, or public structure upon, in or in connection with such front or street, or for any dredging, filling or fixing of lines with relation to said front; any change of any such maps or plans; the location of any public structure upon, in or in connection with, or fixing lines with relation to said front; the location of any public building, bridge, statue or monument, highway, park, parkway, square, playground or recreation ground, or public open place of said city or village. In default of any such ordinance or resolution all of said matters shall be so referred to said planning commission.

The body creating such planning commission may, at any time, by ordinance or resolution, fix the time within which such planning commission shall report upon any matter or class of matters to be referred to it, with or without the further provision that in default of report within the time so fixed, the planning commission shall forfeit the right further to suspend action, as aforesaid with regard to the particular matter upon which it has so defaulted. In default of any such ordinance or resolution, no such action shall be taken until such report is so received, and no adoption, change, fixing or location as aforesaid by said final authority, prior thereto, shall be valid. No ordinance or resolution shall deprive said planning commission of its right or relieve it of its duty, to report, at such time as it deems proper, upon any matter at any time referred to it.

This section shall not be construed as intended to

CARRYING OUT THE CITY PLAN

limit or impair the power of any art commission, park commission or commissioner, now or hereafter existing by virtue of any provision of law, to refuse consent to the acceptance by any municipality of the gift of any work of art to said municipality, without reference of the matter, by reason of its proposed location or otherwise, to said planning commission. Nor shall this section be construed as intended to limit or impair any other power of any such art commission or affect the same, except in so far as it provides for reference or report, or both, on any matter before final action thereon by said art commission.

Section 237. MAPS AND RECOMMENDATIONS. Such planning commission may cause to be made a map or maps of said city or village or any portion thereof, or of any land outside the limits of said city or village so near or so related thereto that in the opinion of said planning commission it should be so mapped. Such plans may show not only such matters as by law have been or may be referred to the planning commission, but also any and all matters and things with relation to the plan of said city or village which to said planning commission seem necessary and proper, including recommendations and changes suggested by it; and any report at any time made, may include any of the above. Such planning commission may obtain expert assistance in the making of any such maps or reports, or in the investigations necessary and proper with relation thereto.

Section 238. PRIVATE STREETS. The body creating such planning commission may at any time, by ordinance or resolution, provide that no plan, plot or description, showing the layout of any highway or street upon private property, or of building lots in connection with or in relation to such highway or street shall, within the limits of any municipality having a planning commission, as aforesaid, be received for record in the office of the clerk of the county where such real property is situated, until a copy of said plan, plot or description has been filed with said commission and it has certified, with relation thereto, its approval thereof. Such certificate shall be recorded as a part of the record of said original instrument containing said plan, plot, or description. No such street or highway which has not received the approval of the planning commission shall be accepted by said city or village until the matter has been referred to such commission under the provision of section two hundred and thirty-six of this article. But if any such street is plotted or laid out in accordance with the map of said municipality, adopted according to law, then it shall not be necessary to file such copy, or obtain or record such certificate.

Section 239. RULES. Such commission may make rules not contrary to law, to govern its action in carrying out the provisions of this article.

Section 239-a. CONSTRUCTION OF ARTICLE. This article shall be construed as the grant of additional power and authority to cities and incorporated villages, and not as intended to limit or impair any existing power or authority of any city or village.

Any city or incorporated village in order to appoint a planning commission under this article shall recite, in the ordinance or resolution so creating the commission, the fact that it is created under this article.

Section 2. This act shall take effect immediately.

CARRYING OUT THE CITY PLAN

State of New York, } ss:
Office of the Secretary of State.

I have compared the preceding with the original law on file in this office, and do hereby certify that the same is a correct transcript therefrom and of the whole of the said original law.

Mitchell May,
Secretary of State.

3

Laws of Pennsylvania, General Assembly. No. 406, of 1913

A SUPPLEMENT to an Act entitled, "An act providing for the incorporation and government of cities of the third class," approved the twenty-third day of May, Anno Domini one thousand eight hundred eighty-nine, creating a City Planning Department, defining its jurisdiction, and extending the same so as to regulate the laying out and recording of plans of lots within the limits of the city, and for three miles beyond the city limits; and to regulate the making and use of certain public improvements until said plans are approved by said department and authorizing the exercise of the powers herein provided by a park or other municipal commission.

Section 1. Be it enacted, &c., That an additional executive department in the government of cities of the third class is hereby created, to be known as the Department of City Planning, which shall be in charge of a City Planning Commission, consisting of five persons, to be appointed by the mayor and councils. In the first instance, one member of said commission shall be appointed for one year, one member for two years, one member for three years, one member for four years, and one member for five years, and annually thereafter a member of said commission shall be appointed for a term of five years. An appointment to fill a casual vacancy shall be only for the unexpired portion of the term. All members of the said commission shall reside within the zone of jurisdiction of said commission, as hereinafter defined. They may make and alter rules and regulations for their own organization and procedure, consistent with the ordinances of the city and the laws of the Commonwealth. They shall serve without compensation, and make annually to the mayor and councils a report of their transactions. They may employ engineers and other persons, whose salaries and wages, and other necessary expenses of the commission, shall be provided for through proper appropriation by councils.

Section 2. The clerks of council shall, upon introduction, furnish to the City Planning Commission, for its consideration, a copy of all ordinances and bills, and all amendments thereto, relating to the location of any public building of the city; and to the location, extension, widening, narrowing, enlargement, ornamentation, and parking of any street, boulevard, parkway, park, playground, or other public ground; and to the relocation, vacation, curtailment, changes of use, or any other alteration of the city plan, with relation to any of the same; and to the location of any bridge, tunnel, and subway, or any surface, underground, or elevated railway. The said commission shall have the power to disapprove any of the said ordinances, bills, or amendments, which disapproval, however, must be communicated to councils, in writing, within ten days from the introduction of said ordinances; but such disapproval shall not operate as a veto.

Section 3. The City Planning Commission may make or cause to be made, and lay before councils, and at its discretion cause to be published, maps of the city or any portion thereof, including territory extending three miles beyond the city limits, showing the streets,

CARRYING OUT THE CITY PLAN

and highways and other natural and artificial features, and also locations proposed by it for any new public buildings, civic centre, street, parkway, park, playground, or any other public ground or public improvement, or any widening, extension, or relocation of the same, or any change in the city plan by it deemed advisable; and it may make recommendations to councils, from time to time, concerning any such matters and things aforesaid, for action by councils thereto; and, in so doing, have regard for the present conditions and future needs and growth of the city, and the distribution and relative location of all the principal and other streets and railways, waterways, and all other means of public travel and business communications, as well as the distribution and relative location of all public buildings, public grounds, and open spaces devoted to public use.

Section 4. The City Planning Commission may make recommendations to any public authorities, or any corporations or individuals in said cities, with reference to the location of any buildings, structures, or works to be erected or constructed by them.

Section 5. All plans, plots, or re-plots of lands laid out in building lots, and the streets, alleys, or other portions of the same intended to be dedicated to public use, or for the use of purchasers or owners of lots fronting thereon or adjacent thereto, and located within the city limits, or for a distance of three miles outside thereof, shall be submitted to the City Planning Commission and approved by it before it shall be recorded. And it shall be unlawful to receive or record such plan in any public office unless the same shall bear thereon, by endorsement or otherwise, the approval of the City

Planning Commission. The disapproval of any such plan by the City Planning Commission shall be deemed a refusal of the proposed dedication shown thereon. The approval of the commission shall be deemed an acceptance of the proposed dedication; but shall not impose any duty upon the city concerning the maintenance or improvement of any such dedicated parts, until the proper authorities of the city shall have made actual appropriation of the same by entry, use, or improvement. No sewer, water, or gas-main, or pipes, or other improvement, shall be voted or made within the area under the jurisdiction of said commission, for the use of any such purchasers or owners; nor shall any permit for connection with or other use of any such improvement existing, or for any other reason made, be given to any such purchasers or owners until such plan is so approved. Where the jurisdictional limit of three miles outside of the city limits, as provided in this section, may conflict with the zone of similar character connected with another city of the third class, the jurisdiction of said commission shall extend only to the point equidistant between the city limits and the limits of said municipality.

Section 6. It shall be proper for said cities to provide, by ordinance, for the exercise of all rights and powers herein conferred upon the City Planning Commission, by a park commission, or kindred municipal bureau or commission, authorized under existing laws. And no person holding office under the government of any of said cities, except the mayor, members of councils, or commissioners, shall be ineligible to serve as a member of a City Planning Commission.

Section 7. All acts and parts of acts inconsistent with this act are repealed.

CARRYING OUT THE CITY PLAN

APPROVED—The 16th day of July, A. D. 1913.

JOHN K. TENER.

The foregoing is a true and correct copy of the Act of the General Assembly, No. 406.

ROBERT MCAFEE,
Secretary of the Commonwealth.

4

LAWS OF NEW JERSEY, 1913. Chap. 72

AN ACT to enable cities of the first class in this State to provide for a city plan commission and provide funds for the same and defining the duties thereof.

BE IT ENACTED *by the Senate and General Assembly of the State of New Jersey:*

1. In cities of the first class it shall be lawful for the mayor to appoint a commission to be known as the "City Plan Commission," to consist of not more than nine citizens of such city, and the terms of office of all of such commissioners shall begin upon the first day of January next succeeding the date of their appointment in such city.

Whenever commissioners shall be appointed under this act, the terms of such commissioners shall be divided into classes of one, two and three years, and the mayor shall designate which of such commissioners shall hold such respective terms under the first appointment, and shall divide the said commissioners, as nearly as may be, into such classes, and said commissioners first appointed as aforesaid shall hold their terms for one, two and three years respectively.

All subsequent appointments shall be for the term of three years, and in case any vacancy arises the appointment to fill the same shall be for the unexpired term.

LEGISLATION AND DECISIONS

Any city plan commission now existing in any such city shall be continued, but with the powers and duties herein provided, until the appointment of new commissioners, under the provisions of this act.

2. Such commissions shall serve without pay, and it shall be the duty of such commission to prepare, from time to time, plans for the systematic and further development and betterment of such city. It shall have the power and authority to employ experts, clerks and a secretary, and to pay for their services, and to pay for such other expenses as such commission may lawfully incur under the powers hereby granted, including the necessary disbursements incurred by its members in the performance of their duties as members of said commission; *provided, however*, that the total amount so expended in any one year shall not exceed the appropriation for such year as hereinafter provided.

The said city plan commission may consider and investigate any subject matter tending to the development and betterment of such city, and make such recommendations as it may deem advisable concerning the adoption thereof to any department of the municipal government, and for any purpose make, or cause to be made, surveys, plans or maps.

3. All questions concerning the location and architectural design of any work of art, statue or other memorial within such city shall be referred to the city plan commission for its consideration and report before final action is taken thereon.

All plats or replats of any lands within the limits of such city shall be submitted to the city plan commission for its recommendation before the same are approved.

4. It shall be lawful for the board or body having

charge of the finances of any city of the first class as aforesaid, to appropriate any amount not exceeding twenty-five thousand (25,000) dollars any year that such commission may remain in existence, for the expenses of such city plan commission, and the moneys required for the expenses of said commission shall be raised by annual tax upon real and personal property as other taxes are raised in and for such city; *provided, however*, that for the fiscal year in which this act becomes effective, such moneys may be raised by said board or body having charge of the finances of such city, by appropriating for that purpose any moneys in the treasury of such city not otherwise appropriated, or by issuing and selling temporary loan bonds or certificates of indebtedness; *provided*, that such bonds or certificates shall be sold at public or private sale, after due advertisement, at not less than par; which bonds shall bear interest at not more than five per centum per annum, and the payment thereof, with interest, shall be provided for in the next tax levy.

5. All acts or parts of acts inconsistent with the provisions of this act are hereby repealed.

6. This act shall take effect immediately.

Approved March 12, 1913.

5

SPECIAL ACTS OF CONNECTICUT, 1907. No. 61

Section 1. That there shall be in the city of Hartford a commission on the city plan, which shall consist of the mayor, who shall be its presiding officer, the president of the board of street commissioners, the president of the board of park commissioners, the city engineer, two citizens, neither of whom shall hold any other office in said city government, one member of the board of aldermen, and one member of the common council board, to be appointed as hereinafter provided.

Section 2. The necessary expenses of said commission shall be paid by the city, but no member thereof shall be paid for his services as such member.

Section 3. Terms of commissioners. . . . . .

Section 4. All questions concerning the location of any public building, esplanade, boulevard, parkway, street, highway, square, or park shall be referred to said commission by the court of common council for its consideration and report before final action is taken on such location.

Section 5. The court of common council may refer to said commission the construction or carrying out of any public work not expressly within the province of other boards or commissions of said city, and may delegate to said commission all powers which the said council deems necessary to complete such work in all details.

Section 6. Said commission may make or cause to be made a map or maps of said city, or any portion thereof, showing locations proposed by it for any new public building, esplanade, boulevard, parkway, or street, and grades thereof, any street, building, and veranda lines and grades thereon, or for any new square or park, or any changes by it deemed advisable in the present location of any public building, street, grades and lines, square or park, and may employ expert advice in the making of such map or maps.

Section 7. Said City of Hartford, acting through said commission or otherwise, shall have power to appropriate, enter upon, and hold in fee real estate within its corporate limits for establishing esplanades, boulevards, parkways, park grounds, streets, highways, squares, sites for public buildings, and reservations in and about and along and leading to any or all of the same; and, after the establishment, lay-out, and completion of such improvements, may convey any real estate, thus acquired and not necessary for such improvements, with or without reservations, concerning the future use and occupation of such real estate so as to protect such public works and improvements and their environs, and to preserve the view, appearance, light, air, and usefulness of such public works.

6

ACTS OF MARYLAND, 1910. Chap. 144

AN ACT to add a new section relating to the creation of a Commission on City Plan to Article 4, entitled "City of Baltimore," of the Code of Public Local Laws of Maryland, to come in immediately after Section 200, and to be known as Section 200a.

Section 1. *Be it enacted by the General Assembly of Maryland,* That a new section be and the same is hereby added to Article 4, entitled "City of Baltimore," of the Code of Public Local Laws of Maryland, to come in immediately after Section 200 and to be known as Section 200a, and to read as follows:

200a. There shall be a Commission on City Plan, to consist of the Mayor of the City of Baltimore and eight other members who shall be appointed by the Mayor in the manner prescribed in Section twenty-five of this Article, who shall hold their offices as in said section provided, and shall serve without pay; one of the said commissioners shall be president of said commission, and shall be so designated by the Mayor; the said commission may elect a secretary, who shall be paid such salary as may be provided for by ordinance and who shall perform such duties as may be from time to time prescribed by said commission. The said commission shall investigate all plans proposed for the construction or extension of public highways in the City of Baltimore and the establishment of a civic centre or other public improvements in connection therewith, and shall report the results of such investigations from time to time to the Mayor and City Council, and shall perform such other duties and exercise such other powers as may be delegated to it or as may be prescribed by ordinances not inconsistent with this Article.

7
Charter of City of Cleveland
Adopted July 1, 1913

Section 77. City Plan Commission. There shall be a city plan commission to be appointed by the mayor with power to control, in the manner provided by ordinance, the design and location of works of art which are, or may become, the property of the city; the plan, design and location of public buildings, harbors, bridges, viaducts, street fixtures, and other structures and appurtenances; the removal, relocation and alteration of any such works belonging to the city; the location, extension and platting of streets, parks and other public places, and of new areas; and the preparation of plans for the future physical development and improvement of the city.

LAWS OF PENNSYLVANIA. GENERAL ASSEMBLY. No. 226, of 1913

AN ACT to create Suburban Metropolitan Districts of the areas within twenty-five miles of the limits of cities of the first class; to provide for the creation of a Department of Suburban Metropolitan Planning and the appointment of Suburban Metropolitan Planning Commissions for such districts; to prescribe their powers and duties; and to provide for assessment upon the cities, boroughs and townships within the limits thereof.

Whereas, The establishment of Suburban Metropolitan Planning Commissions having jurisdiction over territory adjacent to cities of the first class is desirable, in order to provide for its proper development by the coöperation of the various local governmental units in matters pertaining to their common welfare; and

Whereas, It is desirable, that there should be coordination of effort with Urban Metropolitan Planning Commissions, relating to cities of the first class themselves, wherever the same may exist:—

Section 1. Be it enacted, &c., That in order to secure coördinated, comprehensive plans of highways and roads, parks and parkways, and all other means of inter-communication, water-supply, sewerage and sewage disposal, collection and disposal of garbage, housing, sanitation and health playgrounds, civic centers, and other public improvements, as hereinafter provided for, the districts surrounding and within twenty-five miles of the limits of cities of the first class, whether in one or more counties, and in order to prevent waste by unnecessary duplication, the areas included within twenty-five miles of the limits of cities of the first class shall be denominated the Suburban Metropolitan Districts of cities of the first class of Pennsylvania. When any city, borough, or township is partly within and partly without the twenty-five mile limit, the whole of such city, borough, or township shall be regarded as within the Suburban Metropolitan District.

Section 2. There shall be an executive department created for every Suburban Metropolitan District, to be known as the Department of Suburban Metropolitan Planning, which shall be in charge of a Suburban Metropolitan Planning Commission.

Section 3. The Suburban Metropolitan Planning Commission shall be appointed by the Governor of the State of Pennsylvania, and shall consist of fifteen members, who may or may not hold other public office, whether for profit or otherwise, of whom twelve shall be residents of the district involved, and three shall be residents of the said city of the first class, five members to be appointed to serve for one year, five for two years, five for three years; then, thereafter, each appointment to be for three years.

An appointment to fill a casual vacancy shall be for the unexpired portion of the term. Nine shall constitute a quorum.

The Suburban Metropolitan Planning Commission shall make and alter rules and regulations for its own organization and procedure, consistent with the laws of the Commonwealth. From its own members it shall choose a chairman and vice-chairman. Each member shall serve without compensation. On or before January tenth of each and every year, the Commission shall make to the mayor of each city, to councils of each borough, to the commissioners of each first class township, and to the supervisors of each second class township, within the Suburban Metropolitan District, to the mayor of the said city of the first class, and to the Governor of the State of Pennsylvania, a report of its transactions and recommendations. The Commission may employ a secretary, engineers, and other experts and persons, whose salaries and wages, as well as all the other necessary expenses of the Commission and members thereof, shall be provided for as hereinafter set forth.

Section 4. The Suburban Metropolitan Planning Commission shall make, or cause to be made, and laid before the respective governmental authorities of the district, and, in its discretion, caused to be published, a map or maps of the entire district, or any portion or portions thereof, showing any or all systems of transportation, highways and roads, parks, parkways, water-supply, sewerage and sewage disposal, collection and disposal of garbage, housing, sanitation, playgrounds and civic centers, or of other natural physical features of the district; and it shall prepare plans for any new or enlarged facilities for intercommunication, parks, parkways, water-supply systems, sewers, sewage disposal, garbage disposal, land plottings and housing arrangements, playgrounds and civic centers, or any other public improvement that will affect the character of the district as a whole, or more than one political unit within the district, or any widening, extension, or relocation of the same, or any change in the existing township or borough or city plans, by it deemed advisable. And it shall make recommendations to the respective governmental authorities, from time to time, concerning any such matters or things aforesaid, for action by the respective legislative, administrative, or governmental bodies thereon; and in so doing have regard for the present conditions and future needs and growth of the district, and the distribution and relative location of all the principal and other streets, and railways, waterways, and all other means of public travel and business communications, as well as the distribution and relative location of all public buildings, public grounds, and open spaces devoted to public use, and the planning, subdivision and laying out for urban uses of private grounds brought into the market from time to time.

Section 5. Any city, borough, or township, within any Suburban Metropolitan District, may request the Suburban Metropolitan Planning Commission of that district to prepare plans concerning any of the subjects set forth in section four of this act; whereupon it shall be the duty of the Commission to prepare such plans with dispatch.

Section 6. The Suburban Metropolitan Planning Commission may make recommendations to any public authorities, or any corporation or individual in said districts, with reference to the location of any buildings and structures to be constructed by them.

Section 7. The plans so made and laid before the respective governmental authorities by the Suburban Metropolitan District Planning Commission, according to sections four, five and six, shall be considered by such respective authorities, and followed by them in so far as shall be determined by each authority:

Provided however, That the provisions of this act shall not abridge or in any way affect the provisions of an act, entitled "An act creating a Department of Health, and defining its powers and duties," approved the twenty-seventh day of April, Anno Domini, one thousand nine hundred and five; or the provisions of an act, entitled "An act to preserve the purity of the waters of the State, for the protection of the public health," approved the twenty-second day of April, one thousand nine hundred and five.

Section 8. On or before January tenth of each and every year, the Commission shall prepare an estimate of its expenses for the ensuing year, setting forth with as much detail as is practicable the items of which such estimate is composed; and shall cause the amount of its expenses so estimated, after deducting the cash on hand and the unpaid assessments, to be assessed against the cities, boroughs, and townships within the district, in proportion to their respective tax duplicates. The itemized estimate of expenses and a statement of the rate of assessment shall be spread upon the minutes of the Commission, which shall be kept open at all times for public inspection. Each and every assessment, when certified by the chairman and secretary of the Commission, shall constitute a charge on the treasury of the respective city, borough, and township, and its immediate payment shall be at once provided for. The Commission shall have power to secure payment of the assessments by suits of mandamus, or otherwise: Provided, That the rate of assessment shall not exceed one-tenth of one mill.

APPROVED—The 23d day of May, A. D. 1913.

JOHN K. TENER.

The following is a true and correct copy of the Act of the General Assembly No. 226.

ROBERT MCAFEE,
Secretary of the Commonwealth.

LEGISLATION AND DECISIONS

9
LAWS OF PENNSYLVANIA. GENERAL ASSEMBLY
No. 456, of 1913

AN ACT to amend an act, entitled "An act creating an art jury for cities of the first class, and prescribing its powers and duties," approved the twenty-fifth day of May, Anno Domini one thousand nine hundred and seven.

Section 1. Be it enacted, &c., That section three of an act, entitled "An act creating an art jury for cities of the first class, and prescribing its powers and duties," approved the twenty-fifth day of May, one thousand nine hundred and seven, which reads as follows:—

"Section 3. The members of the jury shall serve without compensation; and from their own number shall elect a president and *secretary*, to serve for one year, and until their successors are elected. The jury shall have power to adopt its own rules of procedure and to prescribe regulations for the submission to it of all matters within its jurisdiction. Five members shall constitute a quorum. The councils of said city shall, by ordinance, provide for the necessary expenses of the jury, including the salaries of *such clerk or clerks as may be required and appointed by the mayor of said cities*," is hereby amended so that it shall read:—

Section 3. The members of the jury shall serve without compensation; and from their own number shall elect a president and *vice-president*, to serve for one year, and until their successors are elected. The jury shall have power to adopt its own rules of procedure and to prescribe regulations for the submission to it of all matters within its jurisdiction. Five members shall constitute a quorum. *The jury shall have power to employ a secretary, and such clerks, stenog-*

raphers and other assistants as it may require. All employees of the jury shall be exempt from the provisions of the act to regulate and improve the civil service of the cities of the first class, approved March fifth, one thousand nine hundred and six. The councils of said city shall, by ordinance, provide for the necessary expense of the jury, including the salaries of its employees.

Section 2. That said act is hereby further amended by adding the following:—

Section 7. No construction or erection, in a city of the first class, of any building, bridge or its approaches, arch, gate, fence, or other structure or fixture, which is to be paid for, either wholly or in part, by appropriation from the city treasury, or other public funds, or for which the city, or any other public authority, is to furnish a site, shall be begun, unless the design and proposed location thereof shall have been submitted to the jury, at least sixty days before the final approval thereof, by the officer or other person having authority to contract therefor. The approval of the jury shall also be required in respect to all structures or fixtures belonging to any person or corporation, which shall be erected upon, or extend over, any highway, stream, lake, square, park or other public place, within the city, except as provided in section six of this act. In deeds for land, made by any city of the first class, restrictions may be imposed requiring that the design and location of structures to be altered or erected thereon shall be first approved by the art jury of such city. Nothing requiring the approval of the jury shall be erected, or changed in design or location, without its approval. If the jury fails to act upon any matter submitted to it within sixty days after such submission its approval of the matter submitted shall be presumed.

LEGISLATION AND DECISIONS

APPROVED—The 24th day of July, A. D. 1913.

JOHN K. TENER.

The foregoing is a true and correct copy of the Act of the General Assembly, No. 456.

ROBERT McAFEE,
Secretary of the Commonwealth.

APPENDIX B

EXTRACTS FROM REPORT ON ENGLISH AND CONTINENTAL SYSTEMS OF TAKING LAND FOR PUBLIC PURPOSES

FROM MASSACHUSETTS DOCUMENTS, 1904. House No. 288 of 1904 and House No. 1096 of 1904

THE REPORT OF COMMITTEE

It has clearly appeared, from the evidence submitted to us, that the present system of laying out new streets or widening or altering existing ones, under which only the land actually required for the street is taken, is, especially in those parts of cities which are covered with existing buildings, productive of serious public disadvantages; and a brief consideration of the matter is sufficient to show that this difficulty is inherent in the system itself, and must persist unless some modification of that system can be devised.

The land abutting on any existing street is divided and arranged in lots, which, as well as the circumstances have admitted, are adapted to the street in its present condition, and the buildings thereon are constructed in conformity therewith. Any widening of the street not only destroys the existing buildings, but, by reducing the size of the abutting lots, leaves the residues or remnants of many of them of such shape and size as to be entirely unsuited for the erection of proper buildings, unless and until these remnants have been united with the adjoining properties, generally with those in the rear, which are thus enabled to extend out to the new street lines.

The same condition is found, and frequently even to a greater extent, when a new thoroughfare is laid out through existing blocks covered with buildings.

Hence, when an existing street is widened or a new thoroughfare is laid out under the present system, the lots on one or both sides of the new or widened street are left in such condition that, until a rearrangement can be made, no suitable buildings can be erected thereon, and the public benefit to be derived from the improvement is in great measure lost.

The street may be valuable as a thoroughfare or as one for through traffic, but not for either business or residence purposes; and striking instances of this have been presented to the committee in connection with street improvements in the city of Boston.

Not only is such a situation a great disadvantage to the city, in hindering and sometimes preventing its proper development, but it will easily be seen that this state of affairs renders the collection of betterment assessments extremely difficult, since the benefit to the surrounding property, which should accrue from the improvement, is actually not received until these residues or remnants have been united with the adjoining lots,—a process which, under the present system, may take years.

It often happens that the owners of these remnants, desirous of deriving some income therefrom in the meanwhile, erect thereon temporary structures, unsuited for proper habitation or occupancy; and such structures are too frequently made intentionally objectionable, both in appearance and in the character of their occupancy, for the purpose of compelling the purchase of such remnants at exorbitant prices; with the result that a new thoroughfare, which should be an ornament to the city, is frequently for a long period after its construction disfigured by unsightly and unwholesome structures, to the positive detriment of the public interests. These results, which seem inevitable under the present system, may operate to prevent the undertaking of much-needed street improvements.

. . . .

Furthermore, it is believed that the taking of whole estates, instead of taking the greater part and leaving an undesirable remnant, would not materially increase the initial expense of the undertaking; inasmuch as a city which takes, under the present system, so much of an estate as to leave the remainder unsuited for building purposes, is often obliged to pay for the value of the part taken, and for the damages to the remaining part practically as much as it would be obliged to pay for the whole estate.

What has been said above indicates the public considerations which render a change in the existing system desirable.

There is also, however, another side to the question, viz., that of the private owner, the consideration of which appears to point to the same conclusion. It frequently happens that an owner, the greater part of whose estate is necessarily taken for a public work, would prefer not to be left with the remnant on his hands, and if an opportunity were offered, would voluntarily request the city to take the whole estate. Many people recognize that there is less opportunity for differences of opinion upon the question of the market value of a whole estate than over the more complicated question of the value of the portion which has been taken, and the damages to the remainder by reason of such taking; and hence a system under which the city could acquire the whole estate would be productive of greater ease in the settlement of damages, and less likelihood of litigation over the question involved therein.

This right of the private owner to require the taking of the whole estate, when the residue, after deducting what is actually needed for the public work, is unsuited for the erection of appropriate buildings or is reduced below a certain area, is almost universally recognized both in England and on the continent of Europe. It has also received recognition in this State, in chapter 159 in the Acts of 1867, relating to the widening of Oliver Street in the city of Boston, which act, after empowering the city to assess the cost of the improvement upon the abutting estates, provided that any owner, part of whose land was taken, might before the assessment elect to surrender his whole estate to the city, which should pay therefor its full value as it was before the improvement was made, and should have the right to resell the portion not required for the new street.

The constitutionality of this act was upheld in the case of Dorgan *vs.* Boston, 12 Allen, 223.

With regard to the acquirement by compulsory taking of land beyond the limits of a given public work, we find that two different systems have prevailed:—

1. The taking, in addition to the land actually required for the public work, of all the property within certain bounds in the neighborhood of the proposed work; the rearranging of the lot lines of the property so acquired; and the disposal of this property by sale or lease for the benefit of the city.

CARRYING OUT THE CITY PLAN

2. The taking, in addition to the land actually required for the public work, of such residues or remnants of lots only which, in consequence of the taking for the public work, will be left of such shape and size as to be unsuited for the erection of proper buildings; and also of such portions of the adjoining properties as it may, in consequence of the refusal of their owners to purchase these remnants, be necessary to acquire, in order to make proper building lots abutting on the proposed street.

In favor of the first system, it has been urged that, in consequence of the carrying out of the proposed public work, there will be an increase in value of the surrounding property, caused by no act of its owner, but entirely by the act of the public body, and at the public expense; that it is inequitable that such increase in value should not accrue to the public, to the expenditure of whose money it is solely due; that the method of acquiring the abutting property in the neighborhood is the best method of securing such benefit to the public; that it is far simpler and more equitable than any system for the collection of betterments; and that, if the owners of the abutting property are paid its full value as it was before the improvement took place, they have no cause to complain.

This is the system which, in substance, has been adopted for important street improvements in many cities of Great Britain, Belgium, Switzerland and Italy and has, we are informed, been on the whole successful in its operation, and is believed in certain cases to have materially reduced the cost of public improvements.

As against this system it is urged that the State ought not to dispossess the private owner of his property simply in order that the public work may be carried on at less cost, through resale of the property so acquired; that the expense of public works should be met by taxation, and not by the taking of private property for no other purpose than to benefit the public exchequer by its re-sale; that the power to take property for such purposes as is contemplated by the first system is practically a power to enter into a land speculation, which may result disastrously.

In the case of our cities, there is the further objection that the adopting of such a system might easily carry the initial cost of an undertaking beyond the debt limit of the municipality.

In support of the second system, it is urged that the ends of public necessity and convenience, for which private property may properly be taken, can all be accomplished by limiting the taking, in addition to the land actually required for the public work, to such remainders of lots as are by themselves unsuited for proper building purposes, and by uniting them to the adjoining properties, compulsorily, if necessary; and that the right to take private property should not be extended beyond these salutary limits.

Such is the system which, originally established for the city of Paris, has now been extended to many of the other important cities of France, and under which many of their great improvements have been carried out; and such a system should, it would seem, if fairly and judiciously applied, be ample to our needs.

In the draft of an act herewith submitted we have, in substance, adopted this plan, and believe that it will be time enough to consider adopting a more comprehensive scheme if the plan proposed shall, after a fair trial, be found insufficient to our needs.

It would appear that, in order to give such a system its full value and effect, its operation should be extended to parcels of land comprised within the limits of streets which are discontinued in consequence of the laying out of new streets, so that such parcels could be united to the land abutting thereon.

This has been found to be advisable in the practical application of the law in France; and in the plan for such a law, herewith submitted, we have attempted to make such additional provision.

. . . .

With regard to the provisions as to taking the land of an adjoining owner who does not accept the city's offer to sell to him the parcel which the city has acquired outside of the limits of the proposed public work, it should be added that in our opinion such takings would in practice be of quite rare occurrence. Such owners are usually desirous of acquiring parcels which give them access on new or widened highways, if this can be done at fair prices, but are unwilling to pay the exorbitant prices which are often asked for such parcels. As the very fact that a residue or remnant of a lot had under the proposed act been acquired by the city would show that it had been adjudged that the remnant was by itself unsuited for the erection of buildings, the only uses that could consistently be made of it would either be to leave it open, thus destroying the utility of much of the street frontage, or to unite it with the adjoining property; and, were the owner of the adjoining property to feel that the only possible courses open to the city were either to leave the lot vacant or to sell it to him, he probably would offer but a nominal sum for it.

The purpose of these provisions, therefore, is to

enable the city to receive fair prices for these remnants, and to control the character of their development.

We have been urged to consider, and have considered, the desirability of insisting on certain architectural requirements, to ensure greater symmetry and harmony in the constructions which front on and frame our principal avenues. It has seemed to us that such requirements could not well be embodied in such an act as we have submitted, and were probably beyond the scope of our mandate. We have, however, provided that, in disposing of any land acquired outside of the lines of the new street, the city might impose restrictions thereon; and it is our expectation that in framing those restrictions due regard would be had to ensuring the architectural symmetry of the new street.

It would, in our opinion, often be of great benefit to the city to impose such restrictions for a limited term of years upon all property abutting on a new or widened street; and this might be done, whether any portions of such property were acquired by the city or not; in other words, even were the street to be laid out under the present highway acts. While it might not be desirable to attempt to embody the details of such restrictions in a general act, the power to impose such reasonable restrictions as should be found necessary to ensure the architectural symmetry of the new street might be conferred by a general act, containing provisions for the payment of the damages, if any, resulting from the exercise of such powers.

It should be noted that this question has been successfully dealt with in connection with the new streets of London, by requiring that the façade plans and elevations of the new buildings to be erected thereon should be submitted to the approval of the municipal authorities, which approval, however, is not to be "unreasonably withheld"; and providing for a decision on the plans by an umpire, viz., an architect selected by the president of the Royal Institute of Architects, in case the city and the private owners failed to agree.

The question of the constitutionality of the proposed enactment has of course presented itself, and deserves careful consideration. The committee is, however, of the opinion that it was not the intention of the Legislature, in passing the resolve under which the committee was appointed, that the committee should attempt to advise the Legislature on this important question of constitutional law. The supreme judicial court is made by the constitution (chapter III, article 2) the adviser of the Legislature on such questions, and either branch of the Legislature is given authority to require the opinion of the justices of that court thereon.

It seems, however, proper to direct the attention of the Legislature to the fact that a law which should authorize a municipality to take the whole of those lots, so much of which is actually required for the public work that the remainder will not be of such size or shape as to be suitable for the erection of proper or wholesome buildings, would not be open to such serious or grave constitutional objections as one which, purely for the purpose of effecting a saving in the cost of carrying out a given public work, should authorize a municipality to take private property to a much greater extent than is needed for the work, and, by sale of the surplus, to receive the benefit of the increase in value given to that surplus by the public work in question.

The taking of the whole of those estates the remnants of which would not be suited for the erection of proper buildings may well be deemed a taking for those public uses for which building regulations and those limiting the height of buildings on public areas have been upheld.

Furthermore, the supreme court of this State, in the case of the Copley Square restrictions (Attorney General *vs.* Williams, 174 Mass. 476, 478), has laid down the principle that "the uses which should be deemed public in reference to the right of the Legislature to compel an individual to part with his property for a compensation, and to authorize or direct taxation to pay for it, are being enlarged and extended with the progress of the people in education and refinement. Many things which a century ago were luxuries or were altogether unknown have now become necessaries." And these principles are widely recognized today.

The union of such remnants or remainders to the adjoining properties, either by their sale to the owners of such properties or by the taking of so much of such properties as when added to such remainders will make lots which are suitable for the erection of proper or wholesome buildings, would seem to be essential, if the public ends for which such remainders are taken are to be accomplished; and the right to authorize such takings of adjoining properties would seem to follow, if the taking of the remnants is considered a taking for a public use.

There are doubtless cases in which the Legislature might authorize the taking of the whole of the land comprised within a certain area, and its subsequent resale. It seems to be clear that the right exists, whenever such a course is desirable in order to abate a nuisance or remedy conditions inimical to public health; and that the Legislature may authorize the municipality, after having abated the nuisance or remedied such conditions, to resell the whole or any part of the property as acquired. This power has been frequently exercised, the most notable instance perhaps having been chapter 308 of the Acts of 1867, relating to the Church Street district in Boston, the constitutionality of which enactment was upheld in the case of Dingley *vs.* Boston, 100 Mass. 554.

There may be other cases in which such extended takings would be upheld, but, for the purposes of the legislation which we have recommended, the consideration of such cases would not seem to be necessary.

MUNICIPAL REAL ESTATE OPERATIONS IN CONNECTION WITH STREET IMPROVEMENTS IN PARIS AND LONDON, House Doc. 288 (pp. 53–56)

The experience of Paris and London teaches that it is unwise for a city to attempt to recover a part of the cost of street improvements by taking more land than is required for the streets themselves, with a view to intercepting the increases in value which the improvements may give to the adjoining land. In this respect the experience of the provincial towns of England has not differed materially from that of London and Paris.

Experience teaches that, while the effect of street improvements upon land values often is uncertain, there is, upon the whole, an increase of values that would lessen materially the cost of street improvements, if cities could collect that increase by means of so-called "recoupment." But thus far "failure of administration" has defeated the efforts of cities to collect the so-called unearned increment arising from street improvements.

That failure of administration has resulted from the persistent failure of public opinion to correct the practice of juries of giving awards "contrary to the facts and the law" to the persons whose lands are taken for public use; and from the persistent failure of the Legislature to correct the obvious shortcomings of the law. For this failure of public opinion and of the Legislature there are various reasons. In the first place, it has been entirely impossible to overcome the public sympathy with the private individual against whom the city was proceeding. That sympathy is based largely upon the notion, ineradicable from the mind of the average citizen, that the city, like the State, has large resources upon which it can draw, and which it can replenish without in any way affecting the citizen. This sympathy with the individual and this optimism as to the city's resources acted with all the more freedom from check, since the laws which authorized the cities to go into real estate speculations for the purpose of recovering a part of the cost of street improvements were not enacted in response to any general or compelling conviction of the body of the citizens, that the cost of street improvements must be reduced. The average man takes no permanent interest in the question of the cost of public improvements; and laws of the kind here discussed are enacted only in consequence of the activity of a small body of citizens, who appreciate keenly the necessity of husbanding the city's resources. When such laws, which have been enacted without the support of an intelligent and compelling public spirit, come to be administered by the average juror, the city's interests inevitably are lost sight of, in the desire to do ample justice to the individual whose property the city takes by compulsory powers.

. . . .

Turning next to the question whether the cities whose operations have been examined have been able to sell to the best advantage the lands acquired, the answer once more is in the negative. Baron Haussmann, summing up his vast experience with city activity and private activity in Paris in 1852 to 1869, said that private enterprise had innumerable ways of nursing and developing real estate that the city neither could invent nor imitate.

. . . .

In conclusion, it may be added that in Paris there has been since 1876 an exceedingly intelligent minority which has held that the city should not itself execute any more street improvements, but should leave such operations to private enterprise, subsidizing the latter for that purpose.

In London, the Metropolitan Board of Works was succeeded in 1889 by the London County Council. The latter body in 1890 asked Parliament for permission to supplement the practice of "recoupment" by the so-called American practice of assessing a betterment tax upon property enhanced in value by public improvements. One may, perhaps, go farther, and say that the London County Council was ready to place its main reliance upon the practice of assessing a betterment tax, and to relegate to a subsidiary position the practice of recoupment. Be that as it may, the London County Council, from 1890 to 1898, declined to proceed with any large improvement schemes, because Parliament refused to give it power to employ the betterment system as extensively as it desired to employ it. In 1898, or 1899, Parliament yielded, and the London County Council proceeded with the Strand improvement scheme.

REPORT ON THE FRENCH SYSTEM FOR TAKING LAND BY RIGHT OF EMINENT DOMAIN. House Doc. 288, pp. 44-52

In order to appreciate the system which obtains in France for taking land by right of eminent domain, it should be understood at the outset that the initiative for the construction of public works is rarely taken by the local deliberative body, the municipal council, for instance, but almost always by the executive, or, as they would term it, the administration, the head of which is the chief of the State, with his various ministers, while the prefect in each department and the under prefects and other officers represent the lower ranks of the administrative hierarchy.

This fact explains why the preliminary procedure, which has for its object to determine with careful regard for private interests the exact limits of the land required to be taken, is, even when deliberative in character, considered a part of executive rather than of legislative functions.

. . . .

Provisions for compulsory taking of land outside the limits of the proposed public work:—

By a decree of March 26, 1852, it was enacted that: "In any plan for taking land for widening, relocating or laying out streets in Paris, the administration may include the whole of each lot affected, whenever it shall consider that the residue will not be of such size or shape as to allow the erection of wholesome constructions. It may also include in the taking lots outside of the street lines, whenever it is necessary to acquire them in order to discontinue former public streets which have been deemed useless. The portions of lots which have been taken outside of street lines and which are not capable of receiving wholesome constructions shall be united to the adjoining properties either by agreement or by the taking of those properties."

In order to include in the taking any portion of a lot outside of the street lines, it is necessary, whenever this is practicable, that it should be included in the plan submitted to the preliminary inquiry; and in all cases such proposed takings must be shown on the detailed plan submitted to the second inquiry above referred to, and if the owners opposed the taking, and since 1876, even in the absence of opposition, the decree which determines the limits of such takings is rendered, not by the prefect, as in the case of the property included in the street lines, but by the council of State.

The provisions of law for uniting these portions of lots acquired outside of the street lines to the adjoining properties contemplate a careful appraisal of such portion, to determine its value to the adjoining owner under all the circumstances of the case, the offering of it to such owner at the appraisal value; and if he fails to accept the offer within a week from its receipt, the administration may proceed to take his property for the purpose of uniting the remnant to it, and then reselling the whole.

The provisions of this decree of March, 1852, originally passed for Paris only, have since been applied to most of the important cities of France.

Attention should be called to the fact that under the provisions of the law of April 13, 1850, all the land within fixed limits may be taken whenever required in order to abate a nuisance, or in the interest of works for the improvement of the public health, and the surplus, after completion of the works, sold at public auction.

It is stated, however, that in comparison with the law of March, 1852, that of April 13, 1850, has been rarely applied.

The law of Sept. 16, 1807, contains provisions for the assessment of betterments, according to which private property which has received a marked increase in value from the opening of new streets or squares, the construction of quais and other public works, may be assessed a betterment to the amount of one-half of such increase in value; but this can only be done by an order of the head of the State, passed in State council.

The amount of the tax is determined by a special commission formed for the purpose.

The power to assess such tax seems rarely to have been employed; it is said that not more than twenty instances of its exercise can be found in all France from the passage of the law up to 1886; and, although formerly applied in some instances to cases of street improvements in cities, it seems for the last fifty years, or since the enactment of March, 1852, above referred to, to have been employed only in cases where the special benefit was of an exceptional character, as when arising from the construction of levees, dikes or a series of quais.

. . . .

CARRYING OUT THE CITY PLAN

House Doc. No. 1096, Supplemental Report pp. 4-10

The effect of these provisions and of those of the French law, which place all administrative matters under the control of the administrative courts of which the Council of State is the highest, and remove them from the jurisdiction of the regular courts, is to make the Council of State practically the sole judge of the extent to which these powers should be exercised, and of the size of the remnants which may be taken, and hence the extent to which such takings may be made under the law is almost entirely dependent on the attitude of the Council of State.

There appears to be no question that at present, and indeed for many years past, substantially since the establishment of the present Republic, the attitude of the Council of State has been to limit as far as possible the application of the law which authorizes the taking of such remnants, and to permit any owner who desired to retain the ownership of the remnant of his estate to do so, provided it were in any way possible to erect on such remnant a building which would comply with the requirements of the building law regarding light and air.

This attitude appears to be taken through solicitude for the wishes of the individual owner, and to a theoretical assumption that, as takings by eminent domain are in derogation of common right, they should be restricted, as far as possible, and is doubtless due in large measure to the reaction from the former régime, when private and personal rights were subordinated to the wishes of the administrative government.

The contrast between the position now taken by the Council of State regarding these matters and that taken under the empire may be gathered from a comparison of the size of the remnants the taking of which was formerly authorized by the Council of State, and of those the taking of which it now refuses to authorize.

In 1896 and 1897 there was constructed that portion of the Rue Reaumur connecting the Place de la Bourse with the Boulevard Sebastopol, which lies between the Place de la Bourse and the Rue St. Denis. Although the actual taking of the land occurred in 1894-95, shortly before the construction, the decree which authorized the taking and determined its limits had been made thirty years before, viz., in August, 1864, under the second empire, and that decree authorized the taking of remnants as large, in some instances, as 5,000 square feet in area.

These remnants were resold for building lots, and in some cases the remnant, which had been taken as being too small to allow the erection of a wholesome building thereon, was divided into two lots, each of which was sold by itself for a building lot.

In contrast with this somewhat extralegal method of procedure, should be set the following example of the present application of the law.

The city of Paris has lately, in connection with the development of the land formerly occupied by the Trousseau Hospital, found it necessary to construct some new streets, the laying out of which left certain remnants of estates which the city desired authority to take.

In this case the Council of State refused to approve the taking of those remnants whose area exceeded 650 square feet, while it authorized the taking of those whose area was less than this.

These two instances may fairly be considered as typical of the difference between the former régime, under which the takings in connection with street improvements were often made without regard to the fact that the law only authorized the taking of those remnants which were unsuited for building purposes, and the present régime, where the application of that law is so limited as, in the opinion of some, to defeat in certain cases the purpose for which it was enacted, viz., to ensure that all the lots abutting on the new street should be suited to the erection of proper buildings.

It is important to note that in the case last mentioned (that of the Hospital Trousseau), the request of the city for authority to take those remnants which the Council of State declined to authorize it to take did not appear to have been made for the purpose of securing the profit from the resale of those remnants; nor was the request refused because it was thought to have been so prompted.

That purpose was neither avowed by the representatives of the city, nor would it be inferred from examination of the plan, nor were the members of the Council of State inclined to attribute it to the city or to its representatives.

The difference between the city and the Council of State was rather one of opinion as to the size of the remnant which should or should not be deemed suitable for building, the Council being inclined to place the limit of size lower than were the officials of the city; and it seemed probable that were an opportunity offered to the officials of the city to present their views on this matter before the Council of State, which is not done under the present practice, the standard desired by the city might be adopted.

However this may be, and it would seem that in certain cases at least the limit of the size of a remnant which an owner should be permitted to retain had been placed too low, there appears to be no doubt as to the general consensus of opinion today among those most conversant with such matters in Paris, whether members of the city administration or of the Council of State, that extended takings of land outside of the lines of proposed new streets solely for the purpose of securing for the city the profit from the resale of the land so acquired are neither proper nor desirable.

The increased initial expense involved in such takings was an important reason given for this opinion, and the uncertain length of time required for the disposal of the property another. The taking of remnants properly so called, that is, of such residues of lots as were by themselves unsuited for building purposes, was not considered as open either to these or to the other objections urged against the taking of land solely for the purpose of resale.

The increased expense caused by taking such remnants was, especially where the land had been built upon, but slight.

In any event the land taken for the street had to be paid for, and where part of a building was taken the city was invariably obliged to pay for the whole, the damages to the tenants were the same practically whether the whole estate or only a part was taken, and thus the sole difference in expense between taking the whole estate or leaving a remnant was the difference between the value of the remnant at the time of taking and the damages caused it by the taking for the street, which must be paid if the remnant was not taken, and this difference was not great.

CARRYING OUT THE CITY PLAN

Furthermore, such remnants were found to be readily salable, the adjoining owner almost always being desirous of securing the frontage they afforded on the new street and ready to purchase them at a fair price, which more than compensated for the increased cost of taking them; so that only in rare instances had it been necessary to have recourse to the power of taking the adjoining estate for the purpose of completing a remnant.

. . . .

It seems clear that much of the effort which Paris has made to reduce the expense of street improvements by taking additional land in the hope of profiting by its resale has been due to the lack of a satisfactory betterment law, and now that the attitude of the Council of State is opposed to further takings simply for the purpose of resale the attention of the municipal authorities is more and more directed to securing a satisfactory method for the assessment and collection of betterments.

The present attitude of the Council of State as to permitting the taking of land outside the limits of the street simply for the purpose of profiting by its resale has had a marked effect on the proposals made to the city for the completion of the Boulevard Haussmann, to which reference is so often made.

Until the fact that the Council of State would no longer permit extended takings for the purpose of profiting by the resale of the land so acquired was generally understood, the proposals made to the city contemplated that in addition to the 88,888 square feet required for the street it should take abutting estates of 99,457 square feet in area, the whole at an expense of $10,000,000, for which the city would have become liable in the hope that it might recoup itself by the revenue to be derived from long leases of the surplus land and from its resale at the expiration of those leases. The city was either to advance the bulk of the money required for the new buildings to be erected on those lots or to permit them to be mortgaged for that purpose.

If the expected rents were realized during the period anticipated, the burden on the city would have been little or nothing, while if they were not, the city might have been obliged to bear the burden of the interest and sinking fund charges on the whole $10,000,000, and those on the mortgage also.

It being now recognized that such a taking will not be permitted, the latest proposition made to the city was to the effect that the owners of the most important of the abutting estates were prepared to give to the city 50,783 square feet of the land required for the street, considerably more than one-half, provided the city would build the street, pay the damages to their tenants and release them from any betterment assessment.

The expense to the city was thus reduced from $10,000,000 to about $4,000,000 (the tenants' damages in each case being estimated at about $2,000,000), and though all expectation of profit except from increased receipts of taxes was abandoned, this material reduction rendered it much more possible for the city to undertake the work; and were an assessment of betterments to be made on those estates which did not contribute to the street the expense could be further reduced.

In what has been said above, the present and the

past attitude of the authorities of Paris, and of the Council of State, toward takings of land outside the limits of proposed new streets solely for the purpose of securing the profit from the resale of such land has been considered; but it must not be inferred therefrom that the only purpose for which extended takings of land have been made in Paris in connection with street improvements has been that of securing the profit from the resale of the land taken.

There are many cases where such takings have been made in whole or in part for the purpose of improving the sanitary conditions in the area taken, and where the best method of securing such improvement was by the razing of every structure in the area to be improved and the rebuilding of that area according to modern requirements.

Only actual acquaintance with the conditions which obtain in some of the more ancient quarters of the cities of the Continent can give an adequate idea of how essential such improvement was and in many cases still is, and how impossible of attainment it is by any method short of the total destruction of all the buildings within such area.

The same holds true frequently of small groups of buildings on the line of or in the neighborhood of a projected street improvement.

Where such a case presents itself, the Council of State does not hesitate today to authorize the taking of all the land and buildings in the area to be improved or of the groups of buildings, the demolition of which is required for sanitary reasons, and of the land on which they stand. While in such cases whatever is realized from the sale of such land goes in reduction of the cost of the improvement, the taking of the land is not primarily made for the purpose of effecting that saving, though it would be natural for the authorities, wherever such a saving had been made, to lay stress upon the fact as justifying the method adopted.

In considering the extended takings which have been made in European cities it is important in each case to ascertain whether or not the considerations which prompted the taking of more land than was apparently required for the proposed new streets did not relate primarily to the remedying of unsanitary conditions, as the opportunity which their laws afford of combining in one taking lands required for street purposes and those taken to remedy conditions inimical to public health is often availed of, and in such cases the actual importance of the sanitary considerations does not always clearly appear on the record.

EXCESS TAKING IN BRUSSELS, House Doc. No. 1096, pp. 10–16

In Belgium since 1867 cities have been permitted to take land by zones, as it is termed, either for the purpose of improving sanitary conditions or of improving the appearance of the city, and some of the most notable instances of the exercise of this power are found in Brussels, to satisfy whose needs the law was originally passed.

No limit is fixed by the law for the extent of these zones, and the city is not restricted to taking land within a certain distance of the new highway, as is the case in the Swiss and Italian laws for instance, but may take whatever seems advisable in order to accomplish the purposes for which the taking is made; but, again, the city is not permitted to be the sole judge of how extensive a taking shall be made.

CARRYING OUT THE CITY PLAN

After the city authorities have adopted the plan, the matter is submitted to the Council of the Province, which makes a separate examination of the question by an independent commission, and after both the city and provincial authorities have approved the plan, a royal decree, generally rendered on the report of the Ministers of Public Works and of the Interior, is necessary to authorize the taking.

It is evident that in the Belgian law two matters are united which with us have usually been kept entirely distinct, viz., takings in the interest of public health and takings for public improvement, in the sense of improving the appearance of the city; and a brief statement of the conditions which obtained in Brussels forty years ago will show how this naturally came to pass. (See pp. 122 ff. of this volume.)

. . . .

So far from Brussels having concluded by reason of her trying experience that the taking of land by zones was an error, it is stated by those in authority that since she has had authority to take land in this way she has employed no other method; but, as has already been stated, it would appear that the objects she has in view in her takings, viz., the improvement not only of her highways but of the appearance and sanitary conditions of the city, can be attained in no other way.

Other cities of Belgium, notably Liege, have also employed this method of taking by zones, and, acting under wiser guidance or more favorable conditions, have succeeded in carrying out their improvements without having to pass through the period of "storm and stress" which Brussels experienced, and in the case of Liege especially certain improvements carried out by this method have shown a substantial profit.

ENGLISH AND CONTINENTAL SYSTEMS

It is of interest to note in this connection that the power of taking land by zones conferred on the cities of Belgium is not possessed by the State, one reason for this distinction being that the approval of the Provincial Government required in the case of takings by cities affords a check against the abuse of this power which would be lacking in the case of the State.

As a result of this situation, the State has requested the city of Brussels to make such takings on a large scale in the vicinity of the new central railway station which the State is about to build in Brussels, and has made a contract with the city under which the State agrees to advance the money necessary for the operation and to assume the risk of any loss resulting therefrom.

I am informed that Belgium has no law for the assessment of betterments.

Note as to Certain Differences Regarding Damages in Case of Takings by Eminent Domain

In France in the case of takings by right of eminent domain the damages are assessed by a jury, in Belgium, by the judges.

In France it is not the practice to receive the testimony of experts regarding the value of the land.

(It is said that in the last thirty years there has been but one case in Paris in which such testimony was given.)

In Belgium such testimony in the form of written reports is customarily received.

In both countries the awards for damages to land and buildings, i. e., the damages awarded to the owner, are considered by the city authorities to be somewhat in excess of the market value, but not greatly so.

The law of each country gives damages to tenants in addition to the value of the land and buildings, and permits such damages to be given for loss of good-will, business or custom consequent on being obliged to move to another locality.

It is in connection with the awards of damages for this latter class of injury that complaint as to excessive awards is made, it being considered that the juries in the one country and the judges in the other are more likely to err or be misled regarding the damages claimed for loss of business or custom than as to those which relate to the value of land or buildings.

INDEX

ACQUISITION OF LAND BY MUNICIPALITIES: burden on tax payers, 22; by gift, dedication, or devise, 3, 4; by municipality, limitations of, in United States, 1–2, 14–15; equitable distribution of cost, 1, 22–51; methods of, 1; purchase by cities, 13–17; right to, 1; tax payers protected, 17

ADMINISTRATIVE AGENCIES AND PLANNING, 168–208

ADVERTISING: condemnation costs, 25

ADVERTISING SIGNS: New York court decision on, 151–152

AMENDMENTS TO STATE CONSTITUTION: of New York, 248–249; of Mass., 278; of Ohio, 280; of Wisconsin, 279

APPRAISERS' HEARINGS: granted by court in Minneapolis, 27–28

ART COMMISSION: in Greater New York, 184

ART JURY: power of, in Philadelphia, 184–185

ASSESSMENT BOARD: determines area for special benefit, 90–91; regulation in New York, 90

ASSESSMENT OF BENEFIT: practice of, in Massachusetts, 85

ASSESSMENTS: by jury, in Kansas City, 71–72; committee appointed in Massachusetts in 1658, 58, 60; court decision in Ohio, 62–64; exemption of, for parks, 62; expense of street openings borne by city, 87–88; first special law in United States, 58; general practice of, 86–87; Greater New York parks, 67–68; Kansas City, 70; King's Highway, 91; laws in Massachusetts, 64–65; legislation for, in different states by dates, 59–60; methods of, for street widenings in New York City, 87–88; New York law of 1691, 58; park lands, 60; Pennsylvania laws of 1700, 58–59; policy of figuring by front foot, 57; prior to 1902 in New York City, 87–88; relative taxation on park property for, 61; unfair features of, in Boston, 97–98

ASSESSORS: appointment of, in Minneapolis, to determine tax, 68–69

ATTORNEY GENERAL VS. HENRY B. WILLIAMS, 1899: 174 Mass. 476, 219–221

AWARDS OF COMMISSIONS: in condemnation cases, reform needed in cases of, 51

INDEX

BALTIMORE: topographical survey commission in, 182

BELGIUM: law for excess taking in, 122–125; street system in Brussels, 122–125

BILL-BOARDS, 161–165; dangers from, 164; decisions, 246–248; increase fire hazards, 164; legislation for, 19; license fee discrimination, 162–163; Missouri provisions to regulate, 162–165; opposition to ordinance regulating, 163; regulations for, as nuisances, 164; St. Louis ordinance for, 165; temporary character of, 165

BOARD OF SURVEY: act declared unconstitutional in Boston in 1902, 89–90

BOARDS OF HEALTH: jurisdiction of, for nuisances, 154–155; Massachusetts, practice of, 154–155

BONDS: for land acquirement, 52–55; issue of, for land payments, 52–55; provided by legislature, 52–53

BORROWING MONEY: limit to city's power, in Milwaukee, 53

BOSTON: area of special benefit in, 90; assessment law unfair, 97–98; attitude toward survey board in, 179; benefits of single council in, 189; board of survey appointed in 1891, 89; board of survey in 1891, 177–179; borrowing plan in, 195; condemnation proceedings in, 36; decision against board of survey in, 89–90; exception to special assessment rule, 96; height of buildings on Copley Square, 18, 19; one-way streets, success of, 204; proceedings for street improvements in, 37–38; special assessments prior to 1891, 89; street commissioners' awards, 37–38; street commissioners in, 36–38; survey act unconstitutional in 1902, 89–90; unsuitable land remnants after condemnation proceedings in, 104

BOULEVARD PROPERTY: restrictions governing, 17–21

BOULEVARDS: King's Highway law in St. Louis, 90–91; Missouri ordinance to regulate industries on, 158–160

BUILDING CODES: regulation of, in large cities of United States, 143–144

BUILDING HEIGHTS: Massachusetts acts, 218–219

BUILDING LIMITATIONS, police power, 140–149

BUILDING LINES: designated in streets, 204; establishing boulevards, 211

BUILDING REGULATIONS: city of Köln, Germany, an example, 145; for dwellings, 149–150; German illustration of, 145–146; in Washington, D. C., 142; limitations on height and size, 140–150; New York decisions for, 142; ordinances for, 140–144; restrictions for community benefit, 138–140; type of control of, 138–140

INDEX

BROOKLYN: Furman Street, 17 Wendell 649. 1836, 243-244

BUILDING RESTRICTIONS: community benefits from, 138-140; excess taking and, 136-137

BUILDINGS IN PARKS: not true economy, 6

BUREAU OF SURVEYS: Philadelphia district surveyors, 176-177

BUREAUS: scope of, in Greater New York, 180-181

CALIFORNIA: findings of commission in, 94-95; pueblo lands in, 16; state codes of, 40

CENTRAL PARK: assessment on land benefited by, 65; creation of, in 1853, 65; land cost of, 65; ratio of increase of land value of, 66-67

CHARLESTON, SOUTH CAROLINA: city hall on park site, 7

CHICAGO: acquisition of school house sites, 42; appreciation of lots, 7-8; commission on street improvements, 39-40; Randolph Street taking, 29, 40; settlements for condemnation in, 42

CITY AS TRUSTEE, 4

CITY GOVERNMENT: unit idea in, 186-188

CITY OWNERSHIP OF LAND: public purpose, 3

CITY PLANNING: administrative vantages of unit idea, 188; commission appointed, in Seattle, in 1910, 196-197; controversies over civic centers, 8; councilmen and wards, 186; departments created in Pennsylvania and New Jersey, 1911, 190; disregard of expert suggestions in, 185; functions of commission for, 198-208; future improvements considered, 203-206; necessity for cor-relation in, 200-202; ownership by municipality essential to, 1; police power in, 138-167; politicians' methods, 186; protection needed for, 7; relation of improvements to whole plan in, 201-202, special boards required for, 183; taste and economy in, 6; various methods in, 168-169

CITY PURCHASES OF LAND: supreme court decision on, 54

CIVIC CENTER BONDS: sale of, in East Denver, 77-78

CLEVELAND: city charter, 299; hearings by jury, in condemnation cases, 41-42; condemnation procedure, regulated by state law, 41

COMMISSIONERS: appointment of condemnation in St. Louis, 33; duties of park, in Kansas City, 69; duties of park, in Indianapolis, 78-83; report on parks in Denver, 74

COMMISSIONS: on city plan, limitations of, cited, 200; mayor as exofficio chairman in cities, 190; sum-

INDEX

COMMON LAW JURY: opinions concerning findings by, 48-49

COMMUNITY RIGHTS: scope of, in Germany, 2

COMPENSATION: legislation for, 18-21; method of ascertaining, 48; method of New York constitutional amendment, 48; ordinance governing in Milwaukee, 25-26; commissioners' salaries in St. Louis, 33

CONDEMNATION OF LAND: act of Virginia assembly in 1906, 110; advantages of preliminary tribunal in, 49-50; advertising expenses in, 25; appeals from findings, in Milwaukee, 39, in Minneapolis, 45; assessment of benefits in, 84-102; compensation by jury, 24; compensation for, in New York City, 43-44; Connecticut acts of, 110-111; constitutional clauses affecting, 23; cost of, in London, 126-133; court decisions in Kansas City, 45-46; direct method in Oregon, 30; disadvantages of, to municipality, 104; English and continental systems, reports from, 308-321; estimation of cost in London, 130; excess, 103-137, 268; expenses of, in New York City, 44; findings by jury in Cleveland, Ohio, 41-42; for Denver parks, 75; French system, reports from, 321-330, 333; in Belgium, 331-334; jury findings in Pennsylvania, 93-94; jury proceedings in France, 120-122; jury verdicts in Portland, Oregon, 93; law in Kansas City, 70-73; legal expenses of, 25; legislation in Ohio and Maryland, 110; new act, in Indianapolis, 47; Ohio laws for, 62; opinion of Archibald R. Watson, 44-45; parallel of, in Philadelphia and Portland, 35; park and playground property, 18-19; parks acquired by, 8; payment of compensation, 23-31; Pennsylvania acts of, 111; Pennsylvania jury findings in, 93; procedure in Portland, 35; proceedings in Boston, 36; proceedings in San Francisco, 43; protection cited in Fourteenth Amendment, 23; Randolph Street, Chicago, 29, 40; relation of special assessments to awards for, 92; settlements for, in Chicago, 42; superior court cases in Indiana, 81; uncertainty of jury findings in, 49

CONFLAGRATION RISKS: height limitations for buildings, 140-149

CONGESTION COMMITTEE: appointment of, in New York, 14

CONNECTICUT: condemnation acts of, 110-111; special acts, 296-298

CONTRACT METHOD: advantages of, for land payments, 55-56

COPLEY SQUARE, BOSTON: restricting height of buildings on, 18, 19. See also *Height Limitations*

CORRELATION: Mayor's cabinet in Kansas City an experiment in, 187; value in city planning, 200-202

INDEX

COST OF LAND ACQUISITION: distribution of, 1, 52–102

COUNCILMEN AND WARDS: as affecting city planning, 186

DAMAGES IN CONDEMNATION CASES: findings of jury in Kansas City, 95; hearings on, in Minneapolis, 27–28; jury appeals in St. Louis, 28; objections to rules of, 93–94

DELAWARE PARK, BUFFALO: encroachments upon, 7

DENVER, COLORADO: appraisers in, 32; bonds for land cost in, 75; four park districts in, 73; land condemnation for parks, 75; municipal art commissions in, 200; notice and hearing proceedings in, 28–29; park commissioners' report, 74

DENVER PARK SYSTEM: extension of civic center, 32; findings of appraisers in, 32

DISTRIBUTION OF COST OF LAND ACQUIREMENT, 1, 52–102

DISTRICT OF COLUMBIA: highway restrictions in, 18

DISTRICTS: creation of park, in Indianapolis, 78; principle of separating in Los Angeles, 155

DWELLINGS: building regulations for, 149–150

EAST DENVER PARK DISTRICT: appraisers' report on land damages, 77; ordinance of condemnation passed, 76–77; report of park commissioners, 76; sale of "civic center bonds," 77–78; subdivision of districts, 76

ECONOMY: and good taste in planning, 6; buildings in parks and commons not, 6, 7

EDWARDS VS. BRUORTON: 184 Mass. 529, 245–246

EMINENT DOMAIN: assessors in Washington, 85–86. See also *Condemnation*

ESTHETIC DEVELOPMENTS: restrictions for promoting, 19–21

EXCESS CONDEMNATION, 103–137, 268; adaptability of principles in United States, 116–117; difficulties of, in United States, 133–135; financial results in France, 118–122; financial value of, in United States, 117–118; history of, in United States, 106–111; physical value of, 133–135; relief of, to tax payers, 103–106; substitute for, in America, 105–106. See also *Condemnation*

EXCESS TAKING: amendments for, in Massachusetts, 114–115; amendments for, in Ohio, 114; amendments for, in Wisconsin, 114, 116; causes of failure in London, 131–132; constitutional amendments versus court decisions in, 116; constitutionality in Wisconsin, 116; constitutionality of, 112; constitutionality of, doubted, 114–116; control over remnants in, 134–135; court decision against, in Philadelphia, 112; investigation of, by London county council, 128–132; law for, in Belgium, 122–125; New York amendments for, 114–115; relative increase of property

INDEX

values, 125; restrictions in, 136–137; revenue from remnant sale in France, 119–122; state amendments to, 114–116; supreme court decision on, in Massachusetts, 112–114

EXEMPTIONS: from special assessment, in takings for parks, 61

FIELD COLUMBIAN MUSEUM: decision in case of, 10–12

FIRE HAZARD: increased by billboards, 164

FIRE RISKS: ordinances which regulate, 141–143, 148–149

FOURTEENTH AMENDMENT: protection against condemnation, 23

FRANCE: condemnation proceedings in, 120–122; excess condemnation in, 118–122; remnant appropriation, 119; revenue from sale of remnants in, 119–122

FRENCH COUNCIL: remnant taking, 121–122

GERMAN CITIES: community rights of, 2

GERMANY: building regulations in, 145–146; town planning and municipal ownership, 1

GRANT PARK: and Field Museum, 11–12

HEIGHT AND SIZE OF BUILDINGS: limitations and restrictions in, 140–150

HEIGHT LIMITATIONS: absolute, 242–243; conflagration risks, 140–149; court decision on, 19; German versus American regulations for, 145; Massachusetts act of 1898, 18; Massachusetts court decision on, 147–148; Massachusetts statute for, 146–147; ordinances governing, 140–144

HIGHWAYS: boards of survey for, 171–180; cost to owners, 171; restrictions in District of Columbia, 18

HOUSE OF REPRESENTATIVES, 61st Congress, 1910, 213–218

HOUSING EXPERIMENTS: lending land for, 17

HOUSING PROBLEMS: causes which contribute to, 139–140

IMPROVEMENT COSTS: tax payers' relief from, 56

INCOMES: derived from lease of municipally owned land, 7

INDIANA: acts of, 212

INDIANAPOLIS: advantages derived from park board, 82–83; duties of boards of public works and park commissioners in, 46; four park districts created in, 78; land takings under new act in, 47; park commission in, 37; park commissioners' duties in, 78–83; park law of, 254–267; real estate experts as advisory committees, 82

INDIANAPOLIS PARK COMMISSION: character of, 37

INDEX

INDUSTRIAL DISTRICTS: ordinance for, in Los Angeles, 155–156

INDUSTRIAL OCCUPATIONS: regulations governing, 154–157

INSTALMENT PLAN: method of purchase in Minnesota and Wisconsin, 53–55

JURY DECISIONS: in condemnation, 24; land damage, 24

JURY FINDINGS: uncertainty of, in condemnation, 49

KANSAS CITY: assessment on land benefited in, 64; assessments by jury, 71–72; assessments within city limits, 70; correlation and Mayor's cabinet, 187; division of, into park districts, 69–73; findings of jury for damages in, 95; juries not demanded by corporations, 46; 70; law in condemnation proceedings, 70–73; municipal court on land takings in, 45–46; park commissioners' duties in, 69; park system in, 72–73; rights of corporations in, 28; special assessments, 72; Swope Park appropriations in, 73

KANSAS CITY VS. BACON ET AL.: 157 Mo. 450, 250–254

KING'S HIGHWAY: assessment provision for, 91; instance of excess condemnation, 130–131

KÖLN SYSTEM: building regulations, 145–149

LAND ACQUISITION, 22–51; condemnation and assessment, 248–254; considerations in, 1; issue of bonds for, 52–55; payment for, by cities, 52–57; special assessments for, 83–102

LAND BENEFITS: Kansas City assessments, 64

LAND COST: excessive, 22, 23

LAND DAMAGES: findings by juries, 24; report on East Denver, 77

LAND DEDICATED IN FEE. See under *Minnesota, Ohio*, and other states and cities

LAND ENCROACHMENTS: regulations for, 150–152

LAND FOR SPECIFIC PURPOSES: abandonment of original plan, 5

LAND LOANS: housing experiment, 17

LAND PAYMENTS: instalment plan in Wisconsin and Minnesota, 55

LAND PURCHASE: Wisconsin and Minnesota method of, 53

LAND RESTRICTIONS: governing boulevards, 17–21

LAND VALUES: increase in Central Park, 66–67

LEGISLATION: esthetic considerations, 19; bill-boards, 19; restrictions on use of land, 211

LEGISLATIVE AUTHORITY: limitations of, in benefit districts, for special assessments, 91

INDEX

LICENSE: bill-board fees, 162–163

LONDON: causes of failure of excess taking in, 131–132; excess taking investigation in, 128–132; financial results in, 125–133; land-taking cost in, 126–133; metropolitan board of works in, 125–133; notable opinions regarding recoupment in excess taking, 129; report of county council, 130

LONDON COUNTY COUNCIL: policy of, 128–132

LOS ANGELES: council ordinance in, 26–27; ordinance for residence and industrial districts, 155–157

LOUISIANA: state codes of, affecting condemnation procedure, 40

MARYLAND: acts of, 1910, 298–299; laws of 1908, 269–271

MASSACHUSETTS: act governing height of buildings, 18; acts of 1898, 218–219; acts of 1904, 221–223; acts of 1905, 223–226; acts of 1907, 280–282; acts of 1912, 267–268; acts of 1913, 283–284; assessment committee appointed in 1658, 58, 60; assessment of benefit in, 85; constitutional amendment allowing excess taking of land in, 278; height limitation decisions, 147–148; laws for assessments in, 64–65; limitations on height of buildings in, 146–147; practice of metropolitan park commission, 65; remnant act in, 107–113; revised laws, 213; supreme court decision on remnants, 112–114; various planning commissions in, 193–195

METROPOLITAN BOARD OF WORKS: operations of, in London, 125–133

METROPOLITAN IMPROVEMENT: borrowing plan, in Boston, 195

METROPOLITAN PARK COMMISSION: practice of, in Massachusetts, 65

MILWAUKEE: area of special benefit in, 90; bond issue for improvements in, 53; borrowing method, for improvements, 53–56; instalment plan of purchase, 53–55; jury appeals for land taking in, 39; ordinance governing compensation, 25–26; street opening, docket entries in, 26

MINNEAPOLIS: special assessments for parks in, 68–69; findings in street cases in, 94; instalment plan of purchase, 53–55; park commissioners on damages in, 27–28; percentage of appeals for land takings in, 45

MINNESOTA: land dedicated in fee, 10

MISSOURI: boulevards and industries, 158–160

MISTAKES OF CITIES: sacrificing city owned real estate, 6

MUNICIPAL ART COMMISSIONS: in Greater New York, 184; powers of commission, for Denver, 200. See also *Art Jury; City Planning*

INDEX

MUNICIPAL BOARD: factor in real estate market, 3

MUNICIPAL INVESTMENTS: financial policy of, 56

MUNICIPALITY: public revenue used for, 3

MUNICIPAL OWNERSHIP: in Germany, 1-2; limitations in United States, 1

MUNICIPAL REGULATIONS: industrial districts restricted by, 158-160

MUNICIPAL WASTE: prevention of, by finance commissions, 17

NEW JERSEY: city planning department created in 1911, 190; laws of, 1913, 294-296

NEW YORK: acts of 1911, 249-250; assessment law of 1691, 58; building regulations decisions, 142; congestion committee, 14; cost of school house sites, 16; court decisions on advertising signs, 151-152; laws of 1913, 284-290; nature of amendment for excess taking in, 115; planning commissions appointed in 1913, 190-191; proposed amendment to constitution, 279; provisions of amendment for excess taking, 114-115; regulation of assessing boards needed, 90

NEW YORK CITY: appointment of commissioners for land taking, 43-44; land taking expenses, 44; legislation of 1911 for park land in, 68; policy of assessment boards prior to 1902, 87-88; school house sites, 15, 16; simple method of ascertaining compensation by, 48; special assessment collection in, 96

NEW YORK, GREATER: art commission, 184; decision providing for assessment of parks in, 67-68; topographical bureau in, 180-181

NOTICE AND HEARING: delays of, in Denver, Colorado, 28-29; proceedings in Denver, 28-29; property owners' rights, 25

NUISANCES: boards of health and, 154-155; district regulations for, 154-157; municipal regulations for, 152-165; regulation for billboards, 164

OHIO: acts of 1904, 268; amendments for excess taking in, 114; amendment to constitution, 280; condemnation laws of cities in, 62; land dedicated in fee, 10; legislation for condemnation, 110

OREGON STATE CODE: condemnation proceedings, 30; determination of damages, 30

OWNERSHIP OF LAND: public, 1-21

PARK BOARDS: duties of, in Indianapolis, 46

PARK COMMISSION: in Indianapolis, 37

PARK DISTRICTS: in Denver, 73; local tax on, 61; treated as separate entities, 69

INDEX

PARK PURPOSES: use of land for, cases cited, 8–12

PARKS: acquired by condemnation, 8; acquiring titles in Greater New York, 67; appreciation of contiguous property, 61; assessments in acquiring land for, 60; cost of Central, 65; district subdivision in East Denver, 76; districts in Kansas City, 69–73; Indianapolis law, 254–267; land dedicated in fee, 10; legislation in New York City, 68; Minneapolis assessments for, 68; prohibition of bill-boards near, 162; property exempt from tax in United States, 61; separate districts as entities, 69; sign disfigurement of, 151–152; system in Kansas City, 72–73

PARKS AND BOULEVARDS: state decisions, on objectionable occupations near, 166

PARKS AND PLAYGROUNDS: condemnation of private property for, 18–19; reservation of, for city needs, 205

PARK BOARDS: advantages of, in Indianapolis, 82–83

PENNSYLVANIA: acts of, 1907, 272–275; assessment law of, 1700, 58–59; city planning department created in 1911, 190; condemnation acts of, 111; condemnation by jury, 93; decisions on street planning, 174–175; findings of jury in condemnation cases in, 93–94; laws of 1913, 290–294, 300–307; Mutual Life Insurance Company vs. Philadelphia, 275–278; plan commission created in 1913, 193; road juries appointed in, 33, 34, 35; statutes for street planning, 174

PHILADELPHIA: area of special benefit in, 90; bureau of surveys, 176–177; city hall in public square, 7; decisions on excess taking, 112; land-taking procedure in, 35; scope of art jury, 184–185; street widening in, 176

PHILADELPHIA ROAD JURIES: appeals from awards by, 34–35

PHYSICAL CHANGES: purposes unsuited, 5; uses of land outgrown, 5

PITTSBURGH: markets in public square, 7

PLANNING: agencies created, 280–284

PLANNING COMMISSIONS: appointment of, in New York in 1913, 190–191; appointment of, in unit idea, 190; creation of, in 1913, in Pennsylvania, 193; history of, 190–198; opportunities of, 202–208

POLICE POWER, 138–167; building limitations, 140–149; regulations for nuisances, 152–165

POLITICIANS: methods in city planning, 186

PORTLAND: jury verdict for condemnation in, 93; land-taking procedure in, 35

PRELIMINARY TRIBUNAL: services of, in condemnation proceedings, 49–50

346

INDEX

PRIVATE OWNERS: power limited by municipal regulation, 1; rights in notice and hearing, 25

PRIVATE PROPERTY: control of, for public, 19

PROSPECT PARK: assessment on land benefited by, 65-66; case cited, 9; ratio of increase in value of assessed area of, 66; special assessment district in, 66

PUBLIC CONTROL: private property under, 19

PUBLIC HIGHWAY: regulations to prevent encroachment on, 150-152

PUBLIC LANDS: new use for, 7

PUBLIC OWNERSHIP: of land, 1-21

PUBLIC REVENUE: used by municipality, 3

PUEBLO LANDS: inheritance of, in California, 16

PURCHASE OF LAND: economy in, by cities, 14, 17

RANDOLPH STREET, CHICAGO: finding of commissioners for land taking, 40; widening of, 29

REAL ESTATE: instances of appreciation in Chicago, 7-8; sacrifice of, through error, 6

RECREATIONAL NEEDS: community money appropriated, 2

RECOUPMENT: opinions of Londoners regarding, 129

REMNANT ACT: draft of bill in Massachusetts, 107-110; principles of, 107-111; supreme court decision in Massachusetts, 112-114

REMNANTS: appropriation of, in foreign countries, 107; appropriation of, in France, 119; control in excess taking, 134-135; disposition of, 104-106; Massachusetts act for, 111; near Williamsburg Bridge, 104; policy of French council, 121-122; results of street changes, 103, 104; revenue from sale of, in France, 119-122; unsightliness of, 104-105; unsuitable, in Boston, 104

RESIDENTIAL DISTRICTS: ordinances for, 155-157

RESTRICTIONS: building lines, 211; esthetics promoted by, 19-21

ROAD JURIES: appointment in Philadelphia, 33, 34, 35

RULES OF DAMAGE: objections to, 93-94

SAN FRANCISCO: condemnation proceedings in, 43

SCHOOL HOUSE SITES: acquired by condemnation, in Chicago, 42; minimum price in New York, 16, purchase of, by New York City, 15, 16

SEATTLE: city planning commission appointed in 1910, 196-197

SPECIAL ASSESSMENTS: Boston an exception to rule of, 96; comparison of returns from, 98-99; definition of, 56-

INDEX

SURVEY BUREAU: in Philadelphia, 176–177

SURVEY COMMISSION: work of, in Baltimore, 182

SURVEY LINES: in Brooklyn, 243–246

SWOPE PARK, KANSAS CITY: appropriation for, 73

TAX PAYERS: excess condemnation relief, 103–106; land cost a burden to, 22

TOPOGRAPHICAL BUREAU: in Greater New York, 180–181

TOPOGRAPHICAL SURVEY: Baltimore commission, 182

TOWN PLANNING: German examples of, 1

TRIAL BY JURY: in condemnation cases, 24

TRUST ESTATES: administered by cities, 4; city as trustee, 4; creation of, 4

UNDERGROUND WIRES: municipal regulation for, 152

UNIT IDEA: city planning advantages, 188; in city government, 186–188; planning commissions appointed, 190

VIRGINIA: acts of assembly in 1906, 271; condemnation, in 1906 assembly, 110

WASHINGTON, D. C.: building regulations in, 142

WASHINGTON: eminent domain assessors in, 85–86; state codes of, 50

WATSON, ARCHIBALD R.: opinion of, on condemnation matters, 44–45

WELCH, TRUSTEE, VS. SWASEY, et al., 1908, 234–242

WELCH VS. SWASEY: 193 Mass. 364, 226–234

WILLIAMSBURG BRIDGE: remnants near, 104

WISCONSIN: amendments for excess taking in, 114, 116; amendment to constitution, 279

WORCESTER, MASSACHUSETTS: city hall in common, 6–7

RUSSELL SAGE FOUNDATION PUBLICATIONS

THE PITTSBURGH SURVEY. Findings in six volumes, edited by Paul U. Kellogg. 8vo. Fully illustrated. Maps, charts, and tables. Price per set, postpaid, $10.

> THE PITTSBURGH DISTRICT: CIVIC FRONTAGE. 534 pages. Postpaid, $2.70.
>
> WAGE-EARNING PITTSBURGH. 420 pages. Price, $2.50 net. (In press.)
>
> WOMEN AND THE TRADES. By Elizabeth Beardsley Butler. 2d ed. 440 pages. Postpaid, $1.72.
>
> WORK-ACCIDENTS AND THE LAW. By Crystal Eastman. 350 pages. Postpaid, $1.72.
>
> THE STEEL WORKERS. By John A. Fitch, New York Dept. of Labor. 350 pages. Postpaid, $1.73.
>
> HOMESTEAD: THE HOUSEHOLDS OF A MILL TOWN. By Margaret F. Byington. 292 pages. Postpaid, $1.70.

WEST SIDE STUDIES. Embodying the results of an investigation into social and economic conditions on the Middle West Side of New York, carried on under the direction of Pauline Goldmark. In two volumes. 12mo. Illus. Price per volume, postpaid, $2.00.

> BOYHOOD AND LAWLESSNESS. Illus. 204 pages.
>
> THE NEGLECTED GIRL. By Ruth S. True. 148 pages.
>
> Published in one volume. Postpaid, $2.00.
>
> THE MIDDLE WEST SIDE: A HISTORICAL SKETCH. By Otho G. Cartwright. Illus. 60 pages.
>
> MOTHERS WHO MUST EARN. By Katharine Anthony. Illus. 224 pages.
>
> Published in one volume. Postpaid, $2.00.

SAN FRANCISCO RELIEF SURVEY. Compiled from studies made by six prominent relief workers. Illus. Map. 8vo. 510 pages. Postpaid, $3.50.

WORKINGMEN'S INSURANCE IN EUROPE. By Lee K. Frankel and Miles M. Dawson, with the co-operation of Louis I. Dublin. 8vo. 450 pages. 145 tables. Bibliography. 2d ed. Postpaid, $2.70.

FATIGUE AND EFFICIENCY. By Josephine Goldmark. Introduction by Frederic S. Lee, Ph.D. Appendix containing comparative schedules of hours and extracts from laws regulating women's labor. 8vo. 358 pages. 4th ed. Postpaid, $2.00.

RUSSELL SAGE FOUNDATION PUBLICATIONS

THE DELINQUENT CHILD AND THE HOME: A Study of Children in the Chicago Juvenile Court. By Sophonisba P. Breckinridge and Edith Abbott. 8vo. 360 pages. Postpaid, $2.00.

CO-OPERATION IN NEW ENGLAND: Urban and Rural. By James Ford, Ph.D. 12mo. 260 pages. Postpaid, $1.50.

SOCIAL WORK IN HOSPITALS. A Contribution to Progressive Medicine. By Ida M. Cannon, R.N. 12mo. 272 pages. Postpaid, $1.50.

WOMEN IN THE BOOKBINDING TRADE. By Mary Van Kleeck. Illus. 12mo. 290 pages. Postpaid, $1.50.

ARTIFICIAL FLOWER MAKERS. By Mary Van Kleeck. Illus. 12mo. 280 pages. Postpaid, $1.50.

SALESWOMEN IN MERCANTILE STORES. Baltimore, 1909. By Elizabeth Beardsley Butler. Illus. 12mo. 234 pages. 2d ed. Cloth, postpaid, $1.08. Paper, postpaid, $0.75.

THE STANDARD OF LIVING Among Workingmen's Families in New York City. By Robert Coit Chapin, Ph.D. 8vo. 388 pages. 131 tables. Postpaid, $2.00.

MEDICAL INSPECTION OF SCHOOLS. By Luther Halsey Gulick, M.D., and Leonard P. Ayres, Ph.D. Illus. 8vo. 244 pages. 4th edition, completely revised. Postpaid, $1.50.

LAGGARDS IN OUR SCHOOLS. A Study of Retardation and Elimination. By Leonard P. Ayres, Ph.D. 8vo. 252 pages. 4th ed. Postpaid, $1.50.

WIDER USE OF THE SCHOOL PLANT. By Clarence Arthur Perry. Illus. 12mo. 434 pages. 3d ed. Postpaid, $1.25.

AMONG SCHOOL GARDENS. By M. Louise Greene, M.Pd., Ph.D. Illus. 12mo. 380 pages. 2d ed. Postpaid, $1.25.

A MODEL HOUSING LAW. By Lawrence Veiller. 8vo. 80 diagrams. 352 pages. Postpaid, $2.00.

HOUSING REFORM. A Handbook for Use in American Cities. By Lawrence Veiller. 12mo. 220 pages. 5 schedules. 2d ed. Postpaid, $1.25.

A MODEL TENEMENT HOUSE LAW. By Lawrence Veiller. Working Edition. 130 pages. Postpaid, $1.25.

ONE THOUSAND HOMELESS MEN. By Alice Willard Solenberger. 12mo. 398 pages. 50 tables. Postpaid, $1.25.

RUSSELL SAGE FOUNDATION PUBLICATIONS

THE ALMSHOUSE. Construction and Management. By Alexander Johnson. Illus. Plans and Specimen Records. 12mo. 274 pages. Postpaid, $1.25.

CORRECTION AND PREVENTION. Four volumes prepared for the Eighth International Prison Congress. Edited by Charles Richmond Henderson, Ph.D. 8vo. Price per set, express prepaid, $10; per volume, $2.50 net.

   PRISON REFORM. By Chas. R. Henderson, F. H. Wines and Others. And CRIMINAL LAW IN THE UNITED STATES. By Eugene Smith. Illus. 326 pages. Postpaid, $2.67.

   PENAL AND REFORMATORY INSTITUTIONS. By Sixteen Leading Authorities. Illus. 358 pages. Postpaid, $2.70.

   PREVENTIVE AGENCIES AND METHODS. By Charles Richmond Henderson, Ph.D. 454 pages. Postpaid, $2.68.

   PREVENTIVE TREATMENT OF NEGLECTED CHILDREN. By Hastings H. Hart, LL.D. With special papers by leading authorities. Illus. 430 pages. Postpaid, $2.70.

JUVENILE COURT LAWS in the United States: Summarized. Edited by Hastings H. Hart, LL.D. 8vo. 160 pages. Postpaid, $1.60.

CIVIC BIBLIOGRAPHY FOR GREATER NEW YORK. Edited by James Bronson Reynolds, for the New York Research Council. 8vo. 312 pages. Postpaid, $1.50.

HANDBOOK OF SETTLEMENTS. Edited by Robert A. Woods and Albert J. Kennedy. 8vo. 342 pages. Cloth, postpaid, $1.50. Paper, postpaid, $0.75.

CARRYING OUT THE CITY PLAN. By Flavel Shurtleff. Introduction by Frederick Law Olmsted. 12mo. 360 pages. (In press.)

SURVEY ASSOCIATES, Inc.
PUBLISHERS FOR THE RUSSELL SAGE FOUNDATION
105 EAST 22d STREET, NEW YORK